No Easy Way to Say This

The diary of a (reluctant) carer

With Best wishes
Kate Edwards

Kate Edwards

Kate Edwards

Dedication:

Dedicated to all the care-givers out there
who go unrecognised, unpaid and unheard.

I hear you!

Kate Edwards

Prologue

Spoiler alert! This story has a happy ending – or at least, at the time of writing the ending is happy.

It's a true story – every date, every operation, every treatment is accurate. I kept a diary, partly so that I can record events as truthfully as possible but mostly so that I can retain some semblance of sanity. This book is made up of excerpts from my diary. The names of people and places have been changed to protect identities and preserve privacy. Some of my friends have been amalgamated into just two or three people so as to avoid confusion. Some explanations and bits of back-story have been added in parenthesis but the vast majority of this is as it was written at the time – emotions, expletives and incredulity as it happened. Even the conversations were recorded as soon as possible to ensure their accuracy.

I'm telling you that there's a happy ending because, in 1974 I went to see a film called The Dove. It was subtitled: a young man's attempt to sail round the world single handed. I homed in on the word attempt, assumed that he'd failed because he'd been washed overboard and eaten by sharks, or shot an albatross, become becalmed and died from drinking sea water. I spent the entire film bawling my eyes out in anticipation of something devastating that never happened.

Another spoiler alert: the reason Robin Lee Graham – the aforementioned young man - had failed to sail round the world single handed wasn't because he'd died: it was because he'd fallen in love and moved his girlfriend – and their baby – on board with him.

So, although he succeeded in sailing round the world, he didn't do it single handed.

And therein lies the reason for my warning: this is a story about cancer. Obviously, there are many, many sad bits, untold scary bits, some truly awful bits and (a few) funny bits – all of them absolutely true.

But it's also a story that offers hope – I hope. I don't want readers to focus on the C word and assume the worst. My diary also includes the ordinary, everyday events that need to be dealt with whilst going through probably the worst thing most people will ever experience, dealing with government agencies; technical problems; family disputes; the emotional strain and the financial difficulties that can be devastating to a relationship while you're trying to cope with cancer and chemo and constant fear. Life goes on: it doesn't stop the minute a lump appears.

It's estimated that one in two of us will get cancer in our lifetime and every cancer story is different. This one is ours.

Introduction

Sam and I have both been married before: I have three children, Amy, Alice and Tom and their partners are Chris, Evan and Tilly. Sam has two living children, Aaron and Myles, who has profound learning difficulties and ASD. His eldest son, Frasier, died as an infant of a rare condition called Hirschsprung's Disease – a condition that Sam also had as a child, and which had required him to spend the first six years of his childhood in hospital.

I'd been a special-needs teacher for over twenty years, but I'd always had a burning desire to be a writer. In fact, I'd started writing when I was pregnant with Amy in 1977 and had a stack of rejection letters as high as a house. Then, shortly after my divorce, I had to have major surgery and the three months convalescence gave me the uninterrupted time I needed to knuckle down and get serious about my dream. By the time Sam was diagnosed with cancer, I'd had nine books published and my tenth was out with publishing houses.

Sam had been a social worker but, after Frasier's death, he gave up his job and became a postman. And that's how we met. One morning, I answered the doorbell in my dressing gown to see Sam standing on the doorstep, smiling and holding out a package. At that moment, the little King Charles Spaniel I was looking after for a friend, shot out between my legs and sped off up the road at a gazillion miles an hour. We set off in hot pursuit, Sam with his Post Office bag flapping against his side and me, barefoot, desperately trying to hold my dressing gown together and preserve some modesty. Fortunately, Sam caught the dog.

Sometime later, I got divorced and moved away and didn't see Sam for several years until we bumped into each other in the High Street. By May 2010 we'd been married for five years, Sam was working as a family liaison officer with a Children's Centre and I was working full time as an author.

Part 1

Diagnosis

May 2010 – July 2010

Wednesday May 19th

I was getting dressed. Sam was in the bath. "Kate, come and look at this." I thought he was going to show me a giant tarantula, or some gross plughole gunk. Instead, he pointed to a lump in his neck. It was the size of half a tennis ball and very tender. He said he'd first noticed it on Saturday. Shit! I went cold. Lumps, whether in custard or the human body, are never good news.

I told him he had to make an emergency appointment with the GP - immediately. He insisted on going into work (don't get me started) but has made an appointment for tonight. Feeling very anxious. I've got two friends with cancer at the moment: don't think I could handle it if it struck Sam. Spent the day on the Internet looking up `lumps in neck' - not feeling any better. Please God let it be an inflamed gland or strained muscle or something simple and easily rectified.

Later

Everything is very surreal at the moment. Dr K saw Sam – I went in with him – and she said she'd never seen anything like it before, but he needed urgent attention. By some bizarre stroke of luck there was a mobile ultrasound scanning unit at the surgery. It's a private service and cost £50. Of course, Sam said he'd wait and go to Outpatients for free! I said no way were we waiting, so I went over to the cash point. The scan showed clusters of enlarged lymph nodes at both sides of Sam's neck predominantly at the left where the lump is. There were also clusters in his liver and lungs. This does not look like an inflamed gland or strained muscle. Fuck!

After the scan we went back in to see Dr K and she's sent him for an urgent blood test in the morning and said she wants to see him again on Friday morning when she'll refer him for an urgent appointment with the consultant at St Raphael's. She said he'll get an appointment within 2 weeks or, fingers crossed, sooner.

Sam is freaked out with all the talk of urgency. Actually, we're both freaked out.

Thursday May 20th

1 day since finding the lump

Sam went for his blood test this morning, although we won't know anything yet. He's totally spaced out about it and can't concentrate on anything.

I went over to the lake and had a little cry. I couldn't meditate. I feel as though I'm slightly detached from reality at the moment. *[Most mornings I cycle to a nearby lake and meditate. It helps to ground me for the day ahead.]*

Friday May 21st

2 days since finding the lump

We went to see Dr K in the morning. She didn't have all the blood test results but said she'd phone the consultant haematologist at lunchtime and would phone Sam this afternoon.

Went to watch Aaron play in a football tournament. Aaron and Sam were chatting afterwards and dissecting the matches like a couple of pundits analysing the Champion's League. Then Sam was invited to play in a friendly at the end. You'd have thought he was running out onto the pitch at Wembley, but I think it was a good thing that he played – it took his mind off things.

Just as we were leaving, Dr K rang and told Sam that the haematologist thinks that Sam is extremely anaemic and it's, "Most likely to be cancer." Shit! She's referring him as an urgent (there's that bloody word again) cancer patient and he'll be seen within two weeks. That seems like an eternity right now.

Sam didn't say anything to Aaron, as he doesn't want him to worry until he knows with more certainty what it is and what the prognosis is. Sam was snapping at me all the way home. I told him we had to stick together through all this. He said he was very sorry and we hugged. I want to cry all the time but have to stay strong for him.

Saturday May 22nd

3 days since finding the lump

Neither of us slept well last night. We were awake for hours – talking and crying and hugging each other. Everything is unknown and scary.

7

This evening, while the football was on, I got out my massage couch and gave Sam some Reiki. It's not ideal, giving Reiki while the client's watching football. They don't recommend it on the course but, hopefully, it might make some small difference.

Sunday May 23rd

4 days since finding the lump

We went to see Sam's mum this morning. He's told his brothers and sisters, but he doesn't want his mum to know about the cancer just yet. He was very emotional with her – especially when she said how well he looked since he'd lost weight. Ironic or what? *[In the previous few months, Sam had lost 4 stones, which we'd both put down to his increased exercise.]*

Sam rang Aaron this evening and told him about the cancer. He thought it best that it came from him and not from one of his family. He sounded shocked. He asked a few questions but then said, "All right, Dad. Take care."

Monday May 24th

5 days since finding the lump

Sam phoned the hospital this morning to find out when his appointment is. They said he should have received a letter by now telling him that his appointment was next Tuesday at 4 pm. I know that's still within the 2 week guidelines but it seems like a lifetime away. He asked if there was an earlier one or if he could have a cancellation, but the secretary said he was already on the `urgent' list and no-one cancelled on that list. Stands to reason, I suppose.

We're trying to get on with things as normal, but it's hard. He's going into work, but I work from home and don't have anything to distract me. Plus, I'm a writer so I have an over-active imagination at the best of times. I'm trying very hard to keep my mind on what we know now, in the present moment, rather than allowing it to escalate to the grave side with me in my widow's weeds.

Tuesday May 25th

6 days since finding the lump

It's like living in limbo. I know the doctor said that the scan and blood test results "looked like cancer" but everything seems to have stopped now. It was a whirlwind for the first 48 hours but now − nothing! I'm aware that I'm trying to convince myself it must all have been a bad dream and Sam hasn't really got cancer − it's just a localised infection. If it was cancer, things would be happening much more quickly than this − he'd have been in hospital by now, wouldn't he?

He's been talking about his will and how he wants me to keep an eye on Aaron and Myles. I don't even want to be thinking along those lines. This is just one more challenge for us. Can't help hoping our next challenge might be, how to cope with a £50 million Lottery win!

Wednesday May 26th

1 week since finding the lump. Worst week of our lives.

A letter came for Sam from the hospital. It was his appointment with a leaflet saying, "Just because you've been referred as an urgent cancer patient, it doesn't mean you have cancer: in fact, most of the people referred under this scheme, haven't." He immediately seized upon this and seems to have convinced himself that he's just got an infection. I wish I could agree with him, but I don't think a consultant would have said that the scan and blood test looked like cancer if there was any chance that it wasn't. And that's despite the tiredness, weight loss and nose bleeds. Tuesday can't come fast enough so that we know what we're dealing with.

Sunday May 30th

11 days since finding the lump

Sam has got pain in his lower back and left hip: he's had it for a couple of weeks but whereas he used to assume it was a sports injury, he's now terrified that it's cancer in his bones like my friend Niamh. The bloody consultant appointment can't come soon enough and I've told him he needs to ask for a full body MRI. *[Niamh was diagnosed with breast cancer in January 2009. She had a mastectomy but was told there was no need for further treatment. Nine months later she had back pain and it was discovered that the cancer had spread to her bones, lymph nodes and liver. I believe that an early MRI would have detected the metastases. Who knows?]*

In the afternoon, Sam and I went to the pictures. We had an argument on the way there and another on the way back. The strain is proving too much.

Tuesday June 1st.

Day of the consultation. 13 days after finding the lump.

11 days after referral. Still within the NHS guidelines.

The CSA *[Child Support Agency]* rang this morning. Sam is querying their latest assessment and they've been haranguing him for days. He can't handle it at the moment, so he gave them permission to talk to me.

The woman said that Sam's regular monthly payments were going to be significantly more than before he was made redundant.

I said that we couldn't understand why, when he was earning much less in his new job and Aaron has now left school, the payments have gone up to more than when he was paying for 2 children and earning more money.

CSA: What we do is take his weekly pay, then take 15% of that for one child, deduct £** because he's got shared contact and that comes out at £** per week which, if you multiply that by 52 and divide by 12, gives £***.

Me: I understand that, but can you understand that it doesn't make sense that he was paying £80 per month less than that for two children when he was earning considerably more money?

CSA: Well, what we do is...

Me: I know the equation you use, I'm asking if it makes sense to you that he should be earning less but paying more for fewer children?

CSA: You have to understand that the mother has to have money for her child.

Me: That's not in dispute. My husband adores both his children and does not begrudge paying for them. What we don't understand is why the amount has gone up when the number of children has gone down AND he's earning less money.

CSA: Well, according to the payslip he sent...

Me: I understand how you've worked it out, but it leaves us very little money to live on ourselves.

CSA: Well, you earn I expect. (Bloody cheek!)

Me: That's irrelevant. My income is nothing to do with my husband's child support.

CSA: You have to try to see it from the other party's point of view. (But is she trying to see it from our point of view? Am not surprised Sam couldn't handle this crap.)

Me: Look, I've just worked out the sums you gave me, and I make it £*** a month *[£60 less],* not what you're quoting. Where did your figure come from?

CSA: It's 15% of his weekly wage...

ME: I know how you do it. His weekly payment is supposed to be £**, right? Then multiply that by 52 and divide by 12 and that comes out at £*** a month.

CSA: Sometimes it's multiplied by 48 and sometimes by 53. It depends.

ME: Depends on what? Are you telling me that there aren't always 52 weeks in a year?

CSA: It's the way the schedule is worked out. (God preserve me!)

This went on for 43 minutes round and round in circles. I swear they breed these people on Mars. In the end she agreed the regular payments will be reduced to £***. It's still more than before but I was losing the will to live by this point. No wonder the poor bloke's ill.

Later

Sam's hospital appointment was at 4pm this afternoon. I dropped him off then went to park the car and when I got back to the clinic, Sam was already in with the registrar. He was a strange little man who could be mistaken for a hipster leprechaun any day of the week with his pointy little beard, jack-ups and acres of white socks on display. [He wasn't Irish, by the way.] The Leprechaun told Sam that his lymph nodes were fine and it was nothing to worry about – it was just an infection from when he was ill two months ago. He said he didn't know why his GP had referred him!

Sam was visibly relieved and stood up, heading for the door. He couldn't get out of there quick enough, but I wasn't convinced. Something didn't sound right so I asked him what we could do about Sam's anaemia?

The Leprechaun looked shocked: Anaemia?

Me: Yes, it showed up on the blood test.

Leprechaun: Have you had a blood test then?

Durrr! You'd have thought he'd have checked his notes beforehand! He went on the computer and within 10 seconds said, "Oh I'm so sorry: your blood test shows high levels of kappa para-protein blah blah blah." [Sam's Para-proteins were at 48 at the time. When I asked what the normal level was, I was told they shouldn't be there at all.]

Sam had gone into shock and was sitting staring at the bloke.

Me: So, what does that indicate?

Leprechaun: There's no easy way to say this: it's Multiple Myeloma.

I was shocked at the offhand way he said it. I knew what that meant because at one point they thought Niamh had it. I burst into tears. *[Multiple Myeloma is a cancer that affects the bone marrow. The prognosis isn't brilliant.]*

Then he said, "But it's important not to feel too hopeless, there's lots of things we can do to make you more comfortable and we'll probably transfer you to St Peregrine's because you're young."

Make him more comfortable? Jesus wept! Sam's 46 years old and he's talking about making him more comfortable? He then dispatched us with some forms to have more blood tests, a urine test, a bone marrow biopsy and CT scan. We had no time to process what was happening, we were just bustled off to the blood testing department before they closed at 5 pm.

When we got there, Sam asked the phlebotomist if he could have a specimen bottle for his urine test as the doctor hadn't given him one. All she could do was go on about how it was coming out of her budget. My husband's just been given a death sentence and she's going on about a five bloody pence plastic bottle for fuck's sake!

We both came home and cried. I tried to explain to Sam what Myeloma was, but I think it's too much for him to take in. We rang our families and just held each other and sobbed all night. Aaron is finding this very difficult to handle and keeps phoning up but then putting the phone down abruptly.

Wednesday June 2nd

12 days since referral.

1 day since consultation

We were awake at 2.30 this morning and we're both doing masses of crying. Sam's still going in to work, so I had to take his urine sample up to St Raphael's. There was a total mix up because The Leprechaun hadn't given us a form, so the pathologist didn't know what she was testing for. I'm finding it hard to keep calm with everything that's going on at the moment.

I rang the consultant's secretary and she put Dr T *[Head Honcho: senior haematology oncology consultant: the big boss of the Leukaemia, Lymphoma and Myeloma department]* on the phone and I told him everything. He said that The Leprechaun should never have said that it was Myeloma as it's impossible to diagnose Multiple Myeloma from a single blood test - it needs the biopsy and urine test too. There are several other Lymphomas that mimic MM and because Sam's not presenting typically, he thinks it's more likely one of those, which is a much better prognosis. Anyway, he's seeing us tomorrow to talk to us and explain everything and he apologised profusely for our treatment yesterday.

Feeling a bit more hopeful after speaking to the consultant today but we shall see. It's the bone marrow biopsy tomorrow plus another consultant visit, then the CT scan next week. And, of course, it might still turn out to be Myeloma after all this.

We've had lots of family coming round, which is lovely. Amy and Lily came and Sam's brother and nephew. Then Aaron came round. He was very subdued and asked Sam if he was scared. Sam said, "Of course I'm scared, son." Aaron went very quiet.

Thursday June 3rd

13 days since referral.

2 days since consultation

Sam took today off work because he has his bone marrow biopsy this afternoon. Our landline went down again this morning – this is the 4th or 5th time it's done this. I rang the phone company and told the woman that my husband has cancer and we need to have a landline so that doctors, hospitals and friends can call. They said they'd send an engineer by 1 pm. I told her that we had to leave for the hospital by 1.15 but she assured us an engineer would be with us very shortly. They hadn't arrived at 1, so I rang up and the woman said they'd be there in 2 hours. I hit the roof and told her that there was no point as I'd told her we'd be at the hospital this afternoon.

We had to go to the day unit at St Raphe's for the bone marrow biopsy. It was a different doctor – this one looked like Homer Simpson with heavy features, a five o'clock shadow and pot belly - but without the jaundiced skin tone. Homer Simpson told Sam that bone marrow biopsies are painful and they're even worse for African-Caribbean people because they have more bone density than white people! Why does he need to know that? He has no point of reference, so what difference does it make that he'll be in more pain than I would? What an insensitive numbskull! I was allowed to go into the room although not to actually sit with Sam - but I could hear him groaning and cursing from behind the curtain. He said it was excruciating.

We then went in to see Head Honcho who said that they think Sam has probably got both Myeloma AND Lymphoma! Either that or a very rare cancer that I can't remember. He said that, with aggressive chemo and stem-cell surgery, Sam could have 10 years. That's better than the 2 – 5 years I've read about on the Internet. Either way, it's pathetic when he's only 46. But that's if it's Multiple Myeloma – if it's the 2 primaries, or the other rare one, God knows what the prognosis is. We were both crying again in the unit: sitting in a cubicle, sobbing our eyes out and holding each other but no one came to ask us if we needed anyone to talk to or offered any support. I felt as though we'd been thrown into the Arctic Ocean and left to die of hypothermia. Felt very lonely, lost and frightened. We have cried and cried so much recently, I'm surprised we're not dehydrated.

When we got home the phone engineers had put a note through the door – they'd been at 3 pm! I rang again and said this was not on and the man said that they'd be here by the end of the afternoon. They weren't! Still no landline. How is anyone supposed to deal with all the normal irritations of life when they're trying to deal with the biggest, most terrifying curve ball most of us will ever have thrown at us?

Friday June 4th

14 days since referral.

3 days since consultation

Sam insisted on going in to work today as he's supposed to be DJ-ing for a family fun day. He could barely lift his equipment and was shaking like a leaf afterwards. It's pitiful to see a man who was so proud of his physical strength and fitness reduced to that. I went to the lake and wept.

Still no landline, so I rang the phone company again and went absolutely ballistic. All my pent up anger came out – although I did apologise afterwards. I know it's not the customer services guy's fault. Anyway, he said that the engineers would come this afternoon between 12 and 4. (Like when they were supposed to come yesterday - twice!)

Then I rang the Macmillan service on my mobile and spoke to a nurse called Annie. She was lovely and listened to me for about half an hour. I just wept and wept. I've got an appointment to see her next Thursday and she holds a support group once a month for patients and carers, so I might go to that on 21st.

Saturday June 5th

15 days since referral.

4 days since consultation.

I went to see my friend Liz who used to be a GP. She said it's possible that they might never diagnose what Sam's got. A few patients have cancers that are specific to them and the only thing to do is hope that they can find a cocktail of chemo that has an effect on it. Then I went to visit Niamh whose cancer is now terminal. Am feeling very emotional and totally cancered out!

Sunday June 6th

16 days since referral.

5 days since consultation.

Neither of us is sleeping well – or at all! I went over to the lake, but I can't focus my mind enough to meditate. I had a little cry over there so that I can be upbeat in front of Sam.

Friday June 11th

21 days since referral.

10 days since consultation.

This has been a really difficult week. On Monday Sam got home from work and was very spiky, snapping at everything I said. He went off to do his boxing class where he said he hit the punch bag with such force that all the students gasped and went silent. I can't help thinking he ought to do that more often.

Tuesday morning, he had his appointment with Head Honcho after the MDT [multi-disciplinary team] meeting. Sam told me not to ask questions because, apparently, it's his cancer and I take over. In my defence, m'lud, I only ask questions that I think we need to know. So, I wrote down some things that I thought were important and asked what he wanted to add – which was nothing.

At the meeting Head Honcho said that they thought it was not Myeloma but Waldenstrom's Macroglobulinemia: a low level Lymphoma which wouldn't even require chemo but could just be monitored. He has to have a whole body X ray and a CT scan. Yet, last week, we were told that he couldn't have a CT scan because it involved too much radiation and could exacerbate the condition. I asked again why he couldn't have an MRI but was not given an answer.

Also, the lump in his neck – which is now the size of a grapefruit - doesn't fit with either Myeloma or Lymphoma, so could be another condition altogether. Plus, it's now pressing on his vocal cords and restricting his movement. It needs an urgent biopsy but, because it's so near to major nerves and blood vessels, not many surgeons would be willing to do it. However, a Mr. G has agreed to do it under local anaesthetic on Thursday. Not sure about the local anaesthetic though. Can't think of anything worse than being awake and seeing and hearing them operate on my neck!

On Wednesday, Sam had to go for a whole body X ray, which Homer Simpson had said would take 2-3 hours - but he was in and out in 5 minutes! I began to wonder if they'd done the right one. I have very little confidence in Raphe's. Thursday morning, I saw Annie, the Macmillan nurse, who listened to me but couldn't really offer much else, other than a couple of booklets – I've practically got my own cancer library as it is!

In the afternoon, it was Sam's biopsy. He's been very nervous about this since being told about it on Tuesday but, when we saw the surgeon's registrar, she didn't seem to think there was anything unusual about the lump. When she called in Mr. G, he swanned in like God-I-Am saying that he'd agreed to do the biopsy, because he was helping out his colleagues in haematology. Wow! That's big of him! He said it would be done under general anaesthetic (thank God for that!) on 22nd June – almost 2 weeks away – depending on the results of the bone marrow biopsy. He also said, "So you've got Myeloma (which is NOT what was said on Tuesday) and we often see enlarged lymph nodes in Myeloma." Again, NOT what we were told on Tuesday. I honestly don't think the left hand knows what the bloody right hand is doing.

Sam was furious that he'd psyched himself up for the biopsy under local anaesthetic and the bloke never had any intention of doing it today. He was very snappy with me again – like I had anything to do with it! I tried to contact the cancer counselling service, but no one answered the phone and their website says they're closing down in August due to lack of funds. Sod's law! I feel so sad and so lonely in all this.

We went for the CT scan, which Sam found quite unpleasant and said he thought he was going to be sick halfway through. The radiographer told him that he was luckier than some people she saw because he had time to be with the ones he loved! Talk about tactless – who trains these bloody people?

Saturday June 12th

22 days since referral.

11 days since consultation

Things much better today. Sam is very contrite about how snappy he was last week. I can understand how it gets to him: how terrifying all this is - I just wish he wouldn't take it out on me. We went to bed at 7.30, we were both so exhausted.

Wednesday June 16th

26 days since referral.

15 days since consultation

It's been nice to have a few days without hospitals but then, at 4.10 this afternoon, a man from the Day Surgery Centre rang. He said that Sam's procedure had been postponed from next Tuesday until next Thursday 24th. He said, "But the good news is, it's now only a day procedure." As though this was some sort of party game. I told him it was only ever going to be a day procedure and that I was not happy that it was being put off again. He said he was only the clerk and Mr G had had an 'urgent' case come up, so Sam's operation was having to be put back. Like Sam's case isn't urgent? He gave me several phone numbers to ring but, of course, it was turned 4 pm so everyone had gone home. I cannot believe this. It's now a month since he found the lump and this is supposed to be urgent under government protocols.

I was so screwed up that Sam got out his boxing gloves and pads and I punched seven bells out of them. He said, "You certainly pack a punch. If you learned the correct stance, you could do someone some serious damage." If everyone from Raphe's who's messed us around would like to form a queue...

Thursday June 17th

27 days since referral.

16 days since consultation

When Sam woke up this morning, he tried to move his neck downwards but the lump is now so big that it hurt and he couldn't put his chin on his chest. It's growing daily.

I phoned Mr G's secretary but she's on holiday until next week. (Aren't they always?) I then tried admissions, but they weren't answering the phone – twice! So, then I rang Head Honcho's secretary. I told her the whole thing and she said that this was something that doctors needed to sort out between themselves rather than secretaries. A few minutes later Head Honcho rang from in between patients in clinic. He said he'd speak to Mr G and see what could be done. I said, "I was told that it was because Mr G had an urgent case come up, but my husband is a man of 46, in the prime of his life with a lump which is growing daily and to have it implied that he is NOT an urgent case, is quite frankly insulting." Head Honcho said that as far as the haematology department was concerned, Sam was an urgent case, but he would need to speak to Mr G himself, then he would phone me back. I won't hold my breath.

The secretary then phoned and reiterated everything that Head Honcho had said. I said to her, "While you're on, we haven't heard when my husband's next clinic appointment is." To which she said, "Oh, it's next Monday at 11.05!" (Thanks for letting us know!) Then she said, "But until they get the results of the biopsy there's nothing anyone can do, so the doctors are happy to talk to you, but they can't proceed with any treatment or give a diagnosis yet."

Me: Presumably they've got the results of the bone marrow biopsy and the CT scan and X-ray, so they'll have something more than they had before?

Secretary: Oh yes, they've got those.

I know it's all in a day's work for them, but we are people with feelings and families and lives to live.

I've been looking up Mr God-I -Am on the internet and he does sound like a good surgeon according to his bio: just not good with people who are conscious!

Friday June 18th

28 days since referral

17 days since consultation

I was out this morning and, when I got back at lunchtime, the phone rang. It was The Leprechaun saying that they'd been trying to get hold of Sam all morning: he was needed at the hospital urgently. If I never hear the U word again, it'll be too soon. Sam had been out on home visits but eventually I managed to get hold of him and met him at the hospital. Homer

Simpson saw us and explained that the results of Sam's CT scan showed that there was a large thrombus in his jugular vein on the right side of his neck – the opposite side from the lump – and it would need to be dispersed so that it didn't go to his heart and cause a heart attack. Oh my God! The man's been cycling around like a lunatic with a ticking time bomb in his neck.

He also showed us the CT scan which showed a large mass about 6.5cm x 3.5 cm on the left side of his neck and huge masses of enlarged lymph nodes in both his lungs – each one is about the size of a fist - and smaller clusters in his liver. It seems that, even though they haven't done the biopsy of the lump yet, they think that he's got Waldenstrom's Lymphoma but now there's also this thrombosis in his neck for which he'll have to give himself Clexane *[blood thinning]* injections into his abdomen every day for 3 – 6 months.

We were told to come back on Monday for his appointment at 11.05 and also his pre-op assessment on the same day. Homer Simpson also said that if Sam wanted, he could be transferred to St Peregrine's – a specialist cancer hospital - and Sam said yes, he wanted that. Homer Simpson said that Head Honcho had sent Mr G an email asking him to do Sam's biopsy earlier rather than later but had not heard from him! Now there's a surprise.

Saturday June 19th

29 days since referral

18 days since consultation

Sam bought me a day at a spa as a birthday present. Swam, read, got massaged, then swam and read some more. Not a doctor or scan or antiseptic hand gel in sight. Utter, utter bliss!

Monday June 21st

31 days since referral. The government guidelines for having reached a diagnosis

20 days since consultation

Sam had his pre-op assessment this morning. Both he and I were told that it was at Green Lodge from 8.30am onwards and then he had his clinic appointment with Head Honcho at 11.05.

He went to Green Lodge at 8.30 but was told it didn't open until 9am, so he hung around till then, but a nurse told him that he wasn't down on their records. She sent him over to admissions who told him that his assessment was at the Day Surgery Centre. I would have said that he'd misheard them, but I was there too and they definitely said Green Lodge! Anyway, I joined him at the Day Surgery Unit at 9.20. He had his assessment and then had to go for blood tests. Just as he was called into see Head Honcho, the clinic nurse said to him, "Where are your notes?" As if a patient ever has anything to do with their own notes. Apparently, they've lost all his notes – unbelievable. I didn't think my opinion of Raphe's could sink any lower. I can't wait for him to be transferred.

Eventually, at 11.55, they found his notes and we went in to see Head Honcho. He said they now think it's some sort of hybrid cancer – a cross between Myeloma and Lymphoma – but they still don't know what the lump is in his neck. I said, "Last week you said you'd like to be referred to St Perry's for your treatment, remember?" But Sam said, "It's OK, there's plenty of time for that." I didn't pursue it, but my heart sank.

I spoke to Liz my ex-GP friend and she said that Sam was frightened and angry and I just had to be a saint and not react. Great advice except for one thing – I'm no saint and I do react. OK – two things!

Tuesday June 22nd

32 days since referral.

Three weeks since consultation.

A woman from Admissions rang me because she'd been told that I was not happy about Sam's procedure being delayed. Too right, I'm not happy! She then said it was only 2 weeks since Head Honcho had referred him to Mr God-I-Am, therefore it was still within the government 2 week deadline for being seen by a consultant. Nice moving of the goalposts!

I went round to see Niamh. We talk about everything except cancer. The thing about Niamh is, she never complains – about anything: about having cancer, about being messed about and wrongly diagnosed initially by Raphe's (which could be one of the reasons I have so little faith in them where Sam is concerned), about Bob, *[her husband, unaffectionately known as Bob the Bastard by her friends]* who's buggered off back to Limerick just when she needs support. Nothing. She's dying and yet she's always looking on the bright side and never, ever feels sorry for herself. Now there's a saint.

27

Wednesday June 23rd

33 days since referral

22 days since consultation

I went to a meeting at Raphe's about `Have Your Say.' It was all Myeloma or Lymphoma patients and/or their carers. I told them what had happened to Sam and they seemed to think he'd had a rough deal and the woman running it said that the government guidelines said that a diagnosis needs to be reached within 31 days of referral. I told her that it was now 33 days since referral and they hadn't even done the biopsy yet. She said that they were in breach and she would look into it. Yay! I am not going mad!

Thursday June 24th

34 days since referral

23 days since consultation

Day of the biopsy

Sam was awake from 4am and, as a result, so was I - on and off. We left the house at 6.45 and I drove him to the Day Surgery Centre and then went to park the car in one of the roads nearby to avoid paying for hospital parking. He saw the anaesthetist at 8am, who seemed to think he was having a local anaesthetic! We put him right on that. Then he said this operation could take anything from about 10 minutes to half an hour.

Sam went into theatre at 9.05. I asked the nurses what time he would be back and they said about an hour, so I went over to the lake. When I got back at 10am I told the nurses that I would be in the waiting area if they could let me know when he came out of theatre. At 10.30 Mr God-I-Am walked through in his scrubs, then came back about 10 minutes later. He saw me and came over. He said that he'd got a `large wedge' of the lump (gross) – easily enough for the lab to do a good biopsy so they should know fairly soon what it is. He also said that Sam had bled a lot, probably due to his Clexane and he should have been told to stop having the injections 5 days before the operation. No one told us that and, considering he's only been on it for 6 days, that would have been difficult.

At 11.15 I went back to the nursing station and asked if Sam was back but they said he wasn't. Then Claire, Sam's Macmillan nurse came to see me. We talked for about half an hour. At one point she said that Sam was still within the government guidelines because of the internal referral by Head Honcho to God-I-Am and, provided that he starts treatment within 69 days, they haven't breached the protocol. 69 days! That's nearly 10 weeks. Have they tried waiting 10 weeks with cancer before treatment starts? Anyway, we chatted until it was almost noon and I said I was worried as Sam wasn't back yet and it had been three hours. She went to find out what was happening and said that he was back from theatre. Thank you nurses for letting me know - not!

I went through and he was very groggy and wearing an oxygen mask but said he thought he'd been back about 20 minutes. He had a drain coming out of his neck where he'd bled. I sat with him for a while and at about 12.30 he said he was very hungry so I found a nurse and asked when he could eat. She was very off hand and said, "When he's been out of theatre an hour, he'll be brought food." Ten minutes later he was brought a sandwich and a jug of orange squash. No one up to this point had taken his obs and I'd been sitting with him for 45 minutes. And they didn't do them even then.

As soon as he started eating, he began breathing very oddly then broke out in a very heavy sweat. I've never seen anything like it – it was as though his scalp was a showerhead and water was pouring out of it in globules and streaming down his face. Then he passed out. I went to get a nurse, but she waved in the direction of the nursing station and told me to get someone else as she was busy! FFS! The nurses were all chatting and showed no sense of urgency at all. Then the small nurse who'd been with him earlier came and started opening windows and lowered his bed until he was flat. For the first time since I'd been there, she got a B/P machine. His blood pressure was 80/42 and his blood oxygen level was 89%. They brought a fan and put it on him and put him on a drip and gave him the oxygen mask again. It was very scary and no one gave us any explanation as to why it had happened. I can only assume that, because he'd lost so much blood in theatre, as soon as he began eating and the blood went to his stomach, his blood pressure dropped and he passed out. It took quite a long time for his B/P to get back up to 107/69 and then they sat him up again.

I was not impressed with the standard of nursing care at all until, at 3pm, a male nurse came up and introduced himself as

Tony. The other nurse never came to tell us she was going off duty: she just disappeared. After Tony came on duty, Sam's obs were taken every 15 minutes, which I thought they were supposed to be after an operation. Finally, the surgeons came back at 5.30 and discharged him. Tony tried to take out the drain from his neck but couldn't, so had to call back the SHO to do it and, finally, we were allowed home at about 6.15. What a bloody day! In every sense.

Friday June 25th

35 days since referral

24 days since consultation

Sam was awake very early, probably because he'd been asleep so much yesterday with the anaesthetic. He was being very loving and said he wanted to come over to the lake with me this morning. We just went to the part closest to the car park and sat on our fishing stools to watch the ducklings and fish. It was lovely and warm and absolutely magical. We held hands and it was a truly loving moment. But then Sam wanted to drive back – less than 24 hours after a general anaesthetic! Massive row on the way home – hey ho! I know he's trying to prove that he's OK – but he isn't!

Saturday June 26th

36 days since referral

25 days since consultation

Sam woke up being very loving and apologised for how he'd been yesterday. He then said he was fine to drive today and we'd go to his mum's and then to the supermarket. I pointed out that he could hardly move his neck due to the stitches & dressing and I was concerned that, although he was OK to drive from the anaesthetic point of view, his ability to turn his head to see traffic was still impaired. He got defensive again, but I said, "OK, how about, if you're in the car on your own, you can drive, but if the two of us go anywhere, I'll drive - just until you've had your stitches out?" He agreed. Brownie points for my negotiating skills – Henry Kissinger eat your heart out!

But, in the afternoon, he got upset again. I can't even remember the trigger. He was saying that I was taking over his life and telling him what to do. He was shouting at me but, weirdly, I felt relieved that he was, probably for the first time since he'd found the lump, getting his frustration out. It was just a tad annoying that it was me who got the brunt of it!

Things didn't improve all day. In fact, they got worse. There's only so much breathing into things I can do so, in the end I told Sam that I needed some space. I said I was going to go away but I would ring him to check that he was OK. I booked myself into the Premier Inn, half a mile down the road – my big bid for freedom!

I was very sad and upset but my conscience got the better of me and I came home. It didn't feel right to leave him on his own even though he is being unbelievably difficult at the moment. I went straight up to bed but asked Sam to stay downstairs. I wanted some space from him, but I didn't want him to be on his own either. I know how frustrating and frightening and sad this is. I totally get that. And I understand that he's not physically well enough to go running or knock seven bells out of a punch bag at the moment – just please don't use me as your emotional equivalent!

Sunday June 27th

37 days since referral

26 days since consultation

I went back to the Premier Inn and checked out – what a waste of £75! I didn't even get to sleep in the bed. Sam apologised for how he'd been but at that point his nose began bleeding - a lot. He said it had happened last night too. I said he needed to go to A&E because he had cancer and was on Clexane and he needed to go to hospital and ask for the on-call haematologist just to check out that everything was OK and, if necessary, pack his nose. In the end he agreed, but by the time we got to the hospital it had stopped, so he insisted on coming home. Oh my days! I changed the dressing on his neck and it looks quite clean, but he says it feels swollen. I said I'd keep an eye on it.

It was a pretty grim day. And, when we went to bed, Sam's nose started bleeding again but he wouldn't go to hospital: he said it was just the heat. I felt his head and he was burning up. I said that I thought that needed checking too as he could have an infection. I ran him a tepid bath and he sponged himself down. I put the fan on him in bed but even with the fan on him, he was very hot. Jesus Christ - what now?

Monday June 28th

38 days since referral

27 days since consultation

Sam has gone into work, but his nose was bleeding again this morning. I told him again that he needed to go to Raphe's and get it packed but he didn't. The only good thing is that he took the car and didn't even attempt to cycle - although he's still holding his neck very stiffly and it's very swollen. It looks as though it might be infected but he won't go and get it checked. I worry myself sick about him because he's his own worst enemy at times.

I went to see Niamh this afternoon. She is getting frailer and weaker, but her spirits are still good. We used to be the same height, but I tower over her now and her spine is as crooked as a coat hanger, bless her. That's the cancer that's destroyed her bones.

Tuesday June 29th

39 days since referral

28 days since consultation

Sam had his stitches out at the GP's surgery. Apparently, the nurse said that there was an infection in his neck so called the doctor (not the super-efficient, ultra-competent Dr K, but another of the GPs) who prescribed him Co-amoxicillin, antibiotics.

I was working today - hallelujah! I was in a school doing an author talk and creative writing workshop. It was good for me to get out of the house and get back to the old, writer me rather than the current carer me - although I'm not sure of the quality of my talk and workshop. All these eager Year 8s *[that's 12 and 13 year olds - 2nd year seniors in old money]* were clearly looking to me for inspiration yet, there I was, sleep deprived, creativity deprived and all-round emotional wreck, feeling utterly brain dead. I don't know how I got through it – and the press were there too! Great – Zombie Author Talks to Kids! With a photo to prove it.

While I was at the school, Claire, the Macmillan nurse left a message on my phone saying she'd been trying to get hold of Sam because the hospital had the results of the biopsy – thank God! Now we can find out what we're dealing with. They'd discussed his case with the Perry's team at the MDT meeting this morning and wanted Sam to phone asap to arrange to go up there for his treatment plan. I rang Sam and told him, but he tried all day to get through to the doctors and couldn't. In the end he did get through to Claire and she told him to go up at 10 on Thursday to the Medical Day Unit.

Sam insisted on going to football training tonight but even the kids were worried about him when they saw his neck. In the evening I asked if he'd read the information about his antibiotics and he said he hadn't, so I read it. It said - do not take if you:

a)   have liver problems (they've found a mass in his liver)
b)   have blood cancer (which he has) and
c)   are on Warfarin or blood thinning medication (which he is.)

Bloody useless doctor! Aaaagh!

I said I thought we should go to A&E and ask for the on-call haematologist but, again, Sam couldn't face it, so I rang the out of hours GP service. They rang back and Sam spoke to the doctor who said that nowhere on his computer did it mention blood cancers (It says it on the literature!) and it was OK for Sam to take it because his blood thinning medication was Clexane not Warfarin, and his liver function test was OK - despite having a `mass' in his liver? Then he told Sam to stop taking the tablets anyway until he could speak to a doctor. So, what was he if he wasn't a doctor? Great! That still leaves him with an infected wound the size of a mini rugby ball in his neck and a depleted immune system!

Wednesday June 30th

40 days since referral – 6 long, miserable, hospital-dominated weeks

29 days since consultation

This morning we had another row. I try to walk away but Sam goes on and on and it just seems to get him more upset if I don't engage with him. I am between a rock and a hard place – whatever I do is wrong. Alice rang and was great. She listened to everything and suggested that it might be the cancer that's affecting his brain – which I had thought of and Liz had also suggested.

Sam tried to get hold of the GP about the antibiotics, but they told him to come in at 5.10 tonight. I went with him and we saw Dr K who said she'd never seen anything like the lump on Sam's neck (which now looks less like a rugby ball and more like an aubergine) and that he should continue with the antibiotics. I pointed to an area of discolouration around the swelling and asked if it could be a haematoma? *[Haema = blood; toma = lump.]* Dr K was unsure and said to ask the doctor at the clinic tomorrow. Sam insisted that it wasn't discoloured. Jesus! I know his skin's dark but it's not purple!

Thursday July 1st

41 days since referral.

30 days since consultation

Sam's appointment at the Medical Day Centre.

I went with him. Homer Simpson arrived at 10 past 10 and we went through to a consultation room. He said that, although all the results of the biopsy weren't back yet and weren't conclusive, they'd brought up the case at the MDT meeting on Tuesday with Perry's and it was agreed that it was most probably a low-level Non-Hodgkin's Lymphoma and he probably had the disease at 2 different stages of progression. He said that Sam would be started on chemotherapy next Thursday and would be on FCR *[Fludarabine, Cyclophosphamide, Rituximab]* once a month for 6 months. It was given both intravenously and with tablets. And after 4 months they'd do another CT scan and review his progress.

I asked if the masses in his lungs and liver were also Lymphomas, and he said that, although they hadn't biopsied them, they were making that assumption. I wasn't overly impressed with that answer: this is Sam's life. Don't make assumptions when it's someone's life you're dealing with!

I then asked what effect the blood hyper-viscosity *[the thickened blood that had caused his thrombosis]* would have on Sam and he said that it would affect the flow of blood through the small blood vessels, especially around his eyes, brain and extremities. I asked how that would manifest and he said, mental confusion, lack of concentration & memory loss, blurred vision and numbness in his fingers and toes. I didn't ask in front of Sam, but I'm thinking it could also account for mood swings, which makes it a bit easier for me to deal with when he's being difficult.

Homer Simpson looked at the swelling in Sam's neck and I pointed out the discolouration again. He said he was satisfied that it was an infection rather than a haematoma and told Sam to continue with the antibiotics as they needed the infection cleared up before he could start chemo next week. Again, he asked Sam whether he wanted to be treated at Perry's or Raphe's, and Sam said Raphe's! Nooooo! Deep breaths, Kate: deep breaths!

We got home about 11.45 and Sam was in a tearing hurry to get to work as he had a boxing class this afternoon. I made him some lunch, but he didn't eat all of it. I didn't even mention that it might not be wise to take a boxing class with an enormous lump and stitches in your neck.

In the evening he insisted on going to football training too. FFS! I don't know if he's trying to pretend this isn't happening or what – but it is and he's not making any adjustments to his life.

Friday July 2nd

42 days since referral

31 days since consultation

Sam woke me up at 4.30 am. His wound was bleeding. I mean pouring with blood – everywhere! It was like a blood bath. I drove him to A&E and parked the car in the car park – I paid £4.40 by credit card!

After 4½ hours in A&E he was transferred to the Emergency Admissions Ward – EAW - and told he would need surgery to drain the haematoma in his wound! Haematoma!! I'm not even trained and I could see it was a haematoma! So why couldn't these numpties who've spent 7 years at medical school see it? I am so angry! This could all have been avoided if they'd listened to me.

Once Sam was on the ward, I realised that we'd driven off in such a hurry this morning that I'd left all the windows open, so I dashed home to lock up. But, when I got back to the hospital, the curtains were drawn round Sam's bed and he was surrounded by doctors and nurses. All the strength went from my legs. I ran over there but they wouldn't let me see him. I thought he'd died. I felt sick. Eventually, after about half an hour, a nurse came and took me to see him.

Sam was crying. He said he'd blacked out again and he'd thought he was dying too. He said he couldn't breathe and everything had faded. He was clearly terrified, saying he thought that he wouldn't come round. They put him on a drip again and monitored him regularly. He dozed on and off, but his temperature kept spiking and they said they couldn't operate until it was normal. They moved him into a side ward and put a fan on him. I kept topping up the car park all day – honest to God, that's the last thing we need with everything else that's going on. They just extort money from people when they're at their most vulnerable.

Eventually his temperature dropped and they took him to theatre at just turned 6 pm. I was told to take all his things with me as he wouldn't be going back onto EAW but would be transferred onto a surgical ward, although they didn't know which one. So, I came home with all his clothes, money, phone – everything. The car park had cost us £16.

At home I had to change the bed. The bedroom looked like the St Valentine's Day Massacre: everywhere was covered in blood; sheets, pillows, carpet. Then I had to wash the bedding even though I was shattered. I kept ringing the hospital and, eventually, at 8.15 I found that he was out of theatre and on a ward. The Staff nurse said they'd drained 50mls of blood from the haematoma, dressed the wound and left a drain in just in case it bled again. I asked when I could see him and she said, "Visiting time is 3pm to 8 pm."

Me: Are you telling me that I can't see my husband till 3 o'clock tomorrow despite the fact that he's just had surgery, has no money, no wash things and no clothes?

Nurse: Very well then, you can come up for about 15 minutes in the morning. (That's big of her!!)

She then said that Sam wanted me to pay for him to have some TV and a telephone by his bed and she gave me the PatientLine number.

I rang up and paid £10 and they gave me a phone number so that I could phone him – at 39p per minute off peak. But every time I rang, nothing happened.

Preeti came over, bless her. We sat in the garden, sank a bottle of wine and had a takeaway. It was lovely to see her, but I was exhausted and she left at 10. *[Preeti is like my soul sister: we've been friends for over 25 years.]*

I tried to phone Sam again and an eastern European man answered who couldn't speak English. I rang back PatientLine and they said that the nurses must have given me the wrong bed number. I rang back the nurses' station and they said Sam was in Bed 3. I rang PatientLine and a different man said that I should never have been allowed to pay from a phone that wasn't one of theirs as they had no way of knowing if it was the right number. I told him that my husband had no money on him. I then rang back the ward and spoke to the nurse again.

Nurse: We have nothing to do with the phones.

Me: I know that, but I want to know how I can get hold of my husband.

Nurse: We can't get involved with the telephones at the bedside.

Me: I just want to know how I can speak to my husband.

Nurse: The telephone service has nothing to do with the nursing staff.

Me – now totally exasperated: I know that but I've been up since half past four, we've paid £16 in the car park and now I've paid £10 for my husband to have a phone so that I can speak to him after his operation and it doesn't work. All I want to know is how I can get hold of him and speak to him.

She put the phone down. About 2 minutes later Sam rang on a mobile.

Sam: Why are you having a go at the nurses?

Me: I'm not. (OK – well maybe I was a bit.)

Sam: The nurse has just come to me distraught because you've been having a go at her. The last thing I need is you upsetting them when they're supposed to be looking after me.

Me: She was stonewalling me and I burst into tears. Why are you assuming it's my fault?

Sam: Well, she's letting me use her mobile to ring you because she said you were having a go.

Me: I just wanted to know how you were.

Sam: I'm fine.

Me: Good.

And that was our loving, post-operative phone call – cheers!

Saturday July 3rd

43 days since referral

32 days since consultation

I woke up at 6am – still exhausted. Apart from all the physical exhaustion, there was the emotional exhaustion, too. Plus, I'd been fielding calls and texts from Sam's family all day. I was so over-wound, I couldn't get to sleep until well past midnight. There's knackered and there's this.

I rang the ward and the nurse brought Sam to the phone, he asked me to bring his stuff up. I took it up at 8 and was allowed to stay until 8.30.

Back home I cleaned the house like a lunatic as well as doing the shopping and getting the car cleaned. I was tired but needed to be doing stuff. Gloria *[a counsellor from a specialist cancer counselling charity]* phoned and it was a relief to talk to her about what's going on and how difficult it is and how cross Sam gets. She said it's the hardest thing about being a carer and that's why they have their charity counselling service. I'm going to see her on Tuesday.

Eventually Sam rang and said he could come out at about 3pm. I went to collect him. He said that the nurse had forgotten to take out a cannula from his arm and was going to discharge him with it still in and another hadn't locked his drugs cabinet, so that the door had swung down and bashed him on the head – when he's not supposed to get any knocks because of his blood-thinners! Honest to God, these people beggar belief.

Monday July 5th

45 days since referral

34 days since consultation

We went to bed at about 8.30 and we were both asleep within about 15 minutes. But I had to go and sleep in the spare room – Sam was up and down and in and out of bed, dropping things on the floor, coughing and groaning. I am just desperate for a decent night's sleep.

Tuesday July 6th

46 days since referral

35 days since consultation

I woke up at 6.25 – the best night's sleep I've had for a long time. Sam was agitated from the minute he woke up. He was fretting about getting his dressing changed and saying that it wasn't good enough to expect him to wait till 4.45. I suggested that he go to the walk-in centre at Raphe's. He asked if I would drive him there. I agreed but said I'd need to be back by 10 as I'd got an appointment at 10.30 with my counsellor. Sam said that I hadn't told him – which I had, but he'd clearly forgotten. Then he said he was going to drive himself and off he went. I didn't know if he'd gone to the walk-in centre or the ward or the GP's – or just gone off for a drive!

So, I went to the counsellor on the bus. It's the woman called Gloria who phoned me up. She's very sweet but it was more like a chatting session than counselling. She said how angry and frightened Sam must be, which I know, and said what a difficult life he'd had which, again, I know! She did say that Sam was also entitled to counselling as a patient. Yes please!

When I got home Sam was in bed. He told me that the doctor had shown him a large clot on the dressing and had redressed it with a smaller dressing, which is already showing signs of seepage. He'd said that there was no way Sam should have been put on Clexane before the biopsy had been done and there was no way he should have been told that he had Myeloma before any results were through. He apologised for Sam's treatment and said he'd had a rough deal. He also said that Sam should rest and not use his left arm or shoulder so that the wound was healed by Thursday for the chemo.

I said that I hoped he'd cancel football training tonight, but Sam said no, he needed to go and he'd be fine to drive. (Because of course, you don't use your left arm for driving!) He said he'd sit on the side-lines and let the kids have a kick around. I didn't say anything. I told him what Gloria had said about him also being eligible for free counselling, but he said he doesn't want to be talking about cancer all the time. Join the club, mate!

He went off in the car but came back with blood seeping through his dressing again. He admitted that he's terrified about what's happening.

Wednesday July 7th

47 days since referral

36 days since consultation

I was looking after Lily today so went off to collect her at 8am. I had planned to go to baby swimming with her, but Sam wants to go into work and do his boxing class so needs the car.

I had a lovely day with Lily – what an utter delight in the midst of all this crap. Sam came home and was very tired, so fell asleep on the settee while I took Lily back and then he went up to bed shortly after.

I had book group here tonight, which was lovely. Afterwards some of us were sitting in the garden and we got on to the subject of Sam and the impact his cancer was having on my writing and our life in general. Una started telling me that I should go back to teaching if we needed the money. I said that:

a) I was 57 and had been out of teaching for 10 years and the whole curriculum and education system had changed in that time,

b) I'd hated the job even when I was doing it, so why would I want to go back into it? And,

c) How could I hold down a full time job at the moment? A lot of people have to take time off work to care for partners with cancer, so who in their right mind would employ me?

Then she then suggested I do bar work. I don't even know how to pull a pint! And, again, I'm 57! She then said I was being negative. I pointed out that there was a reality she wasn't looking at. It got quite heated and I just couldn't handle it. I burst into tears. I wanted to scream: I ain't bust so don't try to fucking fix me!

Sam's chemo starts tomorrow so hopefully things will improve. We'll see!

Part 2

Treatment

July 2010 – December 2010

Thurs July 8th

47 days since referral

36 days since consultation

Round 1 of chemo – at long last!

I took Sam to the Medical Day Centre at 9am for his chemo. He said he didn't want me to stay with him. Other people were sitting around on drips with family or friends next to them, but Sam wants to do this on his own, so that's fine by me. Well, it's not really but what can I do? I went off to the lake feeling very alone and sad. I can't focus on anything to do with writing, so don't know what my purpose is in life. Am I just a carer now? What sort of a job is that anyway? Where's the JD? And I know I'd never fulfil the criteria on a person spec.

1) Must be able to stand the sight of blood – NO!

2) Must have infinite patience – NO!

3) Must be willing and able to go without sleep for days on end – NO! NO! NO!

I went to collect Sam at 5.30. He'd been on the drip since 11am and came home with loads of tablets – 22 a day for the next 3 days and then 4 a day from then onwards. The nurse took out his stitches but said his wound was still bleeding slightly. She put suture strips over it and told him to come back on Monday.

Friday July 9th

Chemo +1

Sam insisted that he was well enough to go to work today - less than 24 hours after his first chemo! Unbelievable! He drove himself to a course on Child Protection then came home at 5pm saying he'd been shaking and couldn't focus. And he's surprised? But, I thought, at least there's no sign of blood on his dressing. Famous last words — he started dancing vigorously round the sitting room like a loony and then ran up the road to the ice cream van! And surprise, surprise - his wound started bleeding again! Jesus wept! Seriously?

Sunday July 11th

Chemo +3

We had a talk this morning. I told Sam that I understood that he was frightened and angry that this had happened and I could understand how frustrating it must be for someone as fit and active as he had been and as proud of his physical strength, to be so restricted. He said it was terrifying: he felt like he'd lost control of everything in his life, including his own body and he needed to keep working and keep coaching. He didn't want to just stay at home brooding: he had to do things. We just held each other.

Tuesday July 13th

Chemo +5

Sam insisted on cycling to work today, even though it was raining. He couldn't find his medication and we hunted for about 15 minutes with him getting stroppier and stroppier until he found it in the bottom of his work bag – which means that he didn't take last night's tablet. For crying out loud!

I went over to Raphe's and saw Claire. I told her how difficult Sam was being and how hard I was finding it dealing with his moods. She reiterated what Sam had said to me: that he's feeling as though he's lost control of his life and his body. She said they did have psychologists available, but Sam had to ask for one himself. I said that this morning there was a thing on the news that cancer patients were living longer these days and I'd thought, Dear God! I can't stand another 10 years of this. I felt so guilty, but Claire laughed and said it was funny and quite understandable!

I went to see Niamh this afternoon. She's now lost most of her hair but is quite happy in herself. Honest to God, if she can be so positive, why can't Sam? He went off to football training tonight and admitted that he'd played in defence! I know they're only young kids, but he really needs to let his wound heal before he starts running around. It's like he's in denial.

Wednesday July 14th

Chemo +6

Sam cycled to work again today and I had coffee with Liz who agrees that it's probably Sam's PTSD rearing its head again coupled with fear and anger. *[Sam was diagnosed with PTSD following the death of his eldest son, Frasier, as a baby.]* She's

49

also offered us her holiday house in Devon in August – which, if Sam is ok, will be lovely. But, if not... I'm not even going there.

Claire, the Macmillan nurse, rang at lunchtime. I told her that Gloria had been pretty rubbish as a counsellor, just talking about her own problems, so Claire suggested I speak to my GP and get an appointment for some NHS counselling. She says they're going to test Sam's blood again on Friday, when he goes in to have his dressing changed, to see how his kappa para-proteins are. He's so sick of blood tests, bless him, he says he feels like a pincushion.

I bought him a plastic box for putting his tablets in so that he doesn't get confused. In the evening I got the pill box and, together, we counted out all Sam's tablets. I'd wanted to get one that had days and times, so that there were 28 compartments, but could only get one that had 7, one for each day of the week. His tablets come in 3 different sizes so it should be fairly straight forward.

At bedtime I reminded Sam to have his last pill three times, but he didn't and fell asleep again without taking it. Hey ho!

Thursday July 15th

Chemo +7

This morning Sam got up and realised that he'd forgotten his last tablet yesterday. I told him to leave it and just take today's rather than double up.

Sam: Well, at least I've taken all of today's OK.

Me: Not all of them?

Sam: Yes.

Me: But, Hon, the little ones are supposed to be 3 times a day, not all in one go.

Sam: Shit! You're kidding! I've taken all of them. What does that mean? Have I overdosed?

Me: I don't know. I don't even know what they're for.

There was no leaflet in the box, so he rang the emergency out of hours service and they looked them up on the internet. Apparently, it's his anti-emetic and won't do any harm except that he might feel sick later in the day and his mouth will be very dry. So much for my good idea of buying the pill box to make it easier to remember!

And, today – for the first time in 8 weeks - I did some writing. It felt so good to be creative again.

Friday July 16th

Chemo +8

I woke up at 6am and Sam was downstairs – he said he'd been awake since 3.30. He says he's worried that he's forgetting lots of things. He left his bag at work yesterday and the secretary had stayed behind waiting for him to go back and pick it up. He's at the hospital again this afternoon to have his stitches out (again!!) so I suggested that he speak to them about the confusion and forgetfulness.

Sam phoned at 3.15 saying that he'd been to the unit to have his dressing changed and they'd sent him over to the Pharmacy, but the woman was refusing to dispense his prescription. She said that he didn't have his medical exemption card with him. He asked me to find it for him, which I did but, when I rang back with the number, I could hear her in the background saying that she had to actually see the card and couldn't take details over the phone. Bloody little jobs-worth! He was getting very angry and put the phone down.

I rang the pharmacy. The woman said that Sam had not told her that he was a cancer patient and had refused to give her the information which is why she couldn't dispense the medication. She said she had remained very calm, but he had got extremely agitated and she had had to call her colleague. Eventually, they established that he had cancer and were able to proceed. I said that he also had a condition that causes mental confusion and memory loss and why could she not have asked him why he was exempt? She said he had refused to tell her. That doesn't even make sense on any level. When Sam got back, he totally refuted what the pharmacist had said and wrote a letter of complaint to St Raphael's Complaints Department. We'll see what happens.

Monday July 19th

Chemo +11

Sam went off to work on his bike this morning as I had agreed to have Lily. I was running around doing shopping and tidying before I went over to pick her up from nursery. She is such a ray of sunshine in this quagmire of shit. I brought her home she helped me de-leaf the tomato plants and put the leaves in the big green bag. What a poppet.

Tuesday July 20th

Chemo +12

Amy and Lily are staying over at the moment. Amy and Sam both went off to work and I got Lily dressed and took her to the park and then into nursery at 11.30. Oh, how she cried when I said we were going to nursery. And again when I left her. It was heart-wrenching, but I told her that I'd be seeing her again tomorrow and she was placated.

I was supposed to have a meeting with a bookshop this afternoon about an author event, but I was exhausted so I cancelled. I just lay on the settee and rested for about an hour until Sam got home. He'd been to have his dressing changed at the unit and Homer Simpson told him that he's to have a heart X-ray. He said it was routine, but Sam is worried about what it means. He had more blood taken, yet no one ever seems to give him the results of all these dozens of tests. Or is it because he doesn't ask? Who knows?

Thursday July 22nd

Chemo +14 – halfway through the chemo month

Sam's wound was weeping this morning, so I changed the dressing for him. The nurse said that the other one should have been OK for a week, but it was oozing disgusting yellow stuff all down his chest - after just 2 days!

I went to the lido this morning, which was wonderful. Liz says that Sam's sleeplessness could be due to the steroids. She also said they cause aggression and mood swings – so, all in all, the bugger doesn't stand a chance with his PTSD, cancer related fear/loss of control, hyper viscosity and now the steroids. There's no wonder he's an emotional time-bomb!

Friday July 23rd

Chemo +15

I am absolutely shattered. Niamh and her sister Aoife came to lunch today, which was lovely, but I do just feel as though I need a week of total relaxation. Sam got home at 4.30 and was pleased to be on holiday for a week.

Saturday July 24th

Chemo +16

Sam's wound is weeping yellow stuff again, although he seems to think it's OK. I offered to change the dressing and he said perhaps later. Sam was saying how much he loved me and how nice it was to be getting on again and, I must admit, I felt very loving towards him. Fingers crossed it continues.

Sam collected Myles for his week's holiday with us.

Sunday July 25th

Chemo +17

Sam woke up at 4.30 and then got up and began tidying the house. As long as he uses these steroids to do housework and other productive things, long may they last!

Monday July 26th

Chemo +18

Sam did his catheter this morning and said, "I feel like a walking hospital with my catheters, my syringes, my tablets, my dressings and everything else I have to do. I'm more like an eighty year old than a 46 year old." Felt very sad for him. *[Sam had a collapsed urethra some years ago as a result of having so many operations as a child in Great Ormond Street and has to self-catheterise twice a week.]*

Thursday July 29th

Chemo +21

This evening I had a meal with my book group friends. Halfway through I got a text from Sam thanking me for being such a support and inspiration since his cancer had been diagnosed. A good day, all round.

Friday July 30th

Chemo +22

In the afternoon we took Myles into town. We watched some street performers and Sam was invited to join in with one. He absolutely glowed and was clearly in his element performing in front of the crowd again. *[In his youth, Sam used to perform doing street dance, juggling and balancing.]* Myles enjoyed watching him but when the next act came on, he was bored and Sam got irritated with him. He loves Myles to pieces and would never normally get annoyed with him. It all got a bit tense and I felt upset for Myles who doesn't have a clue what's going on with Sam. On the way home he kept saying, "I lub

Dad." But Sam was telling him off all the time. This is not Sam at all – he adores Myles and will put his life on the line for him, so this is definitely not normal behaviour. And poor Myles was very confused. I feel so, so sad. I know he's ill and I know all the myriad reasons why he's like this, but it doesn't make it any easier to live with!

Saturday July 31st

Chemo +23

I went over to the lake in the car this morning and as I was driving, I made sure the windows were up and screamed my lungs out to vent my frustration. Felt much better afterwards. When I got home, I was cleaning out the freezer and Sam came and put his arms round me and gave me a big hug and a kiss. I really wanted to reciprocate but I couldn't: I'm so on edge all the time waiting for his next mood swing. When it was time for Myles to go home, I gave him a big hug and he said, "Lub you, Tate." Which reduced me to tears.

Sunday August 1st

Chemo +24

Woke up feeling very sad and low. I went over to the lake in the car but didn't even want to get out and sit by the water. I just sat there crying in the car park. I went through a mental list of people I might talk to, but I feel so desolate about how difficult things are at the moment I don't want to burden any of my friends.

I drove over to Amy's, but they were all in the park, so I went over there and met up with them. I told Amy what was going on and I cried on her shoulder - in the middle of the park: just standing there sobbing in public. I feel so miserable.

Monday August 2nd

Chemo +25

I changed the dressing on Sam's neck – it's still open about 1cm x 1cm and very red in the centre and the old dressing stank. It's almost 6 weeks since his biopsy and it's still not healed.

Tuesday August 3rd

Chemo +26

Sam is on a day trip today with the low-income families from work, so I made him a packed lunch. He said he needed to leave the house by 8.30 but I'd just got to the lake when my phone rang: he couldn't find his keys. *[Sam's memory was so poor that he was losing his keys, phone or wallet almost daily. He was also leaving his keys in the outside of the door as well as his car keys in the ignition probably about once a week.]* I said I'd come straight back but we needed to talk about how to resolve his memory difficulties. OMG! Wrong thing to say!

I went up to town to meet Penny for lunch. I'd been looking forward to seeing her and just letting off a bit of steam, but she was incredibly judgemental saying, "So how long are you going to put up with this, Kate?"

I said, "What do you mean how long am I going to put up with it? He's got cancer!"

To which she replied, "That's not your problem."

Actually, Penny, it is!

Thursday August 5th

Chemo +28

Sam seemed in a good mood this morning. He was laughing and cracking jokes. He has his blood tests this morning and he's seeing the doctor but then has to go into work for their Sports Day.

I cycled over to join him at the unit but, on the way in, I bumped into Homer Simpson. I asked if I could talk to him and he (reluctantly) agreed. He said Claire had spoken to him and he had heard what was going on but what Sam was exhibiting was quite normal for cancer patients. They exhibited one of 3 things:

1. They become withdrawn, refusing to speak or communicate,
2. They become very passive just doing whatever anyone said, or
3. They become aggressive and angry.

He said Sam presented as very calm on the outside, but he suspected that he was putting all his energy into going to work and carrying on as normal and avoiding addressing his illness.

Homer Simpson: He never asks questions: you do, but he doesn't and, until he does, I cannot answer them. And, if he wants to be left alone, then I would advise you to leave him alone.

(So that's me told then!)

Me: I am quite happy to leave him alone but what I am not happy to do is to put up with his very challenging behaviour, doctor. Sam is being very difficult with both me and his disabled son and that is not acceptable. I've even wondered if there is anything physiological going on in his brain to account for it.

Homer Simpson: Of course, there is. Everyone with cancer has something physiological going on in their brain.

I consider my wrists well and truly slapped!

Later Sam phoned and said that he had spoken to Claire and the doctor, and he'd told them that he was depressed and not sleeping and had been taking it out on me. They'd suggested a sleeping tablet that also contained Serotonin to help with his depression and he's also been referred to a psychiatrist to see if there's something underlying his anger.

Am feeling pretty hacked off at the moment what with Homer Simpson (he who couldn't even recognise a haematoma when it was practically squirting blood in his face!) minimising what was going on and putting me in my place and Penny being a judgemental bitch. I'm feeling very alone. Who's there for me? Or is it just me being weak and not handling it well? Feeling very sad – just for a change.

Friday August 6th

Round 2 of chemo

This morning I went over to the lake and had the most amazing meditation. I felt quite overwhelmed and got an enormous sense of gratitude for being given this opportunity to learn about myself and my authority - and my shadow side. It was very moving.

When I got back, I drove Sam to his chemo and then went on to do the shopping. I'd no sooner got home than Sam phoned and said that he'd forgotten to take any packed lunch, could I make him some sandwiches and take them to him? *[They did provide patients with one round of sandwiches and a yoghurt or piece of fruit, but Sam has always had a healthy appetite.]* I made him a sandwich and took it up with some wine gums and chocolate. I cycled over there feeling very loving and grateful to be doing something to support him but, when I got there, he was very frosty again and I came out feeling pissed off – so what's new? But I cycled over to the lake – twice in a day - and sat and did another meditation and got in touch with who I am and what I want and felt much more positive again. Let's hope things are OK when I go and get him tonight.

When Sam was finished, I drove over to collect him but he said that the pharmacy had run out of Fludarabine *[one of his chemo drugs]* and wouldn't have any more for 10 days! He has to ring up at 10am on Monday August 16th to see if they were in yet. I could not believe that a teaching hospital with a specialist cancer unit could run out of one of the main chemo drugs!

Me: OK, but we're going on holiday on 16th. *[Taking up Liz's offer of their house in Devon.]*

Sam: Well, we'll have to set off later after lunch then.

Me: (Feeling a bit niggled.) It's a 6 – 7 hour drive. I was hoping to leave early.

Sam: Well, what do you expect me to do about it? I'm only telling you what they told me. (Ouch!)

I thought it best to leave the subject, but I cannot believe that they've run out of his chemo drug.

Later I was looking through Sam's blue chemo book (something he's not let me do before) and I noticed that his diagnosis is down as CLL (Chronic Lymphocytic Leukaemia) and not Non-Hodgkin's Lymphoma. But when I asked Sam about the discrepancy, he started to get agitated again so I left it.

I did check the leaflet on the sleeping tablets they've given him and my heart sank when it said, 'Possible side effects include: irritability, aggression and depression.' Like we haven't got enough of those already!

Saturday August 7th

Chemo +1

We both woke up at 5.30 and Sam was like a furnace. I took his temperature and it was 38.2o the temperature at which chemo patients are supposed to phone the hospital but Sam refused. I told him that I'd take it every hour and if it didn't go down, he'd have to ring them and not go to the open day at work. Very slowly it did come down to 37.4 – which is still high!

I went over to the lake but, when I got back, Sam was staggering around the sitting room holding his right side and groaning in pain. He said his abdomen kept going into spasm. When I felt it, there was a hard lump just below his rib cage on the right where his liver is. I got him to lie down on the settee and gave him some Reiki. I could feel `fizzing' and rumblings under my hands and this solid lump. I said I thought it might be the chemo working on the lymphomas in his liver and, unless it got much worse, we'd work on that theory. He then began to cry out in pain as his fingers kept going into spasm too and then the muscles in his cheeks kept doing it as well. We're assuming that it's the chemo, but I was not happy about him going in to work today - but he was adamant.

Niamh has been in Perry's for a week now with a temperature and chest infection and I said I'd visit her today but, when I came to leave, Sam couldn't find his keys - again! We had the whole palaver of turning the house upside down looking for them. In the end I got out the spare set I'd had cut yesterday and told him to take them instead.

I went to see Niamh. She was asking about the young woman across the road who, aged 31, had found a lump in her breast when she was pregnant with her second child. She died 6 weeks ago when the baby was 2 months old, but I'd avoided telling Niamh until she asked. Niamh looked as though she was going to cry and just said, "Hold me, please."

What is it with this bloody disease? I'd had virtually no experience of it until Niamh got it 18 months ago and now, just about every other person I come across has it in one form or another. Slight exaggeration, but it seems like it sometimes.

When Sam got home from work his temperature was back up to 38.3. I told him he needed to speak to the on-call haematologist. He argued and protested until about 6 o'clock when he did finally ring. The on-call haematologist spoke to him and told him to come up to A&E and they'd be expecting him.

But then Aaron came round at 6 and they had pizza! No sense of urgency at all. At 6.40, we took Aaron home and then went to Raphe's. Sam registered and was sent straight through to A&E where he was told they'd be waiting for him. A nurse did his obs and said his temperature was still high. She gave him 2 Paracetamol and said the medics would be through to see him soon. Two hours later no one had arrived, so I went to the nurses' station where loads of nurses and doctors were milling around chatting. I asked a nurse when someone would come but she turned her back on me. Another nurse said that the shift was just changing so they'd be some time. I went back and told Sam, so he got dressed. He said, "If I stay here, I'm going to lose it." So we left. *[Every visit to A&E is traumatic for Sam as that's where his son, Frasier, was pronounced dead after failed efforts to resuscitate him.]*

When we got home, I rang Raphe's again and asked to speak to the on-call haematologist but the telephone operator said they'd all gone home at 4.30. I said that was impossible as my husband had spoken to one at 6pm and she said, "No, he can't have done, not at this hospital." She then put me through to

A&E. I went through the whole thing to a man who said, "Two hours is nothing. You expect to wait longer than that in A&E."

Me: My husband is a cancer patient with a high temperature and it's taken me all day to persuade him to even go to hospital. He was told that a doctor would be waiting for him and we waited 2 hours with no sign of a doctor and just 2 Paracetamol which I could've given him at home.

Man: There's been a lot of emergencies tonight and if your husband went through triage, he can't have been judged an emergency.

Great! What are the chances of Sam going to hospital again if he's got a temperature? Nil, I would imagine. I wish to God, he'd opted for Perry's instead of that shithole! There's no wonder it comes bottom of all the league tables. When I see the treatment Niamh gets now she's transferred to Perry's - it's a million time better.

Sunday August 8th

Chemo +2

Sam's temperature was down to 37 today but he said he would stay in bed as he was so stiff that he could hardly move his arms and legs. He said his whole back and right across his shoulders was rigid and painful. He slept most of the morning and came down at about 2pm but could hardly walk. He was shuffling like an old man. It's pitiful to watch.

Monday August 9th

Chemo +3

Sam's temperature was 36.4 this morning so he went into work. I told him to take the car and he said he was too weak to cycle anyway. At 1.30 I got a voicemail saying he'd gone up to the Day Unit because his temperature was back up and he'd had the rigors at work. He'd been shaking so much he was dropping things and knocking things over. He'd been going to come home and sleep it off but decided to go to hospital and get checked over instead. Thank God for some common sense at last!

I got a lift over there and he was already on a drip. His temperature was over 40! Claire said that he's got sepsis and, if he had come home to sleep it off, he might never have woken up! Jesus Christ, I went cold. She said to him that he was silly to have left A&E on Saturday and impressed upon him that he could die with a high temperature. She also said that it was a good job his Fludarabine (it's the manufacturer who'd run out of it and not the hospital apparently, so I'll take back my judgements on that score) had not been available as that really knocks the immune system for six and he could have died. I also asked about the CLL diagnosis in his chemo book, but she said that because his diagnosis has been 'a bit woolly' the nurse had probably assumed that because he was on FRC chemo that he had CLL but he definitely has a form of NHL as we were told.

They put him on intravenous antibiotics and he was taken up to Jupiter Ward – a geriatric ward for men with dementia! It's in the old part of the hospital and has no TV or bedside phones. As he's got sepsis, they said he really should have been in isolation in a side room, but it was the only bed available. It's not just the patients who are geriatric: it's the ward itself. It's like something out of Dickens! Awful.

Sam was sobbing and sobbing like a child. I held him and he was saying how sorry he was for his moods and he realised he'd been difficult and would I please forgive him. He said this was his Karma and he was terrified. I tried to calm him down, but it was very distressing to see him like that. I'm also freaked out by all the talk of sepsis and how he 'could die.' I'm also worried that, if he does die, we don't even have enough money to pay for a funeral. But I daren't let my mind go there. I'll cross that bridge if/when we get to it.

I left feeling numb and sad and totally spaced out. Alice came over after work and we stayed up talking till 1 am – which was lovely.

Tuesday August 10th

Chemo +4

Day 2 in hospital

Woke up at 6.15 and rang the ward. A nurse said that Sam's temperature had gone down slightly yesterday evening but then, during the night, it went even higher. Last night they'd taken him down for a chest X ray to try and see if he'd got a lung infection, but he said he got hardly any sleep because the old men were calling out and roaming around. They've got security guards patrolling the ward because some of them can be aggressive – just what he needs.

I bought him a portable DVD player because there's no TV on the ward and, when I got home, I rang Preeti. I told her what had been going on with Sam and how I was terrified with what was happening with his health but also pissed off about his behaviour: I wished I could be stronger and more understanding. She was amazingly non-judgemental (take note Penny!). She said that sometimes our minds go places that we don't want them to and it didn't make me wrong or a nasty person. I felt so much better.

Sam rang to say that the food was disgusting and would I make him some sandwiches and take them up along with a paper and a change of clothes. I went up to visit him at 2.30 when the ward opened. He looked much better than yesterday and his temperature was fairly stable at 36. He was very grateful for the DVD player and the DVDs - I'd taken all comedies - and had just started to eat his sandwiches when his brothers arrived, followed by Aaron, followed by his sisters. I just wanted some time alone with him – hey ho!

Sam rang in the evening and said he'd gone to the loo and the nurse had unplugged his cannula from his drip, but she hadn't capped it and it was spurting blood all over the floor and his clothes. He called for help, but she said, "You should have put pressure on it to stop it bleeding!"

Has she ever had a cannula in her hand? Does she know how painful they are?

Then the sister came over and told the nurse off for not capping it. She said, "Don't you realise how distressing this is for a patient?" Too bloody right!

I was exhausted and spent the evening fielding calls from his family again before crashing out at about 10.

Wednesday August 11th

Chemo +5

Day 3 in hospital

Another broken night last night. I kept waking up and thinking Sam had gone downstairs – totally forgot he was in hospital. He'd also had a broken night with other patients calling out all night long.

I was looking after Lily today, so I told Sam I'd be along to visit him in the evening. I'd go from 6 – 7.30. He sent a whole list of things for me to get him again. I had a lovely day with Lily then I drove her home and got back at 5.15, with just enough time to make Sam some pasta and put it in a wide necked thermos, gather up some more DVDs, his shaving stuff, ear plugs and eye mask, then I drove over to the lake where I parked (to save money) and walked down to the hospital.

As I arrived Sam's brothers were just leaving. They stopped and chatted for about 10 minutes and I was relieved that they were going so that I'd have some time with Sam on my own. But, when I got to his bed, Aaron was sitting there. He and Aaron were laughing and chatting and sharing jokes about Family Guy and The Simpsons that I was not a party to and, although I was pleased that he was enjoying some time with his son, I felt very much like a spare part. Then Sam said, "Will you record the football for me tonight? It starts at half past seven."

I said, "That's when visiting time finishes. You're booting me out early so that I can video the football?"

I tried to make a joke of it, but I was gutted. Although I suppose I shouldn't grumble because Sam seemed really happy. He said to me, "I've had a fantastic day today, seeing so many people. It's been great."

Thursday August 12th

Chemo +6

Day 4 in hospital

I rang Sam at 6.15am after another broken night – I had hoped that with Sam in hospital I might catch up on my sleep but it's just not happening. Sam had also had a dreadful night with 2 old men screaming and shouting and swearing all night from 2.30 onwards. In the end, almost everyone on the ward was shouting at them but the nurses didn't do anything.

Later I rang back to ask him to check with the doctors what medication he's had while he's been in there so that we know where we are with all his tablets at home. If they've been giving him his anti-gout and anti-emetics etc we don't want to double up. But he said he trusted them to be doing the right thing. Well, there's the difference, because I don't. I know I was a bit abrupt with him. I am so utterly exhausted. I drove over to the lake and screamed in the car all the way there till my voice has almost gone. I sat by the lake and sobbed. Luckily no one came onto the little promontory where I sit.

When I got home there was a text saying that the doctor said he'd been given Fludarabine and antibiotics! How can he have been given Fludarabine when there's supposed to be a world shortage?

Sam then phoned and said the pharmacist had been to see him and wanted to know if he'd got all his drugs there. I said, as far as I was aware he had. I'd gathered up everything I could find. She said she'd get his medication ready and have it up on the ward for him to be discharged this afternoon. Yay!

At 1.30 I rang to ask what was happening. I can't settle to anything in case I have to go up there to pick him up. Apparently, the doctor said they'd like him to stay in another night to have more blood tests, but Sam said he needed to get some sleep and also, he was worried about catching something. He said a friend was going to visit him at 2.30 and another after that so would I go up at 5 pm? I know he's pleased to see people but I'm beginning to feel like someone to be slotted in between other visitors. It's all self-pity on my part, I know that. Even so, I just wanted some time with him.

We waited and waited for Sam's medication to be brought up so that he could go home. A doctor came round and took some blood, but no medicines appeared. At 5.30 Sam got dressed but still no tablets and the pharmacy was closed, so the nurse gave him enough medication for tonight and tomorrow morning and told him he'd be phoned in the morning to go up and collect his prescription from the ward. But, when he asked for his medicines from home to be released from his locker, the nurse said they couldn't allow that as he didn't need them: if he needed them, the doctor on the ward would have written them up! Jesus wept!

Me: But the doctors on the Medical Day Unit wrote them up.

Nurse: Well, that's not up to us. We can only let him have what the doctor on the ward has written him and he clearly doesn't need these anymore. Do you have gout, Sam?

Sam: No.

Me: Gout is one of the long term side-effects of chemo and those tablets are to counteract both that and the sickness.

Nurse: Well, I don't know about that, so we'll have to speak to one of the doctors from the MDU in the morning and check up with them.

God preserve me – do none of these people have common sense? These were his medicines from home, prescribed by specialist doctors who know what they're doing (OK, so that's debateable) so why the fuck won't they release them? Give me strength!

We finally left at about 6pm without either his antibiotics (other than 2 doses) or his other medicines! Sam went straight up to bed and slept most of the evening. I woke him at 10 for his tablets. And again at 10.05; and again at 10.10 – until he finally took them at 10.15. Hallelujah!

We both went out like lights, but Sam woke up just before midnight gagging and saying he was going to be sick. He drank some water and stood by the loo for a while then came back to bed but said he felt very dizzy and nauseous. Probably because they haven't been giving him his bloody anti-emetics!

Friday August 13th

Chemo +7

I had my weigh-in at Weight Watchers and I'd lost 3 lbs, which was brilliant. Will have to step it up a bit though if I'm to lose another 2½ stones by December 11th when Tom gets married.

The hospital didn't ring, so Sam rang the MDU and no one from the ward had even contacted them, so they said they would ring the ward and sort out the medication situation. It got to 12.30 and still nothing, so I rang the ward.

Me: Hello, I'm the wife of Sam Edwards who was discharged yesterday and I was wondering if his medication is ready for collection yet?

Nurse: Hold on. (She went away for quite a while until I thought she'd left the phone off the hook) The Staff Nurse says you were told that you'd be telephoned when they're ready.

Me: Yes but...

She put the phone down on me.

I told Sam and he rang the pharmacy at Raphe's. The pharmacist said that they'd only just received the document from the ward. It was sent to them at 12.10 today – this is from 12 noon yesterday! She said she'd send it up to the ward, but Sam told her not to as they'd cocked up too much already. He said that I'd go up and collect it. She said that was highly irregular but if I asked for her by name and gave his date of birth, she'd make sure they were ready. When I got there the ward had also sent down his own tablets so we're back on track again.

I then had to go over to the MDU to pick up some mouthwash and Nystatin drops to prevent thrush (no doubt because of the antibiotics) which I did. But then the nurse said that the Fludarabine wouldn't be in until lunchtime on Monday. Really? So how come they've apparently given it to him on the ward? Plus, we're supposed to be going down to Devon on Monday. Who needs a holiday anyway? It's not like I'm totally knackered or anything!

When I got home Sam was groaning in pain. He said his abdomen was going into spasm again and his fingers were cramping up and he was getting pins and needles. I gave him all his stuff and he tottered into the bathroom to do his mouthwash, but he looked so dreadful – like an old man. I want to weep for him. He says he feels too weak and in too much pain to come downstairs – yet he's still insisting on doing his DJ gig on Sunday. I give up!

Sam's temperature dropped to 35 this afternoon and I was worried about him getting hypothermia, so I got him to put on more clothes. He was in a great deal of pain all day and didn't get out of bed. Homer Simpson rang in the afternoon and said not to worry about the Fludarabine on Monday – just go on holiday and they'll sort out his dosage when he gets back, even if he has to go down to 3 weekly cycles instead of 4 weekly. Yay!

Saturday August 14th

Chemo +8

Sam's temperature kept dipping down to 35o today, which was worrying. He did come down and wrapped himself in blankets on the settee and put his woolly hat on. In the end, he said he was too uncomfortable on the settee so went back to bed.

I went round to get the keys to the Devon house from Liz. At one point she was talking about her disabled father and said, "It makes you grateful for your freedom, doesn't it?" Then she paused and said, "Not that you've got any at the moment." I felt a wave of self-pity overwhelm me and almost burst into tears on the spot.

Sunday August 15th

Chemo +9

I cannot put into words how exhausted I feel – and I've got a 6 – 7 hour drive tomorrow. I pray to God I get some sleep tonight.

It's Amy's birthday today and I went to meet her, Chris and Lily for lunch while Sam did his DJ-ing at a centre for adults with learning difficulties. He is so stubborn! If prizes were given out for obstinacy, mules wouldn't get a look in! In the evening I suddenly came over with a dreadful sore throat and temperature. Great! That's all we need for Sam to catch something from me just as he's getting better.

Monday August 16th – Thursday August 19th

Our holiday in Devon.

I felt pretty grim with my cold so kept my distance from Sam. The drive was 6½ hours and I was exhausted by the time we got there. Obviously, I drove as Sam is as weak as a kitten but he was in good spirits and kept me company all the way there rather than being asleep. I had to unload the car as the cases were too heavy for him to lift, which must be difficult for him: his physical strength is so important for him. The view is magnificent from the cottage! Sam said he'd go and get fish and chips while I had a bath but there are so many steps into town, and they're so steep, that he was exhausted by the time he got back. We crashed out by 8.30 and slept like logs with the curtains open and all the lights flickering across Torbay. Wonderful!

Sam made breakfast but the house is on 3 floors with the kitchen in the basement, so he was knackered by the time he got up to the bedroom with it. Then, as he was in the bath, he washed under his arms and a whole load of hair came out in his hand. I'd noticed that his eyebrows appeared thinner but didn't want to say anything. He went very quiet – Homer Simpson had said that the chemo wouldn't affect his body hair – but then, Homer Simpson couldn't recognise a haematoma when it was staring him in the face!

Sam is in constant pain in all his joints and muscles and can hardly carry any weight. I know he was warned about all this but it's one thing to know something's going to happen and another to be faced with the actuality. He went very quiet and, when I went to cuddle him, he just put his head on my shoulder as if to cry, although he didn't actually shed any tears.

We decided to go down to the town and have lunch, but the walk really took it out of Sam. We sat on the harbour wall and I had a jacket potato and Sam had fish and chips again. Then he was exhausted so we went back to the house. In the afternoon, I read while Sam just went from one chair to another with the binoculars watching boats and people along the harbour. In the evening, we pulled out the bed settee and lay on that watching TV. Sam fell asleep, so I went up to bed at 10 and left him sleeping. He came up to bed in the night but didn't wake me up, thank goodness.

On the Wednesday we decided to go to Liz's beach hut. I went swimming in the sea which was amazing and Sam sat on a deckchair wrapped in a mountain of coats and blankets. There was a brief shower but his coat was waterproof, so he said he was fine to stay out while I swam in the rain – fabulous! It restores my soul to swim in the sea, especially when I can feel the rain on my head. Utter, utter bliss.

In the evening we went out for dinner to the restaurant where we went on our first visit there 5 years ago. We're now probably horribly overdrawn, but I'll sort that out later. When Sam looked at the menu there was nothing he fancied, so I called over the waitress. I said, "I'm sorry, we have a bit of a problem because my husband's on chemotherapy at the moment and it's affected his taste buds, is there any chance he could just have a piece of plain cod?" She came back and said yes that was fine, so he had grilled cod, new potatoes, steamed vegetables and a side salad. What a lovely evening. But 2 trips down the steps into town was a bit much for Sam and it took a long time to get home. When we did, we went straight up to bed. It's been a lovely visit but very short – I could've done with longer.

Friday August 20th

Chemo +14

I woke up exhausted, so Sam said he'd make breakfast, but the tray was too heavy for him to carry.

He rang the MDU and they told him to go over there at 2pm. I drove him and dropped him off. Of course, there's been a new rotation of doctors as it's August so he doesn't know some of them and one guy told him to go in next week for his next chemo instead of September. Sam said that it wasn't possible as he had his son next week and we were going away.

New doctor: Well, you didn't come in for your last lot so...

Sam: Hold on a minute! It wasn't that I didn't come in – you didn't have it in stock, so don't try to make out it was my fault that I didn't have it.

He said the doctor looked taken aback and walked off then another guy came and took over. The cheek of it! Anyway, he's booked in for the first week of September – I don't know how they're going to catch him up on the missed Fludarabine though and I don't know if the fact that it was missed out of the cocktail last time could account for his pain and lethargy this time round.

He rang me to collect him at 4.30 and said they'd done more blood tests but think that his weakness and pain are connected to the chemo – although his blood is slightly thick again, but nothing to worry about. He's to go back on Monday for more blood tests and he just started crying again. I feel so helpless. I held him and we both wept.

Saturday August 21st

Chemo +15

Sam decided to stay in bed for as long as possible today. Amy and Chris brought Lily over at about 10 and then went off to a wedding. She was absolutely no bother, but I was very aware that I was exhausted. After lunch I put her in the buggy and walked her down to the woods. She fell asleep and I parked her by the pond, put my jacket on the grass and lay down next to her. I didn't actually go to sleep, but the rest was wonderful. She woke up after about half an hour and we fed the ducks before coming back through the woods. Sam was still in bed when we got back, although he did get up at about 3.30. I gave Lily her tea then we took her in the car to pick up Myles at 6.30.

Monday August 23rd

Chemo +17

I made breakfast and then Sam said he was fine to drive himself to Raphe's this morning. He parked down the road and walked to the MDU. He said he took it slowly and managed it without being too out of breath and without sweating, which is a huge improvement. He got back at about 10.30 and said they'd taken more blood and would let him know the results this afternoon.

The doctor phoned at about 5.15 and said that his liver functions and kidneys were fine, which is a relief – although Sam hadn't realised they were checking those! There was no mention of his para-proteins though, but I suspect that if there'd been a problem, they'd have told him.

We had a quiet evening: Sam went to play on the PS with Myles but was too weak to get up. He had to shuffle his way to the front of the settee and then, with my arms under his arm pits, I had to haul him to his feet and steady him before he could totter across the room. I moved Myles to the stool so that Sam could sit on the chair. As they were playing, Sam's hands were so painful that he could hardly press the buttons on the console, but Myles thought it was a joke and started copying him. It hurts to see him like this – and Myles not knowing what's happening and not comprehending the severity of the situation. I could weep. And do - frequently!

Tuesday August 24th

Chemo +18

As we were driving down the road, Niamh was being picked up by the Perry's transport to go to the hospital. I pulled up and Sam wound down his window, but he didn't recognise her. She is so tiny now – probably no taller than 4'6" or 4'7" and she had a sun hat pulled right down low to cover her almost non-existent hair. Her cheeks are also sunken and her skin, sallow. Sam was shocked at the decline in her since he last saw her before Easter. He'd been saying that he wanted to go round and talk to her as he thought it might help him to come to terms with his condition, but her appearance upset him so much that he now says he doesn't want to.

Saturday August 28th

Chemo +22

There was a letter from Raphe's this morning in response to Sam's letter of complaint about the pharmacist. It was apologising for Sam's treatment in the pharmacy on July 16th and said that the matter had been fully investigated: the whole team has had training on the matter and the woman in question was going on a customer service course. Yay!

In the afternoon I went to see Niamh who's looking well – relatively speaking. Having witnessed her gradual decline, I'm used to it and she's always so bright and happy, she's great to be around. I know it had come as a huge shock to Sam to see her as she is now but let's not forget, three months ago, no one thought she'd even be here at the end of August. So, there's a lot to be thankful for. She's even talking about going to Ireland when she finishes her current chemo run at the end of October.

At 5.30 I started to pack Myles's bag to go home but, as I bent down to pick up something from the side of his bed, there was one of Sam's Clexane syringes on the floor. I went cold. I took it down to Sam immediately and he was also shocked. He says that sometimes he lies on the little bed to do his injection and must have dozed off or forgotten about it. I have offered to do his injections for him, but he is adamant that he wants to do them himself. It's something that he can be in control of – even though, at the moment his hands are too painful to push in the plunger and it can take him several attempts. But his level of consciousness about disposing of them afterwards is frightening. This must be the 3rd or 4th time I've found needles lying around the house – in our bedroom and even downstairs in the sitting room. He's got a special sharps box in the bathroom, but he forgets to use it. It's very worrying. I don't know what to do about it. Niamh was saying today that a community nurse comes to do her white blood cell injections and I've even suggested to Sam that he applies for one, but he won't.

Sunday August 29th

Chemo +23

Sam is very cold most of the time, even though I've put the heating on – in August! He wraps himself in blankets and wears his woolly hat in the house. In the evening he brought down the duvet and curled up under that. His hands were freezing and he's getting terrible shooting pains down his right arm and hand.

Monday August 30th

Chemo +24

Sam is wracked with pain in his hand and arm and often screams out with it. It's very distressing. He's also lost lots more weight and his trousers now regularly fall down over his bum and hips and sometimes even down to his knees and ankles. I changed the dressing on the wound on his neck again, but it's still not healed. That's 10 weeks now!

Tuesday August 31st

Chemo +25

Back to some sort of normal routine today. I went swimming this morning, which was bliss and Sam went into work. He can't cycle but he said his hands were OK to drive – we're going to investigate a route by public transport in case they get so bad that he can't hold the steering wheel.

But, tonight, coming home from work, Sam witnessed an articulated lorry running over a young woman. He was in shock and had obviously been crying. He said 6 of the 10 wheels had gone right over her and she was lying in the road with her friend screaming hysterically. The lorry then had to carry on driving because some of the wheels were on top of her. Horrendous!

What is the Universe playing at, putting him in a place to witness that when he's got cancer and is constantly thinking about death anyway? We had some time to talk about it and then I gave him Reiki and he slept for about an hour listening to Louise Hay – which is so good.

Wednesday September 1st

Chemo +26

Penny rang this morning and we had a conversation in which she denied saying that it wasn't my problem that Sam had cancer. Then she told me that she found me 'devious' for not having told her I was upset at the time! WTF! I need friends like that like I need a bloody neutron bomb between my eyes.

Thursday September 2nd

Round 3 of chemo

I dropped Sam off at 10.10. He's very anxious about this round of chemo as he's been in so much pain after the last lot and is dreading the fact that it might have a cumulative effect.

I had lunch with Niamh today then I went to collect Sam. He was tired but OK. He said that no doctor went near him today; in fact, the young doctor that he'd told off for insinuating that he had missed his chemo, kept a noticeably wide berth! The Leprechaun and Homer Simpson were both there but neither went over to him and he said he felt as though he didn't really matter and no one gave a toss about him.

Friday September 3rd

Chemo +1

I said I was going to go for a short jog this morning and Sam said he wanted to go with me. The day after chemo! It was just round the block and he did jog all the way - although mine was more of a power walk as my knee was playing up. Then we had a lovely breakfast sitting on the patio in the warm September sun – it was wonderful.

After my weigh in at Weight Watchers (a gain of 2½ lbs!!!) I got home to find that Sam had mowed the lawn and started on the ironing. I told him not to overdo it, but he wanted to come with me to order his birthday cake for next week. After ordering the cake we did some shopping but, halfway round the aisles, he doubled up clutching his chest. He said he's getting the same spasms as he gets in his hands but now in his chest and abdomen. I told him to go and sit in the car, but he refused – he says he's scared that he might die on his own. I asked if he wanted us to go home but he said the pain was subsiding and to carry on. It's like living on a knife edge.

As I looked at the photos of our holiday in Devon, I thought: is this going to be our last holiday together? And, doing the shopping, my mind was thinking, Will doing the shopping be the last thing he does? I feel very sad most of the time and every now and then it bubbles up to the surface. I was fighting back the tears all the way round Sainsbury's.

When we'd unpacked the shopping, he went up to bed to lie down and I'm here feeling flat and low and miserable again and the sun is shining and the weather is mellow and I want to be happy but it seems like an impossible dream at the moment.

Sam stayed in bed most of the afternoon. He's having spasms in his chest and liver, as well as both hands – and in particular his right arm. He dozed on and off and came down later for me to give him Reiki which I did. I could feel lots of activity going on in his head, chest and liver, although not so much in his arms.

During dinner Sam was finding it increasingly difficult to move his arms and said his head was pounding again. I took his temperature and it was 37.8! Oh my God, I can't believe it. Only .2o away from the danger mark and I've had 2 glasses of wine, so won't even be able to drive him to A&E if it goes any higher.

Later

I walked up to the High Street and got some money out of the cash point in case we needed to take a taxi to Raphe's. He was in excruciating pain with his hands, arms, neck and liver all going into spasm. It was terrifying because his right arm became immoveable and he thought he'd had a stroke and was paralysed. His temperature went up to 37.9 so I sponged him down with a damp flannel and put the fan on him and, thank God, it started to go down. This is every time he's had chemo, his temperature has shot up. Don't know whether it's infection or just a reaction to the drugs. Am exhausted.

Saturday September 4th

Chemo +2

Our 6th wedding anniversary.

Sam's temperature was down to 36.4 this morning, phew! Although I had another very bad night, wandering round the house from 1am till 3. I listened to my iPod and meditated and made warm drinks and counted sheep – I am knackered again - or still - or just plain always.

Sam stayed in bed till noon, then we wandered, very slowly, up the High Street to the deli and had some lunch. We are absolutely flat broke – with less than £200 to last us till the end of the month and 4 birthdays coming up. But I thought, sod it! You have to seize the moment and we don't even know if he'll still be here for our 7th anniversary, so let's push the boat out. It cost £12, which was not the end of the world and it was lovely to sit in the sunshine and relax.

When we got back, he went straight back to bed while I did the ironing - for 3 hours! And it's still not finished. It's household things like that that mount up and get to me. There are dust balls like tumbleweed under the bed - and in the sitting room - but I have neither the energy nor the time to give the house a thorough clean. I go over the surfaces that other people see. God! I wish we could afford a cleaner – but that's not going to happen!

Sam came down at about 5.30 and we had a candle-lit dinner. During dinner I got very upset seeing Sam in such pain. Just trying to reach out to pick up his drink or stretch across the table to take my hand causes him to cry out. Our financial situation is also a great cause for concern for me. Sam doesn't seem to understand that I feel utterly useless for not earning anything at the moment, yet I don't know what I can do. I can't go back to teaching – who would want me – plus I hated it even when I was up to date with educational policies. I've got 4 projects out with publishers and/or TV companies yet no one's biting at the moment. And I haven't got a single schools' visit in the diary. A sign of the recession or a sign that I'm past it? I've thought of other jobs but with Sam ill and me needing to take time off every now and then to look after him, what could I do and who would employ me?

Sunday September 5th

Chemo +3

A whole 8 hours sleep - wonderful! I woke up at 6am feeling refreshed but soon started to think about money and became very tearful again. The whole conundrum of me feeling guilty for not contributing yet believing that I'm unemployable goes round and round and I get very distressed about it. Sam talks about taking on another job but that just compounds my guilt. I know I do the housework and look after Sam and all that `female' stuff but I really don't want to be a housewife and carer. I WANT TO BE A WRITER! I want to be creative. *[With the wisdom of hindsight, I now realise that, although I moaned constantly about NOT writing, I was writing – almost every day. It was writing down my thoughts and feelings that got me through.]* Sam really, really doesn't seem to understand that it's not just about him taking on more work and earning more money – it's about ME and MY sense of self-worth and MY creativity and MY contribution. I went over to the lake and had a little weep and realised it's Sunday, so not a thing I can do about it anyway. So that was a waste of energy.

I went to pick up Amy and Lily to go to the Country Fair up the road. Sam stayed in bed all day. It would have been a great day out except that Lily hated all the: dogs, horses, donkeys, tractors and musicians! So, we came back here and had a glass of wine!

Sam is in so much pain – down both arms and shooting into his hands and fingers. I went up to see him and suggest that he comes downstairs for a while, but he was crying. He said he'd been crying on and off all day. I held him and we both wept. I feel so helpless seeing him so helpless. I suggested that he ring the on-call doctor and ask about painkillers. He came down but I had to help him put on his pyjamas as he can hardly move his fingers and his hands are semi clenched all the time and held across his chest, as though he has some sort of disability.

He rang Raphe's and got through to Homer Simpson who said that there is no way he should be like this on the chemo that he's on. (Sam has twice told the new junior doctor about the pain in his hands and has been dismissed both times and told that it's normal.) Homer Simpson said it was OK to take Tramadol and he would speak to Head Honcho tomorrow about Sam's condition. Sam took 1 Tramadol, but it made little difference and at 8 o'clock he said he wanted to go back to bed because at least if he's asleep he can't feel any pain. He cried again and we just held each other on the settee and wept together. It all seems so hopeless.

Tom rang earlier and has been talking about his wedding, yet I find it hard to drum up enthusiasm when this is going on and we don't even know if Sam will be well enough to go. I'm so happy that he's getting married but I want to turn back the clock and make all this wretched cancer go away. I want Sam to be well and us to be happy and me to be writing and everything as it was. I know no one knows what the future holds but ours seems even more uncertain. Sam doesn't fit any recognisable pattern with either his symptoms or how he's reacting to the chemo. Plus, he said today that he has only about 70% confidence in Raphe's – and, if I'm being honest, I have even less. I do so wish he'd gone to Perry's – or anywhere but St Bloody Raphael's!

Monday September 6th

Chemo +4

This morning I found Sam's Fludarabine from yesterday! He hadn't taken his bloody chemo – again! Honestly, it is so frustrating. When I got back from the fair, I asked him if he'd taken his tablets and he said, yes! I don't know what effect it will have that he forgot them.

Sam went to the MDU on the way home from work. He's just rung – they're referring him to a neurologist for the fizzing and shooting pains in his hands and arms as they say it's not the chemo. Oh my God! Not something else? I can't bear it.

Tuesday September 7th

Chemo +5

Sam said he was going to cycle in again today but, just as he was getting dressed, he threw up violently. I suggested he ring the MDU and ask whether to take his tablets again as he'd only just taken them when he was sick. They said to leave it as he's no idea how much had been ingested.

He went back to bed and kept feeling nauseous on and off all day. I found a letter on the table which was a referral letter stating the reason for referral was 'Immunoglobulin-related neuropathy' so at least I know now: it's related to the para-proteins in his blood and not the chemo.

I had an assessment with a new NHS counsellor at 11 this morning. After I'd been talking to her for a while she said, "Do you realise you've been talking to me for over 40 minutes and you haven't told me a thing about yourself? You've told me all about your husband and his condition but nothing about you." I told her that was the problem: I'd lost all sense of me and who I am and my job and MY life. I've become swamped with all Sam's issues and his cancer. I cried and cried and cried. She said, "What is it you want from us?"

Me: I haven't a clue. I want my life back.

Counsellor: It looks to me as though you need support to find yourself again. (Understatement of the decade!)

When I got home, Sam was still in bed and he asked me how it had gone but when I said I didn't want to talk about it, he got upset and said I was shutting him out. I ended up crying again and came downstairs and just sobbed and sobbed. How can I tell him that his illness is ruining my life? I can't. In the end, I went back up and tried to explain how desperate I feel and how frustrated. I think he understood a bit better.

He looked dreadful today – very ill. He's now starting to look like someone with cancer, thin and pale and drawn and his trousers hang off his bum like an elephant's skin.

Wednesday September 8th

Chemo +6

I made Lily a card for CBeebies birthday shout-out and posted it off today. I do hope they read it out on her birthday. Then I went over to the lake and had a little cry again. I don't know if it's just that I have no moral fibre or what? Do other people find it so difficult? I don't remember feeling this depressed when Mum and Dad and Max *[my late brother]* were all ill and dying – and I had 3 young children to look after. But I managed and, in fact, from what I remember, I handled the whole appalling business brilliantly – and it went on for years and years with me dashing up and down to Yorkshire and still having time for my own family down here. I do remember being ill quite a lot though, and I think having the children around me really helped.

The woman from the NHS Counselling Service phoned and said that, after careful consideration, she thinks I'd benefit from being part of a `carers group' rather than 1:1 counselling as this is a long term thing. I felt so upset and angry – she said I would get support to be ME and I AM NOT JUST A CARER – I AM A WOMAN AND A HUMAN BEING AND A WRITER AND I WANT SUPPORT TO BE THE PERSON I USED TO BE. I used to write comedy books for crying out loud! I was organised and capable and creative. I WAS NEVER CUT OUT FOR NURSING OR CARING AND IF I WAS I'D HAVE CHOSEN NURSING AS A CAREER! There!

Sam got home at 5 and looked awful. He slumped on the settee but is still in so much pain. We decided to go to bed early but he couldn't get up again. I had to stand in front of him and put my arms under his arms and then, after three, heave him to his feet. It took three goes and, when he did get to his feet, we just held each other and wept into each other's shoulders. He said he just wants a new body. He doesn't know how much more he can take.

Thursday September 9th

Chemo +7

Sam still looks very drawn and ill and he's hunched over and clearly not well. He was supposed to be referred to the psychological service over a month ago, but we've heard nothing – and he was supposed to have a heart X-ray over a month ago, but again nothing. I don't know what's going on. Perhaps I should ring Head Honcho's secretary again. Sam keeps telling me I'm taking over and it's his life and his illness, but he doesn't follow things up, he forgets things and gets muddled. Surely one of us has to be on the ball?

In the end I emailed Claire and told her that I had no point of reference as to what was normal for Sam's condition and reading all the leaflets in the world could not have prepared me for this. I also asked her to follow up the psychologist, X-ray and neurologist appointments as I understood that doctors were only human and forgot things.

I started filling in the form to apply for a grant from a charity that supports authors. I feel dreadful writing to them, but I can't think of any other way to make ends meet at the moment. We could downsize of course, but just the thought of going through all the turmoil of selling and packing up and moving makes me feel ill.

Friday September 10th

Chemo +8

I went off to the lake to have a cry – just for a change! Honestly, it used to be a place of peace and serenity for me: a place where I meditated and sent healing around the world but now it's turned into a place where I go to sit and weep. Dog walkers and fishermen must think that's all I do – come to think of it, at the moment it is just about all I do.

Saturday September 11th

Chemo +9

Sam's birthday celebration tonight. We went over to a Chinese restaurant and met up with all his brothers and sisters. I was not looking forward to it at all. I don't like Chinese food and I felt very low and tired - I just wanted to slump in front of the TV then go to bed but, in fact it turned out to be a really good evening. There was lots of stir-fried vegetables and fresh fruit salad – both of which I love. And it was so nice to see all Sam's family together.

Monday September 13th – Sam's 47th birthday.

Chemo +11

I made Sam a huge veggie fry-up for breakfast and took it up on a tray with all his cards.

Then he had to go into work, which was a shame. He had to do rhyme time but, when he sat down, he said to the kids, "Today is a very special day. Do you know what day it is today?" When they shook their heads he said, "It's Christmas Day!" He meant it was his birthday of course but he said Christmas instead. The poor children were totally bewildered. Word confusions like that happen all the time and it worries me that there's some permanent brain problem. Hopefully, he'll see the neurologist soon.

I went over to the lake and had a much better morning. The party on Saturday really lifted my spirits and I do feel much better. Sam finished work at lunchtime and we went to the pictures in the afternoon, then I cooked us a candle-lit dinner. It was lovely.

Tuesday September 14th

Chemo +12

Sam rang to say that he'd just spoken to Homer Simpson who said that he had made a referral to a neurologist but hadn't heard anything back yet, so there was nothing more he could do. Follow it up perhaps? Jesus wept!

Claire the Macmillan nurse phoned. She said that Sam could apply for Disability Living Allowance provided that he no longer does his sport. I told her that he couldn't cycle any longer, but he had tried to jog a couple of weeks ago but had been ill afterwards. She thinks I could be entitled to Carers' Allowance too. She said that the neurologist has been contacted and asked if he'll see Sam on the MDU to expedite his consultation. I asked about the psychiatrist, but she said that Homer Simpson had said that it had been agreed Sam didn't need it anymore! (WTF?) She'd told him that wasn't the case, so that's now gone ahead too – five weeks late! Honest to God!

When Sam got home, I talked to him about DLA but explained that he would have to stop going to football training: he wasn't well enough to coach football at the moment anyway and he certainly couldn't claim DLA if he was going off there twice a week. He said he only stood on the side-lines: he didn't run about. I know it's one of the things that keeps him going: he loves the coaching and the kids – it means the world to him. So sad!

Wednesday September15th – 4am!

Chemo +13

I couldn't get to sleep until turned midnight. Sam was very good listening to me. I told him I felt uncomfortable applying for the grant from the charity: it's like begging. He was very compassionate and said it was a fund for writers who have landed on hard times: I am a writer and I am suffering hardship, therefore I am entitled to apply and it's up to them to decide whether or not I'm worthy of receiving anything. I felt a bit better. But then I woke up at 3 worrying about the neuropathy in Sam's hands and wondering if it's a permanent thing. I'm down on the computer now – at 4am. I've been researching it and it looks as though it is irreversible. I can't bear it. I won't tell Sam – I don't know what he'll do if he finds out it could be like this for the rest of his life. He's in so much pain. And it does say one of the causes is chemotherapy – although not the particular drug cocktail Sam's on.

Thursday September 16th

Chemo +14

I got a flat tyre on my bike yesterday and Sam said he'd mend it last night. In the end he was too tired, so I said I'd take it to the bike shop today - but he was having none of it. He went down at 8 o'clock and started to mend my bike. I could hear spanners being dropped and he was cursing and swearing but he did do it – although it took him about an hour. His hands are so bad, he can't even take the top off his yoghurt or turn the tap or lift the breakfast tray, let alone use a spanner.

3.30 pm

God! What do I do all day? Nothing! I am so shattered and my head is thumping. I've tried to do some writing but my brain just doesn't function. I was going to sort out the sitting room but I just don't have the energy. I can understand when people 'collapse with exhaustion.' I am beside myself.

Sam came home early today. He's got an appointment with the neurologist tomorrow at 2 pm in the MDU. Hopefully they'll sort out about his hands. I said I'd walk over there and meet him but he said he didn't want me to go. I felt gutted. I'm sitting here with a bloody great label round my neck that says `CARER' but then he excludes me from knowing what I'm supposed to be dealing with. How does that work? I don't know why I'm so upset because I sure as hell don't want to be a carer. But I'm here crying my eyes out – AGAIN! I feel sad, lonely, useless, unwanted – good enough to nurse him when he's ill but not good enough to be included in any of the consultations or important things. What is my role in all this? What am I - just somebody to make his food and clear up after him and change his dressings?

I went back in and we talked about it and Sam said, "All right then, if you want to come, you can." I know he's had a lifetime of doing things on his own but it would have meant so much more if he'd wanted me to go with him, rather than saying I could go if I wanted to. I wanted him to want me there, but the bottom line is, he doesn't.

Friday September 17th

Chemo +15

Sam made breakfast this morning which was lovely – of course it's 2 weeks since his chemo, so he's building up strength again, although his hands are still painful and weak and he can't do fine motor things or anything that requires upper body strength.

He asked me to take off his dressing and, at long last, after 3 months, his wound has healed. We were both over the moon. I cleaned up the surrounding area with surgical spirit and, apart from the scar, it looks great.

I walked over to the lake at lunchtime and met Sam in the car park, then we went to the MDU for 2pm to see the neurologist. At 3pm the sister said she'd tried to ring him but he wasn't answering his bleep and his secretary wasn't answering the phone. I started to get an ominous feeling. At 4pm the haematologist came over again and said that the neurologist was seeing Sam on his ward rounds and, finally, at 4.30 Dr George Clooney Look-a-Like, consultant neurologist, came over. He started talking to Sam then looked at me and said, "Oh, you've brought a friend with you." Jesus wept! It's the C21st – is it beyond a doctor's comprehension that a black man can have a white wife?

Dr George did lots of tests on Sam's hands, arms and feet and said that he also had weakness in his left foot and leg and that it was caused by the lymphoma or at least by the para-proteins and NOT by the chemo. I asked if it was reversible and he hedged saying, "Like with any nerve damage, once the nerves are stretched, it can sometimes take them a while to get back." He asked Sam if he was having any visual problems or difficulties with words or mental confusion but Sam said no. Aaagh! He's having all three! But I kept my mouth shut: best not to contradict him in public. Dr George prescribed some different tablets.

Sam was OK about the diagnosis, although the fact that the doctor didn't say that the pain and numbness would go away eventually obviously played on his mind. It sounds silly, but just sitting there with him for two and a half hours made me feel useful: I didn't do anything but sit and read, but I was there and with him and not sitting on my own at home feeling about as much use as a milking machine on a fish farm.

Saturday September 18th

Chemo +16

This morning I went to the open air pool again. I had so much to do – tidying and cleaning the house, shopping, washing but I thought, What would I really like to do? So I went to swim in the open air. Fabulous! On my way home Sam rang putting on a silly accent. It's little things like that that make me laugh and love him.

Sunday September 19th

Chemo +17

Today was the local arts festival. I wanted to go but Sam said he didn't and he didn't want me to leave him on his own either. He said he felt very vulnerable and frightened when I went out. I said that he was well enough to go to work and we couldn't be joined at the hip 24/7. It all ended in a row again. He has so many wonderful qualities: he can be funny and kind and generous and thoughtful and quirky and zany and attentive and loving and I do love him for all those things, but he can also be extremely bloody challenging.

Monday September 20th

Chemo +18

I slept on the settee last night which did not help my insomnia – or my back! At 10.30am Sam phoned from work to say he was sorry and was deeply ashamed of himself. I told him that he needed to follow up the referral to the psychiatrist as he needed to have some support other than me.

This afternoon I went to the Macmillan support group and it was actually quite therapeutic. We did relaxation and visualisation.

Tuesday September 21st

Chemo +19

I woke at 6 feeling alive and vibrant. I did 20 minutes meditation then did ½ hour of yoga before breakfast. I felt so full of energy. I cycled to the lake and did some distant healing.

When I got home, I looked up on the Internet to check Sam's salary had been paid in – but they'd only paid half the normal amount. When I did finally get through to him at work, he rang the wages department. They said he'd had the wrong tax code and so they'd adjusted the tax – and that was all he was going to get! It didn't even cover our direct debits for council tax, gas, electric, insurance and water, never mind the CSA, car, food and anything else. FFS!

He spoke to his boss who has agreed to lend him some money till next month but that would mean that next month he'll only get £200! I don't understand. Of course, he's so confused mentally at the moment that he's probably got it wrong (I hope), but I am in a state of shock. I've been writing out my CV to apply for teaching jobs again. What the fuck is the Universe playing at? Haven't we got enough problems at the moment without making us destitute too?

So, guess what? Having had 24 hours of feeling on top of the world (for a change) I'm now crying again. FFS! Sent out my CV to a teaching agency and applied for 2 jobs.

Wednesday September 22nd

Chemo +20

Sam rang the tax office and apparently someone has put the wrong tax code on his pay slip. "But it'll be sorted out next month, with back pay." Great! But how does that pay this month's bills?

This afternoon I took Niamh up the High Street to look at the Art Festival. I can't believe how well she is. Honestly, 6 months ago, Raphe's had written her off but, now she's at Perry's, they put her on a drug trial and she's doing amazingly well. She did get tired after about 45 minutes, so we had a cuppa and then came home. She said a friend of theirs has an agency who work with hard to reach teenagers in all sorts of subjects, so I said I'd pop my CV round with a view to doing some ad hoc work – which would be so much better than contract work; what happens when Sam's not well and needs attention? I can't just keep taking time off from a new job – so the 'as and when' work would be much better for me at the moment. And Elaine's told me about internet copywriting and how much money you can earn. Will give that a go too.

Tuesday September 28th

Chemo +26

Sam's at the hospital today for his pre-chemo blood tests but he wanted to go on his own, so I'm going to work on the copywriting stuff Elaine sent.

When he got home, Sam said that Head Honcho told him that the neuropathy needed to be seen by another neurologist at a specialist hospital, although he wasn't sure which one. He forgets so much and doesn't seem to hear a lot of what is said to him, which is why I'd much rather be with him when he has consultations but he's having none of it at the moment. Apparently, HH told him that the cancer seems to be destroying the myelin sheath, the layer of tissue that protects the nerves, and it's irreversible. He said it was very rare and he'd only seen 2 cases like Sam's. He also said that he would have to have all 6 sessions of chemo and couldn't get away with 4 as they'd previously hoped. Sam was very down. I was aware of being very matter of fact and unemotional as he told me, but inside I wanted to scream.

Then, as we were watching television, Sam said to me, "How's your arthritis?"

Me: Arthritis? I don't have arthritis.

F: In your hands.

Me: I don't have arthritis in my hands, hon.

F: I mean eczema. Eczema! Sorry, I said the wrong word.

This type of thing happens dozens of times a day and yet, when the doctor asked if he had mental confusion, he said no!

Wednesday September 29th

Chemo +27

Sam was very subdued this morning. I think he was shocked about what Head Honcho said yesterday – he'd convinced himself that it was the chemo that was causing the pain in his hand and that it would stop once the chemo stopped. Even though Dr George Clooney Look-a-like told him otherwise, Sam was still telling everyone it was the chemo!

I went over to the lake but couldn't meditate. It was raining and I just sat and went over things in my head trying to make sense of everything. Why is this happening? I know Sam can be awkward and I know he's got a lot of anger from his childhood and losing his son, but he's got a good heart. He cares about people and communities and he dedicates himself to trying to help others. It's so unfair. And look at Niamh - what has she done to deserve it? Cancer is so bloody indiscriminate.

I felt so sad again today I just really needed to talk to someone – someone I feel safe with: someone who'll listen to me and hear my fears but as I went through my phone book, I could only find Aunty Christine – who was out. All my other friends were working and I no longer trust Penny with my feelings. I miss my mum so much and I miss not having a sister to talk to. I'm feeling very sorry for myself again, I know that. I'm very aware that I need to do something to pull myself out of this mire.

10pm:

Aunty Christine phoned back and it was a relief to talk to an older female. I do find being the family matriarch quite heavy at times. I know I haven't actually seen her for about 40 years but she's older and wiser and has known me all my life. It was good to talk to her.

Thursday September 30th

4th round of chemo

I took Sam to the Medical Day Unit at 10 for his chemo and came home and pigged out on a massive cheese and tomato sandwich. So much for losing ½ stone! Then I started to clean the sitting room like a demon – furniture pulled out, settee cushions washed. I blitzed it. Sam rang at 3.30 and said I could go up and he'd be ready in about 10 minutes.

I got up there and waited and waited and waited. All the doctors came out; Head Honcho, Homer Simpson, The Leprechaun and another doctor I haven't seen before. There must have been some big meeting. None of them recognised me - or if they did, they didn't acknowledge me.

Eventually, at 4.10, Sam came out – he was very subdued. He said they'd wanted to take more blood as his para-proteins are still high and it's giving the doctors cause for concern. Apparently, they shouldn't still be this high after 4 sessions of chemo. He'd told them about the chest pains he's been having and they said it's the hyper-viscous blood that's finding it difficult to pump through his heart. He was clearly very depressed.

Sam went up to bed early and I made some phone calls. I spoke to an old friend, Rita, but regretted it. She is such a bloody know-all. I breathe into it but what I really wanted to say is: Rita, you know fuck-all about cancer – you are a teacher, so just shut up and listen to me – stop trying to tell me how I should be and how Sam should be! But I didn't.

I then spoke to Tom about the wedding, which was lovely and happy and uplifting. A nice note to go to bed on.

Friday October 1st

Chemo +1

We went to the cinema this afternoon to see Made in Dagenham. It was lovely to get out of the house and do something and not talk about the `illness.' It took me back to the 60s with the fashion and the music and, although Dad didn't work at Ford's, he worked at a factory that made components for Ford's. I remember the knock-on effect the strike had. Dad was a security officer, so he wasn't affected, but the factory was closed as a result.

It was a great film and a lovely afternoon but, as we came to leave, I noticed that Sam was shivering. When I felt his arm, he was burning up again. I'd been aware of him wincing throughout the film with pain in his hands but when I felt his skin, I could tell he had a temperature. My heart sank.

When we got home, I took his temperature and it was 38o. He wouldn't phone the hospital but, when it got up to 38.2o he did ring Head Honcho. He said that he was probably OK unless it got to 38.5o and then he'd have to go in. It got up to 38.4o and I felt sick at the thought of spending another weekend in that place. We went up to bed at 9.30, by which time it had gone down to 38.2o again, so fingers crossed.

I am very aware of wanting to burst in to tears all the time. It's like there's a huge water balloon just under my sternum and it won't take much for it to pop.

Saturday October 2nd

Chemo +2

Sam's temperature was down to 36.3o again this morning, so normal. Breathe a sigh of relief.

I went over to the lake – it was a glorious morning and all the Michaelmas daisies are out all round the pond. They were the first flowers I grew as a child. We'd planned to go to the Imperial War Museum today but Sam really wasn't up to it. So, we stayed in. He's still very weak.

At about 5pm there was a ring at the doorbell and it was Niamh – her first solo trip to the shops since before Easter. She was wearing her wig and had colour in her cheeks and was excited about being out on her own. She said I was her first point of call. Sam came out into the hall and invited her in. She didn't stay long but Sam was, again, very shaken by her appearance. He kept saying, "I hope I don't end up like that. She looks so old and so small and so ill." Of course, I see her regularly, so can see the small improvement in recent weeks, whereas he's comparing her to how she was when we went to theirs at New Year and she was dancing the night away like a one of Pan's People!

Monday October 4th

Chemo +4

I checked our bank balance today and was shocked to see that we have only £173 to last us till the end of the month. Plus, I've used up nearly all the money in my tax account, so that I can't even pay my income tax when it's due in December. I went into total panic. I went on to TES *[Times Educational Supplement]* website immediately as well as various teaching agency sites and uploaded my CV. I applied for 5 jobs – although I haven't heard back from the others I applied for 2 weeks ago. I've usually got a trickle of royalties coming in and a fair few schools' event lined up, but my royalties have all but dried up and I haven't got a single event in my diary – and not a drop of creative juice in my brain to write anything new. *[Writers of fiction don't earn very much – unless you hit the big time - so the schools' events were my biggest source of income.]*

I have never in all my life had to live hand to mouth like this. I put my CV on other sites too – for admin work – although a lot of them wanted data inputting, which I can't do, and Excel, which I don't know. I'm fine with word processing. I wish I could get my head round Elaine's copywriting stuff but it's about being creative again and that just isn't happening at the moment. God, this is just shit.

I phoned the NHS Counselling Service and said it was now 4 weeks since I'd been assessed and hadn't heard anything. The woman took my number and said someone would ring me back today. Not that having counselling will help our bank balance one iota!

An agency rang me this afternoon and I've got an interview next Tuesday to do supply teaching. I feel very heavy about it, but it has to be done. I rang Sam and told him and he was very tearful. He said he'd come back to talk to me but when he got home he looked dreadful – very thin and drawn. He's felt sick all day and he said he'd been in so much pain he'd gone into a church at lunch time and talked to the minister. He said he didn't think he could go on much longer and had even thought he'd been better off if he wasn't here. The vicar told him about a 20 year old girl who'd had lupus and had been in 10 times more pain than Sam (how does he know?) and she'd never given up so Sam mustn't. But in the end, the girl died. Cheers, Vicar! Great bit of comfort there! And, the bottom line is, some people do commit suicide due to constant pain.

I was very tearful about our finances and about Sam's mental state. Sam said he would apply for a new job with more money but A) his boss has been very good to him and another place might not be and B) who would take him with Stage IV cancer? Now it's down to me to support us. I hate teaching and absolutely do not want to do it, but it's relatively good money - £125 per day gross and it's variable, so I don't need to commit to going in every day if he's ill.

We also filled in the form for the DLA *[Disability Living Allowance]* today – all 39 pages of it. Jesus! What a palaver. They want to know how far Sam can walk in 1 minute and whether he walks normally, or slowly or very slowly! How the hell are we supposed to gauge that? How long does it take to get in and out of bed? How many minutes are spent reminding him to take his medication? (How long have you got?) The Macmillan nurse told us to fill it in as if he were on his worst day, so we did. I wrote it in pencil because Sam can't hold a pen anymore and we'll take it up to the Day Centre tomorrow to get Claire to check it out and fill in her page.

We were both very emotional tonight. It breaks my heart to see him in so much pain and so depressed. There's a photo of him on the mantlepiece, running a 10K last July – only 16 months ago. I can't believe it's the same man.

We went up to bed and Sam was crying. He says the pain is now starting to affect his left foot too. He says if it continues to progress he won't be able to walk and will end up in a wheelchair. He said the taste coming up from his stomach 'tastes like death.' I know it's the chemo, but this is the first month it's really affected him like this. I feel so utterly useless.

Tuesday October 5th

Chemo +5

I drove Sam to work. As he went through the gate, he looked so small and vulnerable and thin. I wept as I drove away.

I'd asked Claire if she could find out which hospital Sam was being referred to for the pain in his hands as he still hadn't had his appointment. She'd sent an email saying it was St Dymphna's: a specialist centre for neurological conditions. I rang them up but they hadn't even got Sam registered with them. I told the woman that was unacceptable as it was weeks since he'd been referred. The woman went away and came back saying she'd found his referral and 'was just going to do it' (how convenient!). Anyway, his appointment is October 22nd at 9.15.

And then a letter came from the NHS Counselling Service saying that my first session would be next Monday from 3 – 4.30. Again, how convenient that it should come the day after I phone up. Do these people think we're all idiots?

Niamh called round on her way to the shops again on her own. She asked about Sam and I burst into tears. Honestly, how selfish of me! With all her own problems and there I was blubbing on her shoulder! I kept saying sorry but she said she was OK about it. She said to have another go at Sam and ask him to be referred to Perry's but I told her the more people try to get him to go there, the more he digs his heels in. She said (and I agree) that, had she stayed at Raphe's, she wouldn't be here now! It was a relief to talk to someone and let it all out but I did feel bad that it was Niamh, although she said she could fully understand because she's been there, which is true.

I met Sam from work and we went straight to the Day Unit. I parked in the car park at the lake, which is only about 300-400 yards from the unit and Sam walked really slowly, yet he was sweating by the time we got there. He sank down in a chair utterly exhausted. I got him some water but he looked very pale all round his eyes and across the bridge of his nose.

When he felt better, we stood by the nurses' station. There were 2 nurses and Homer Simpson sitting there. No one even looked up for several minutes, then one nurse asked if we were OK. (Obviously not, as we were standing waiting!) We said we had an appointment with Claire at which point Homer Simpson turned round, looked at us then turned back. He didn't even acknowledge us. This is the man who has been treating Sam for 5 months and he can't even give him a nod or say hello! I was disgusted.

Claire came over and checked the form. She said we'd done a good job, then she filled in her part. She said that she'd rung St Dymphna's and they hadn't received Sam's referral, so Homer Simpson was writing another now and would fax it across. I told her that I'd also spoken to them and his appointment was October 22nd. She was shocked and annoyed that they'd found his referral for me but not her. I told her that I'd said it was not acceptable and she'd gone off and found it. Claire then called across to Homer Simpson that the referral had been found but, again, he didn't even acknowledge us. Claire did say that she thought that 22nd was a long time away and she'd phone them again tomorrow and see if there was an earlier one available. She also said that, in future, we should park outside the unit rather than expect Sam to walk down the road. She said we could apply for a blue badge for him and Carers' Allowance for me.

We drove home but Sam feels so sick all the time that he said he didn't want anything to eat. I told him that he needed to eat to get well, but he said the taste in his mouth is so disgusting he can't face food. I said that I was worried about his mental state after what he'd said yesterday but he assured me he wouldn't do anything silly. I told him that, having been a Samaritan a few years ago, I would respect his wishes if he did decide to take his own life, but I would appreciate it if he would let me know so that it didn't come as a shock. We were both crying. He told me again that he would do no such thing.

I filled in the DLA form in ink and asked Sam to sign it, which he did with a great deal of effort. I'll post it tomorrow.

Wednesday October 6th

Chemo +6

I've got blooming cystitis! Talk about it never rains but it pours!

I woke up at 1.30 am and couldn't go to sleep again. When I took breakfast up to Sam, he said he'd been having nightmares all night about death. I told him it was just his unconscious fears coming through.

I went to the doctors and got some antibiotics for my cystitis and asked for some more Amitriptyline for Sam. *[It was a doctor who's known me for 30 years and Sam for over 20 years.]*

Dr: So, apart from the cystitis, how are you in yourself?

Me: Not good.

Dr: Ok, then here you go. Take one, twice a day.

Why ask if he's not going to follow through? I then asked for Sam's medication.

Dr: How is he doing?

Me: Not good. He's been referred to St Dymphna's. They thought the pain was as a result of chemo, but they now think it's the cancer that's destroyed the sheath around the nerves.

Dr: And is the Amitriptyline helping?

Me: A little but he's in a great deal of pain all the time.

Dr: Here you go then – tell him to take one at night. Is that everything?

How to make your patient feel like a valued human being – not!

One bright spot today – a cheque from the Macmillan Fund for £380! What a relief. I wept - and not in a bad way, this time. At least that gets us out of trouble for this month.

Thursday October 7th

Chemo +7

Claire phoned this morning, she's managed to get Sam's appointment brought forward to the 18th at 9.15 which, at least, is 4 days earlier. She was on the phone for about ½ hour. I told her how low Sam was but she said, because they never see that in clinic, Homer Simpson didn't believe it, so he ***still hasn't***

referred him to the psychiatrist!!! This is since the first week of August! He told Claire that the referral had to come from his GP, which Claire disputes and says it can be consultant to consultant. I told her we were in OP clinic on Monday, so she said to make sure and ask for either Head Honcho or a different doctor that I've never heard of. We must insist on seeing the consultants, and not be palmed off with an SHO or Registrar. She said she'd come over and see us there. She also said she was feeling frustrated as the team didn't seem to think that Sam was a priority. I told her that emotionally, he was a priority but he was also a proud man who found it hard to admit to pain or weakness, so no doubt, presented as someone who was handling everything, when, in fact, he was coming home and collapsing in a heap with the pain, biting my head off and seeking out priests. She said, "Sam's a fighter." And I said, "But that's what concerns me: it's like he's lost his will to fight these last few weeks." She said there was a meeting this afternoon of the whole team and she'd have another go about getting him referred. I thanked her for everything she was doing – especially the Macmillan grant. What a life saver.

Tomorrow is Lily's birthday and I needed to get the video recorder set up in case the card I made is featured on CBeebies. Sam and I spent a good 2 hours trying various combinations of TVs and video recorders but couldn't get any to record from the cable channels – either upstairs or downstairs. But what was nice was to see Sam applying himself to trying to sort it out – regardless of hurting hand, tiredness or depression, he was a man on a mission and it was a joy to watch. Sadly his mission didn't succeed, so he suggested that I video the TV on the camcorder.

Friday October 8th

Chemo +8

Sam woke several times in the night coughing. I don't know what this is – he's been coughing on and off for about 3 days now.

Yay - Lily's card was shown on CBeebies! At 10.30! I'd got the camera set up and I recorded it. I felt so ridiculously excited about it and went round phoning everyone and putting it on Facebook. Anyone would think it was my birthday, I felt so chuffed. Am so pleased – it was like confirmation that good things can and do happen. Now let's focus on a cure for cancer – and maybe 6 numbers! Or is that just being greedy?

4pm

Just heard that *[my latest manuscript]* has been rejected AGAIN! It's such a bloody good book, why will no one publish it? I plummeted again. I went up the High Street this afternoon and felt very spaced out. The only other time I've felt like this was after Mum died: as though I was walking through porridge and not really of this world. I'm aware of feeling very tearful again. Jesus! Please let us get some significant money before Tuesday when I have my supply teaching interview. I so do not want to go back to teaching. I try and be positive and think, well, it'll keep me in touch with my target readership and it'll bring in the desperately needed money and it'll get me out of the house and talking to people other than medical people or other cancer sufferers. But, the bottom line is: I DON'T BLOODY WELL WANT TO DO IT!

I broke down when Sam came home and he was very good and supportive. He has such faith in me as a writer, it's very touching.

Monday October 11th

Chemo +11

Sam had his outpatient appointment this morning. It's to assess the effectiveness of the chemo and whether or not to change it. I parked in the car park simply because of the time factor – and it was £2.50 which didn't break the bank thanks to the Macmillan grant. At least if Sam gets a blue badge, it'll be free!

He was called in to see Jessica Rabbit, a female consultant with masses of red hair cascading over her shoulders. She was very nice but told us totally different things from Head Honcho to the point that we even queried if she was looking at the right notes! She said the CT scan showed:

- No sign of enlarged lymph nodes in the neck. (The ultrasound AND the CT scan we were shown, showed enlarged nodes all around the neck and one enormous one on the left – the one that was the size of a melon that the biopsy was taken from!)
- No enlarged nodes in the chest cavity. (We were shown 2 large masses - one in each lung)
- Enlarged nodes in both arm pits. (We've been told several times that there were no enlarged nodes under his arms.)

- Enlarged nodes in both groins. (Again we've been told there were no enlarged nodes in his groins.)
- Spleen, liver and kidneys were clear. (We were told – AND shown – smaller masses in the liver and stomach, although none in the kidneys or spleen.)
- Evidence of the disease in the bone marrow at level 15-20. (This has never been mentioned before but she did reassure Sam that under 10 was considered normal, so 15 – 20 wasn't very high.)

When I said that those notes were not my husband's she waved her hand dismissively and said, "It's of no consequence." No bloody consequence? Sam's entire treatment programme has been based on an inaccurate report! That is pretty much OF CONSEQUENCE if you ask me.

She said that Sam had a `low level' B Cell lymphoma but when I said that Homer Simpson had said Sam had the disease at two different stages of progression, she said she didn't know what he meant by that and Sam should ask him. She's supposed to be a bloody consultant!

I left feeling angry and even less confident in Raphe's than I was before. Sam said he was relieved that it was `low level' (although that only means slow growing and not that it's benign) but said he was totally befuddled with all the contradicting information. Homer Simpson had told Sam they were concerned that his para-proteins were still high, but Jessica Rabbit didn't seem particularly bothered and said that at least they were coming down.

She also said she could find no evidence of a request for another CT scan having been made so wrote out another referral and told Sam to take it across to the main building and ask if Homer Simpson had made an appointment; if not, hand it in. Needless to say, when we got to the CT department, no appointment had been made. He's to go back to OP in one month.

Decided to write a letter to Head Honcho about the discrepancy in Sam's notes. Really want to get to the bottom of what's going on and what his condition really is. Appalled at the dismissive wave of the hand when I pointed out the irregularities. Such arrogance.

And now I've got my bloody NHS Group Therapy this afternoon. And I DO NOT WANT TO GO!

I walked up to the group, only to find it was run by a woman I used to know and was attended by only 2 others – a very nice woman who is caring for her mother with dementia and an extremely needy woman who is tending to her 91 year old father and who totally dominated the entire session. Fortunately, the woman who runs it said to me at the end that it was not appropriate for me to continue as she knows me and I told her that I agree. She's going to go back to the team leader and suggest that I have 1:1 – which is what I asked for back at the beginning of August – and it's now halfway through October.

A couple of things did come out of this afternoon though:

- As I was telling them about my situation, the needy woman said, "So, if it's incurable but not terminal, that means you have no idea how long this is going to go on for. And he's so young. You could be living like this for years and years with no light at the end of the tunnel."
- The facilitator said, "In the last 6 months, your life has completely turned upside down; although this is happening to your husband, it's had an even bigger impact on you and yet you're not ill. It sounds as though you've lost yourself in all of this, so what you're going through is a grieving process for your life and your dreams."

Both quite depressing statements, but both absolutely true. And, bizarrely, I felt better just for having that acknowledged.

Sam came to pick me up, which was lovely but, when we got home, I went into total meltdown. I just collapsed in floods of tears. Poor Sam— as if he hasn't got enough on. I'm the one who's supposed to be supporting him, not the other way round. All in all, not a good day.

Tuesday October 12th

Chemo +12

Got my passport photo taken in the chemist - £4. Gathered up my CRB clearance, passport, proof of residence, birth and marriage certificates and headed off for my interview with the supply agency - £6 fare.

When I got there, I started to go into a panic attack and had to stop and consciously do `yoga box breathing' *[in for a count of 4, hold for 4, out for 4 and hold for 4]* to calm myself down. I made it to a very run down building and was shown up to an extremely small and shabby office where a woman who was streaming with cold, interviewed me. After 20 minutes of questions such as, "How do you like to arrange your classroom?" and, "How would you describe your style of teaching?" (I mean, let's be honest, who in their right mind is going to say `military' or `Adolf Hitler'?) she told me that if all my references came back OK and if I got CRB clearance again (I have to pay £50 a time!) then they would put me on their books but, at the moment, they had no teaching jobs whatsoever registered with them. She then said that I'd be paid through a 3rd party company and I would have to PAY THEM `a small amount' each week for the honour of being paid! She then said would I be interested in doing exam invigilation? I said yes, how much does it pay and she said: it's just expenses really – it works out about one pound an hour! Fucking hell – the National minimum wage is £6 per hour. She did say that I might get some amanuensis work at £9 per hour. With a maximum of 6 hours in a school day that's £54 a day! And that would be in south London – 1½ hours away and about £8 on the tube. And then I've got to pay the `small (conspicuously unspecified) amount' to the payment company + tax + N.I. Jesus! This sucks. Trying to look for positives: I suppose it's teaching me humility. I came home and wept - just for a change. Only good thing of the day – I bought my coat for Tom's wedding – in the Salvation Army Charity Shop – dark blue velvet Country Casuals and looks as though it's never been worn. Gorgeous!

Wednesday October 13th

Chemo +13

Met Tom's future mother-in-law for lunch and had a really lovely day. We wandered our way up to meet Tilly at work. She was showing us styles of wedding dress and fabric and lace and we were talking about menus and guest lists and bridesmaids – and it was soooooooooo wonderful to be talking about happy things.

At about 7pm, a woman from the writers' charity phoned. She said the committee had agreed to award me £3000! Plus – pay off our credit card debt and bank loan totalling £4,700!!! How amazing is that? I wept – but with relief and gratitude. I felt as though the weight of the world had been lifted from my shoulders. Just the debts being paid off will mean an extra £200 per month.

Thursday October 14th

Chemo +14

I went to the Health Centre where I underwent a medical for a Caring for Carers Pilot Scheme. I've asked for help with losing weight, support with ironing and gardening and time for myself to have some free pampering sessions. If I do get all that, I'm thinking being a `carer' isn't quite as bad as I thought - joke! Unfortunately, during the medical the nurse discovered that I've still got a urine infection – that's even after 7 days of antibiotics, so I had to ring up and get another prescription for stronger ones.

Held my Reiki sharing group tonight. Lovely peaceful energy in the house.

Friday October 15th

Chemo +15

I went over to the lake and then straight to yoga this morning, which was wonderful. I feel alive and refreshed and really grounded again.

When I got home there was a message on the answer phone from Jessica Rabbit saying she'd read Sam's letter to HH and would he phone her? Actually, it was my letter, trying to clarify the wrong notes in Sam's file. I passed the message on to Sam.

The DLA people had rung Sam and asked for an exact date when the neuropathy had started, so that they could backdate the money. They said his case was being discussed at panel this afternoon and he should hear in 2 – 3 working days, which I think is remarkably quick. I was expecting it to take weeks.

I had lunch with Niamh and her sister, which was so nice, although my new antibiotics say I mustn't eat dairy products, so the cheese was out. It's so good to see Niamh dashing around the house like she used to do. She's still quite bent at the top of her spine and considerably smaller than she used to be, but a million times better than she was a couple of months ago. She asked if I'd feed the cats for her while she's in Ireland for 10 days, so I agreed. It is a bit of a tie but, if I don't do it, she's got no one else to ask and she'd worry herself sick if she had to put them into a cattery.

When I got home, I rang Sam and asked how he'd got on with Jessica Rabbit and he said that she'd told him that no doctor could tell him everything about his case, so she'd speak to Head

Honcho about how much information the doctors had told him. (NOOOOOOO! That does not solve anything!) She said that the important thing was that Sam was making good progress (NOT what the other doctors had said!) and that he had to keep his eye on the bigger picture. I asked him if she'd explained why there was such a discrepancy between what we'd seen on the CT scan and what the report said but he said, "The important thing is I'm getting better, so I'm not worried about the rest."

OH MY GOD! How are we supposed to have confidence in them when they fob him off with crap like that? If they can get the results of the scan so wrong, how can we believe them about anything? Felt my good mood beginning to ebb away.

Monday October 18th

Chemo +18

Sam and I had another row last night. We didn't speak either last night or this morning. I went round to feed Niamh's cats and got back at 8am just as Sam left for his neurological appointment – we didn't exchange a word. He didn't want me to go with him and I was happy to have some time for myself.

I am at a loss to understand what goes on with Sam. One minute we're fine and loving and romantic and then, for absolutely no reason that makes any sense to me whatsoever, he flips. Yesterday morning, we were cuddled up in bed and I thought, did I tempt fate? We have periods of wonderful, happy, relaxed, harmony and then, suddenly, out of the blue, he'll go into one of his moods again. I feel very unstable and insecure whenever this happens. I suspect it was because he was anxious about today but I am nobody's doormat and I do react. I do try to breathe into things, in fact I must have the lung capacity of a pearl diver by now, but there are also limits to my patience.

I phoned the haematology department this morning: last week Sam told Jessica Rabbit that he was on 5 mg of Amitriptyline but, when I checked the box, it's actually 50 mg, so the 'increase' she recommended to 15mg will in fact be a decrease. They said they'd pass on the message. And the DLA want to know how many hours he has to be supervised taking medication!

Jessica Rabbit phoned back and said 50 mg was OK and she was happy with that. She said she'd spoken to Sam and repeated what she'd told him. I said, "The problem we both have, Doctor, is that when Sam had his CT scan, we were shown his actual scan on the screen and what we saw did not, in any way, correspond to the report you read out last week. We were concerned that the wrong report had been put in his notes, as it's not uncommon for Samuel Edwards to be confused with someone called Edward Samuels."

She said that Sam's notes were like an encyclopaedia and he couldn't possibly be told everything there was to know and he shouldn't concern himself with 'minor unimportant details' (scan results, minor unimportant details? FFS!) and he should just concentrate on the important things such as getting his neuropathy sorted out and the fact that his condition was improving. Jesus wept!

Again, I can't help but think she's missed the point. How can we have any confidence in her or the other doctors when we SAW the scan and yet the report bore no relation to what we saw with our own eyes? I just said thank you and put the phone down feeling frustrated and not remotely satisfied or reassured.

When Sam came home, he apologised for yesterday but then started to justify how he'd been. And that was it – I erupted. Vitriol like volcanic ash spewing in Sam's direction. I went ballistic until I was practically hoarse.

This is spiritual `Reiki Master' Kate at her most unspiritual! What's the point of doing all that meditation and processing and yoga when I totally lose it like that? And why do I lose it so enormously? I've no doubt I'll do some processing and get to forgiveness. Then we'll lurch forward for a while before something else crops up and I lose it again. It's so exhausting. I so wish I didn't react. Why can't I use the skills I've learned? Why can't I be the bigger person? I know he's got cancer. I know he's in agonising pain in his hands. I know it's the anniversary of his son's death. I just feel as though I'm running on empty and have no resources left.

Later

Went to the Macmillan Support Group this afternoon. It was about `Dealing with Uncertainty.' At one point I said I also had uncertainty around my own life because I wasn't able to write at the moment. *[See previous comment about the fact that writing was probably ALL I was doing, although I couldn't see it at the time.]* I explained that we needed money and I'd tried to get back into teaching to no avail. I repeated what the counsellor had said last week – that Sam's cancer had had more of an impact on my life than on his, in many ways. Oh MY God! I then got a whole heap of `advice' from people who don't know me or my life from Sweet Fanny Adam, `telling' me what I `should' do. Aaaagh! One woman suggested doing voluntary work and then the whole group jumped on the band wagon. Dear Lord – I've probably done more voluntary work in my lifetime than all the rest of them put together and I don't want to do it anymore! I WANT TO WRITE! I'd created my ideal life before Sam got ill – I was doing what I loved. And there are these people telling me to do voluntary work because I'd get a lot out of it! Jesus wept! Why do people think they know how other people should be? "Oh if you were doing voluntary work, it would be a way into paid work." Durrr! "You'd find yourself meeting other people and finding the funny things that people do and say would inspire your writing." "Why don't you write when your husband's out at work?" BECAUSE I CAN'T! And – a small point, but a pertinent one I think – does voluntary work solve the, `I'm not earning anything' problem? I don't think so! I was almost in tears with frustration. A male nurse could see how upset I was and asked if I was OK. I said, "No, not really." But he just took my cup and walked off. So why ask? I walked out and cried most of the way home. Something that's supposed to be supportive felt like a very unsafe place this afternoon and I don't know if I'll go back.

When I got home, Sam was already back. He said he was very sorry: he'd been totally out of order. I was still angry – not only with Sam but with the whole group thing this afternoon. With hindsight, I probably shouldn't have gone but I really thought that 'coping with uncertainty' would be useful and would have had some sort of philosophical or emotional or spiritual guidance for actually coping with uncertainty. Little did I realise it would be a free for all for people who think they know how I should live my life when, in fact, they know Jack Squat. When I've calmed down I'll probably ring the woman who was 'leading' (not!) the session because I don't believe it supported anyone the way it was run. There needs to be more structure and direction from a proper facilitator who knows what they're doing.

Anyway, my conversation with Sam was OK and he told me about the hospital this morning. The doctor had put electrodes on his hands and arms and tested his nerves. They'd also got him to register heat and cold by pressing buttons. In the end the doctor said that he had 'slight neuropathy' but that it didn't account for the amount of pain he had, which was probably associated with the chemo. He said he'd have Sam back in January when his chemo has finished and retest him.

Tuesday October 19th

Chemo +19

I woke at 12.30am and couldn't get back to sleep. I was upset about the (un)support(ive) group and also because the cheque hasn't arrived from the charity yet and we're horribly overdrawn again. Plus, these antibiotics cause insomnia apparently, so I'll be glad when I've finished them tomorrow. I just hope they've hit the cystitis on the head this time.

Sam brought up breakfast, which makes such a difference. I know it sounds silly but it's the accumulation of little things that really gets me down: the fact that he can't do breakfast most of the time, or dinner and he can't help with the hoovering or ironing or mowing the lawn or doing the washing up or emptying the bins or any of the other things he used to help with. It did used to take two of us to keep on top of things but now it's just me and I'm exhausted. Plus, the fact that I don't have use of the car now is really, really limiting. It was wonderful yesterday morning just to get in the car and pop out to do the shopping. Most of the time, I feel marooned here with only my bike or public transport - and how much shopping can one person carry on a bike?

I cycled over to the lake but it was a huge effort, I'm so tired. Then I fed the cats – I love Niamh to pieces but I could really have done without this at the moment. But, as Sam says, either do it with a good heart or don't do it at all, so I'll shut up and just get on with it.

Then my agent rang with news of another rejection! One manuscript has now had 4 rejections and another has had 5! It's hard not to get disheartened and wonder what the hell I'm doing or not doing at the moment.

And then – THE CHEQUE ARRIVED! Hallelujah. I am so relieved. Can now breathe easy - for a few months, anyway. And who knows, I might have had something accepted by then.

And I still haven't finished my tax return. I really do need to get on top of that because I think there'll probably be a rebate from it – at least I hope there's a rebate. I'm stuffed if there isn't as

I've had to use most of the money I've put aside for tax to bail out our current account!

Sam told me that today he'd tried to walk to a home-visit and the family lived almost 2 miles from work. He hadn't wanted to drive as the car is low on petrol and he can't fill it up because his hands aren't strong enough to use the pump. But then, of course, he had to walk all the way back and he was exhausted – and it poured down. He got soaked and had to rest for 2 hours when he got back to the office.

Wednesday October 20th

Chemo +20 - Day of the CT scan

Woke up at 5.50am. I told Sam that if he wanted anything to eat, he should say so now as he wasn't allowed to eat after 6.00 but he said he was fine and he'd wait till after his scan. Then, at 7.20 he decided he'd like a slice of toast. I told him he was too late and he grumbled like mad.

I drove Sam over to Raphe's for his scan at 10. He'd had to drink a litre of water and was in a bit of a state because, of course, his bladder isn't the strongest! There was another man there who was kicking up a stink about having to drink so much water. I said to him, "Think yourself lucky you're not pregnant, with a baby kicking at your bladder when you've got two litres of water in it!" He wasn't impressed.

When we got home there was a letter from the DLA people – Sam's been awarded the highest level for mobility and the medium level for care – so he'll get almost £100 per week and I can now apply for Carers' Allowance. Talk about relief. What an amazing society we live in that we can get this money. There must be people all over the globe who live in countries where there is no welfare state who are struggling to make ends meet and dying in poverty as a result. I know Sam's ill, but our financial worries are over for the time being and I do feel very, very humble and enormously grateful. Such a relief.

And now I've got the charity grant, I can afford to tax the car – and get it serviced. And we desperately need a new washing machine. Ours is 14 years old and making the most terrible grinding noises. Words cannot describe how freeing it is to know that I can pay for these things without going into debt again.

When Sam got home, he was clearly in a great deal of pain again/still, wincing and flinching and crying out. I filled in the application for a blue badge for him, but it needed 2 passport photos, so I drove him up to the chemist to have them taken: he was frozen despite having on his anorak, big fleece-lined boots, woolly hunting-type hat and thermal gloves. He could hardly keep a limb still with shivering. He's saying he doesn't think he can handle it if this pain doesn't go away. He's also fretting because Jessica Rabbit said that the disease was in his bone marrow – he said it's been preying on his mind ever since we saw her. He was very low, which invariably brings me down too.

Friday October 22nd

Chemo +22

I went to feed the cats, then cycled over to the lake. I had a lovely session and felt such a wave of gratitude for everything that's in my life at the moment. I was thanking the geese and the trees and the sky – I sometimes think I'm turning into one of those eccentric old women that kids laugh at behind their backs. It was such a glorious morning – I watched a flock of about 20 – 30 long tailed tits bob and bounce from the big oak on the island to the little sapling birches on the bank. It was a wonderful moment.

When Sam got home, he put on some music and we slow danced around the sitting room. It's so wonderful to be held. He said he'd help to tidy up but kept having to sit down after every couple of minutes.

Saturday October 23rd

Chemo +23

A bit of normality today – we're hosting a supper party tonight. Well, Liz and Bill are coming over. I started cooking and prepping early. Sam was really brilliant – he kept doing brief bursts of tidying and cleaning and then crashing out for about an hour. When I told him to rest, he said, "It's important for me to feel useful. I'm not an invalid and I don't want to be treated as one." Fair enough.

Liz and Bill arrived at 7.45 for supper. It's so nice to be doing normal-ish stuff. We let Myles stay up till almost midnight and he was very good, watching TV and playing his games. It was really lovely to entertain again.

Sunday October 24th

Chemo +24

In the afternoon, I went out in the garden and cut the lawn – it was like a meadow out there – tidied up the last of the vegetable pots and did some cutting back and weeding, then started on the north face of the ironing basket. I ironed for about 2 hours but was still only halfway through – and I had to keep sitting down every 15 – 20 minutes to have a rest. Have been on my feet for the last 3 days, almost without a break, so feel shattered but it's a healthy tired rather than the emotional exhaustion of late.

Sam's still in a real state with his hands. Even the slightest brush of fabric has him screaming in agony and there's not a thing I can do. We went up to bed early and Sam went out like a light. He says it's the only relief he gets from the pain.

Tuesday October 26th

Chemo +26

I told Sam I wanted to go to the hospital with him this morning. He said he wasn't sure, but I was adamant: I'm hoping they'll have the results of the scan back. It was the most glorious sunrise today – crimson and breath-taking. I went over to the lake but it had already faded into a grey drizzly morning. My meditation didn't go very well today – all my stuff about Penny is still coming up. I really need to complete with her – I don't want this hanging over me and I don't want someone who behaves that way in my life. She said she'd ring when she got back from holiday and that was 3 weeks ago, so it's all mind games and I'm really not in the mood for that.

When we got to the Day Unit, Head Honcho came up and said he'd got Sam's letter (my letter!) and it was nothing to do with him – he rarely saw the actual scans: it was down to the radiologist to interpret them! What a pack of bullshit! He looked at it with us!

Me: I'm sorry doctor, but that doesn't make sense to me. You called Sam and me over to Outpatients' in Area 1 and the three of us sat round and looked at the actual scan. Do you remember? (He nodded.) And on it we could see large white areas where there were enlarged lymph nodes or masses all around Sam's neck with a particularly large one on the left; 2 large ones one in each lung and smaller ones in his liver. There was nothing in either arm pit or groin. Yet the report that was read out was almost the exact reverse of that. So perhaps you can understand why we are confused and, to be honest, don't know how you can make a comparison with the 2nd scan, when the report on the first one was so erroneous.

He ummed and erred and tried to fob us off again saying he saw so many scans (contradiction of what he said earlier about not seeing them!) that he couldn't remember Sam's. I was quite insistent and, in the end, he said he'd go and bring up the scan and compare them both and report back to Sam on Thursday when he's having his chemo. Which I'm a bit annoyed about as I won't be there and Sam really doesn't ask questions or pursue things with them. Anyway, at least he's said he's going to look at them again. And, when he'd gone, Sam did turn to me and said, "Thank you for that." Yay! Recognition for my persistence!

While the nurse was taking Sam's blood, I noticed one of the nurses who'd been in the MacMillan Support Group meeting, so I leapt up and went after her. I told her that I thought the sessions were usually great and very supportive but I'd found last week's quite unsafe and had left feeling very upset. I said I'd been looking for some sort of practical guidance about handling uncertainty (because, let's face it, everything in life is ultimately uncertain) but, instead, it had turned into a free-for-all of people trying to tell me how to live my life and I felt judged and unheard. I told her that if there was another session like that I thought it needed more careful facilitation so that people didn't jump in with their own ideas on how to fix others. She thanked me - and then asked if I'd help with that! Hang on: this is something that's supposed to be run for me, not by me.

Then Elaine came round for me to do some typing work for her – and she paid me a tenner, which was very much appreciated.

I fed the cats and put Niamh's heating on for her to come home to tomorrow: the house is like an ice box. After dinner I reminded Sam that I was going to my craft group tonight and Sam's energy visibly deflated. I was sorely tempted to blow it in, but it's almost a month since his last chemo and he's relatively well at the moment. And I do need to keep doing the things that support me and not totally give up my life to care for him and his needs.

The hospital have increased his Clexane to 130mg a day now – and it comes in huge syringes with wobbly needles. He says it's quite tricky to inject but is adamant that he doesn't want me doing it for him as long as he can do it himself. Just as I was about to go out, the NHS counsellor rang up. I told her I wasn't impressed with the service and told her my experiences. She sounded a bit put out, but I didn't exaggerate or lie: they were all genuine shortcomings on their part. Anyway, she's booked me in with herself next Tuesday morning. It's now 3 months since I first went to the GP in crisis – I could've topped myself in the time it's taken them to see me.

Sam was asleep when I got home. I just watched him breathing – bless. He's had such a crap life, I do want to make it all better for him and of course, I can't. I hope he does get through this and we can go on and live a long and happy life together. I have a dream of walking hand in hand along the beach when we're 75 & 85. I need to hold on to that and not get morbid.

Wednesday October 27th

Chemo +27

As we were talking this morning Sam said that he was going to rest fully on Friday after his chemo – which will be a first.

Me: Well, you can stay in bed all morning because I've got a woman coming from the Caring for Carers.

Sam: What's she coming for?

Me: To find out what I need.

Sam: And what do you need?

Me: I don't know what's on offer. I've asked for some pampering sessions and perhaps someone to help with the ironing and gardening. (OMG! BIG mistake!)

Sam: No way! I don't want that.

Me: Hon, it's not about what you want. This is about what I need.

Sam: No. I don't want strangers coming into this house. I can do the ironing and gardening.

Me: Hon, you can't. It hurts your hands to hold the iron and you haven't the strength for the gardening.

Sam: The garden's not important (it is to me!) and I'll power through the pain and do the ironing.

I didn't want a row, so I got up and went and ran the bath. Everyone else can see that I'm exhausted and getting overwhelmed by things piling up, but he can't. OK, so I could have done the ironing instead of going for a walk the other day but, for God's sake, I need to do normal things and not just stay in these four walls doing bloody housework. I need to talk to people other than medics or people who are ill. Anyway, he came through to the bathroom and apologised.

Need to go and feed the cats now. Niamh's home today, which will be a relief. I know it only takes about 10 minutes twice a day to feed the cats, but it's seemed such a burden this time. Right now, I haven't even got the energy to cycle over to the lake. And that's after a good night's sleep! And I think I've STILL got a urine infection. I need to take a sample to the doctors. God knows what that's about – I've had 2 lots of antibiotics. Louise Hay says it's about being pissed off – well you don't need a degree in psychology to work that one out!

I started on my tax return today. God! What a palaver. I ended up speaking to 5 different people before I finally got it done – and, hopefully, I should get a rebate. Yay! Which is good because it means we'll have some more money to play with, but bad because it means I earned so little!

Preeti rang and asked if she could meet up with me tonight but it's the night before Sam's chemo and he gets very anxious. I suggested she come here instead and we can sit in my study for a while – she sounded very low. I'll light a fire to cheer her up and get some wine and nibbles.

Then I decided to take the bull by the horns and phone Penny. She was asking about Sam and I filled her in to date. Then:

Penny: I don't know what to say to you.

Me: You don't have to say anything. I just rang to complete with you.

Penny: OK - if that's what you want but will you still keep me up to date with emails about how you're doing and how Sam's doing?

Me: (after a pause while I tried to decide whether or not I want to email her.) The problem for me is that I don't believe you really care about how Sam's doing.

Penny: That's not true. Obviously I don't care as much as if he were a friend – I've only met Sam a couple of times. The same as you wouldn't care if it were Pete.

Me: I would care about him on a human level.

Penny: Well, of course I care about Sam on a human level.

Me: But that's my point. I don't get that. (Like - how long is it since you got home from holiday and have you bothered to phone?)

Penny: I resent you saying that.

Me: I know you resent me; it's very obvious.

Penny: You have to remember you've rung me up sobbing several times.

Me: Yes, I'm not denying that, but you've judged me and Sam in a very difficult time and that's why this no longer serves me.

Penny: I'm sorry I'm obviously not qualified to support you properly. (Smell of burning martyr!) I feel that you're judging me for not being the way you wanted me to be.

Me: It's not about that – or, in fact, maybe it is. I wanted friendship and support and not to be judged or have Sam judged but I didn't get that. But actually, I think this conversation is in danger of going downhill, which I don't think would benefit anyone so perhaps we should end this here.

Penny: Fine. Bye.

I put the phone down and was trembling but felt such a relief. It's like the old Chinese proverb says: friends are like leaves on a tree: as old ones drop away, new ones blossom and grow. We were in similar places in our lives when we became friends and now we're not – simple as that. I felt as though a concrete yoke had been lifted off me.

And then I started to fill out the Carers' Allowance form. OH! MY! GOD! Why does everything to do with the government have to be so complicated? I'd got 2/3 of the way through when I came across the `self-employed' bit! Durrr – I've been trying to fill in the employment part! Now have to find some Typex and re-do the whole bloody thing.

Had to go to GP and give a urine sample to see why infection's not clearing up – but do you think I could pee? Squatted in the loo for over 20 minutes and managed to produce about a millilitre! Sod's Law. Then took the key back to Niamh and had a cup of tea – she looks so well. She'd had a great time but starts her next batch of chemo tomorrow, bless her.

Preeti arrived about 7.30 and we had such a lovely evening. She's so precious to me. She stayed until just turned 10. When I went to bed, Sam was quite anxious about his chemo, so we chatted until about 1am. He was saying what a good life he's had and how being with me has been like a dream (and sometimes a nightmare, I think!) but it was very moving. We held each other and cried a bit. He's still in so much pain and is terrified that the news might not be very good. I've said I'll go early to pick him up and we'll see the doctor together and he was OK about that.

Thursday October 28th

Round 5 of Chemo

Sam had a very bad night. I made breakfast and took it up and afterwards we made love – first time since chemo began. So lovely just to be close like that.

I dropped Sam off for his chemo and he said he was very anxious about getting the results of the scan today. He asked the nurses when the doctors would be coming round. They said they'd be around in the afternoon, so I said I'd go back at 3 and wait with him and he said that was fine. I drove off to the lake and gave thanks for my life and Sam and the NHS.

When I got home, Sam phoned up – Homer Simpson had been to see him! He said the first thing he said was, "Where's your wife?" No doubt relieved that I wasn't there! Anyway, first of all he apologised and said that the report in Sam's notes IS the wrong one! He said he'd challenged the radiologist about it and he'd apologised for writing up the wrong notes. That must be a first - but it also means that somewhere in Raphe's is another patient who has Sam's scan report in his/her notes. And, how do we know that Sam's been given the appropriate chemo for his actual condition if they were basing it on a report that said he had it in his bone marrow and arm pits and groins, but not in his lungs, neck or liver? Could that be why he's in so much pain with the neuropathy? Anyway, I mustn't go there. He then went on to tell Sam that the scan last week showed that he is in `almost total remission.' God! I hope they haven't made a mistake on that one too! I was so relieved, I cried. I won't totally believe it till I've seen it with my own eyes, but so, so, so relieved. Apparently, there's one small mass still in the centre of his chest and the last 2 chemos should put paid to that; then he'll be transferred to Perry's (yay!) for a PET scan and `watch and wait' - which is monitoring. Apparently, he'll be on drugs to keep the lymphoma suppressed and might need stem cell surgery at some point but they're very pleased with him. Wow!

So much good news recently. Spent the rest of the day phoning and emailing people with the news. Thank you: Universe, God, Allah, Yahweh, Jehovah, Life, Divine Spirit, NHS and anyone else out there.

I went up to the hospital at 3pm and sat with Sam for the last 1½ hours of his chemo. All the doctors were in a meeting. Claire came over and spoke to us but none of the doctors did – even though Homer Simpson had said he'd speak to me when I came up. Never mind – was just so relieved and pleased that Sam's almost clear. He'd sent me a text saying that this was the beginning of a new life for him and he was going to be kind, generous, loving, humble and accepting of everyone and everything from now on. A pretty tall order, but at least the intention is there.

Friday October 29th

Chemo +1

Woke up at 6.30 and did our first meditation together for months. I cycled over to the lake and shed a few tears – of gratitude and relief this time, rather than sadness and fear. Got back and the woman from the Carers' Support Service came over. Not quite sure what she, or her service, does but she was here for about an hour and I'm booked in for pampering in January and they also do yoga on a Monday and Mosaic Art on a Tuesday, which might be quite nice to do. She chatted about herself and what she'd done on her day off and how she'd got her law degree and her son who's 27 and lives in Manchester – she even took a phone call from him in the middle of our talk - but she was very nice and said, "If the NHS counselling isn't any good, we do counselling too." Wish I'd known that in August when I was in crisis, instead of 3 months down the line when I'm feeling so much better. No mention of the ironing or gardening services I'd hoped for, but because I'm feeling better, I'll probably be better able to keep on top of things.

Saturday October 30th

Chemo +2

I drove over to the lake this morning rather than cycling – lazy, I know! It was glorious again: all the colours shimmering and golden. There was a cormorant with a white breast and, at a distance, it looks for all the world like a penguin! I had to do a double take. It reminded me of when Amy was about 4 or 5 and she came running in, all excited, "Mummy, Mummy there are eight penguins sitting on the fence!" Wasn't sure if it was the beginning of a joke or if there'd been a mass break out from the zoo. Turns out they were magpies!

The sun was so warm and the colours so vibrant, I could have stayed there all day. It's like a mini holiday: every time I go over there I feel so refreshed. How lucky we are to have all that nature and beauty right on our doorstep.

On the way home I saw a friend. I told her about Sam and she said, "Oh yes, I've had Non-Hodgkin's Lymphoma for the last 13 years. I had 18 months of chemo and now I just go up to Perry's every so often and they keep an eye on me." I felt so heartened hearing that – mind you, she doesn't have the neuropathy, which is the biggest problem at the moment, but nevertheless, a real success story.

It was a gentle day. It doesn't sound much but I really revel in quiet domestic times: not having to dash here or there or do things – just 'being' – it's wonderful.

Sunday October 31st

Chemo +3

I woke feeling rested and full of energy. I did yoga, then I drove over to the lake. It was raining, but I sat in my jacket and watched all the muted colours – definitely from the ochre and umber end of the palette – and the waterfowl diving and ducking for fish. Even in the rain, I love it over there. My dream would be to have a house overlooking a lake like that, with a veranda where I could sit, and a jetty where I'd have a rowing boat that I could row out on the water. It would have to be clean water, of course, so that I could swim, something like they have in America and Canada. And the cottage would have roses and honeysuckle round the porch and wood burning stoves and an Aga in the kitchen. There'd be a vegetable plot at the back and enough rooms for all the grandchildren (of which there'll be loads) to come and visit and a soppy old dog will be sitting by my feet. Hopefully Sam will be chopping wood for the stoves and reading his papers in a hammock. And we'll rock together on our big swing on the veranda watching the sun go down across the water. Golden Pond comes to London! Hey ho. If you don't have a dream, how you gonna have a dream come true?

When I got back Sam wasn't feeling well. He felt very sick and was trembling from head to foot, although no temperature – which is a first after chemo. He dozed on and off all morning in bed. He felt very demoralised again. Plus, he's freezing cold all the time even though it's very mild today AND I've put the heating on for him. I made him a couple of slices of toast and jam for lunch – it's all he could face he feels so sick all the time. And he says he can feel the chemo burning up inside him, particularly on the sites where his lymphomas are/were and in both his hands.

Sam did manage to eat some Quorn mince and potatoes for dinner but all he did all day was lie on the settee, he felt so ill. When he did his Clexane, he drew blood which upset him – it's never happened before.

Monday November 1st

Chemo +4

Woke up at 6 am feeling refreshed and wide awake - like I used to. Sam woke at about quarter past and we did our meditation together again, which is so lovely and bonding. I told Sam not to go into work if he still felt crap, but when I got back from the lake, he'd gone. I knew he would: it's like work is his reason for being.

I cycled into town for the Caring for Carers' yoga from 11 – 12 but when I got there, I was told the time had changed to 12 – 1! I was not well pleased. Decided to try on some dresses for Tom's wedding in the mistaken belief that it would be something nice. OMG! Talk about mega stress. First of all the assistant was unbelievably bossy: "That's cotton; I won't even allow you to take it into the changing room for a wedding outfit!" Then she was going along the rails picking out the most inappropriate dresses for a woman of my age. When I picked out one I really liked she said, "Really? Black for your son's wedding? I don't think so, do you?" I'm like, hello! It's got silver beading and embroidery all over it. Anyway, I took 6 dresses and started to get changed. I HATE changing rooms with a passion, but at least this had separate cubicles. I took off my glasses and put them down on my bag to take my jumper off but then, do you think I could find them again? Oh my God! I had everything out of the changing rooms, my handbag, my shopping bag, my bike basket – everything – about 4 times and they were nowhere. I felt quite sick with panic. Anyway, Miss Pushy kept saying, "Oh they'll turn up – here try this on. It's the next size up." Which didn't help as every single dress at size 16 was TOO SMALL and I refuse to wear an 18. How depressing is that? In the end I said I needed to find my glasses and lose a stone and I'd go back later but she started to say that I hadn't been wearing them when I'd gone in – Durrrr! Then why did I have to take them off when I got changed? I was on the verge of submitting to hysteria when I saw them hanging off the strap of my bag. I grabbed them, shoved the dresses back at her and told her I'd be back when I've lost weight. Better get a move on as the wedding's in 5 weeks!

Then I went back to the yoga class. I'm not sure what I was expecting but certainly not that. The yoga teacher, an elderly Indian woman, asked if I was new to yoga.

Me: I'm new to this class, but I've been practising yoga for over 20 years. Over the years I've done Astanga, Iyanga, Svinanda and Hatha. What type of yoga is this class?

Teacher: Oh well you're quite an expert then. We're very basic here. I just teach what I learned on an Ashram in India about 40 years ago.

Me: That's OK. Would you mind if I sometimes did the progressions to the asanas?

Teacher: Well I'd rather you just stayed within the boundaries of the class, so that the others don't get confused and think they have to do complicated asanas.

That put me in my place!

The rest of the group arrived – 5 of us altogether: 2 elderly Asian women – one with a brain tumour and heart disease; a youngish black woman and an elderly Canadian woman wearing the type of clothing not normally seen outside Lapland, who talked and giggled the entire time. `Basic yoga' didn't go halfway to describing the session. `Stretch and breathe' would have been better, but at least it was exercise and relaxing. At first, I found myself getting irritated by the Canadian woman, but I breathed into it and decided that was my challenge to accept her and her chatter and just be with the moment and not judge the class as being disappointing: it was just different. And it worked. Once I got off my stuff and was just with the movements, I quite enjoyed it for what it was. As they say on Star Trek., "It was yoga, Jim, but not as we know it!" I probably won't go back again.

Sam came home looking yellow around the eyes and exhausted. He slumped down on the settee in the study but, when I went to comfort him, he put up both hands: "No mothering! No mothering, thank you!" I told him that I wasn't going to mother him: I wanted to comfort and care for him, so he said, rather grudgingly, "Oh, all right then," and let me sit next to him. He said he'd felt sick all day and was utterly exhausted. He said he can't walk up the stairs to his office without stopping several times and he used to run up them. And the pain in his right hand is very bad all the time. He was very low again/still.

In the evening, every time he needed to get up off the settee, I had to either hoist him under his arms or push him from behind.

Tuesday November 2nd

Chemo +5

I felt bright-eyed and bushy-tailed despite having a broken night. Meditated together, then I did some sun salutations before cycling to the lake. I was skidding on all the mud but had a wonderful meditation. I cycled up to the counsellor, but she was ten minutes late and not particularly friendly. I told her again that I wanted help to get back in touch with me and my life and my career and she's seeing me again in 2 weeks, so we'll see.

Wednesday November 3rd

Chemo +6

Another dreadful night for Sam. I don't know what to do – he's already on sleeping pills AND Amitriptyline. Of course the problem with all sleeping type tablets is that the body becomes immune to their effects and needs stronger and stronger doses

– and before you know it, you're addicted to prescription drugs. He is totally zonked. I worry about him driving when he's so tired but he's adamant that he's OK. I went to cuddle him but the whole top left of his body around his shoulder and upper chest is so tender – that's where the biggest lymphomas were and the site of his biopsy. He says he can feel things going on in his body: bubbling, boiling, fizzing sensations and it freaks him out. If I'm slightly too enthusiastic with my hugs, he screams out in pain. And he was freezing when he woke up. I took his temperature and it was down to 35.2o – very near hypothermia level again. He did warm up after he'd had a bath but I worry all the time.

Book group tonight at Preeti's. I got Sam his dinner, got dressed, dried my hair and put on some slap. At 6.30, I was just cooking the rice for Alice and my tea (due to eat at 7pm) when the phone rang.

Me: This had better not be Alice saying she's just leaving work.

A: Hi Marzie, I'm really, really sorry but I've got held up and I'm just leaving work. (!!!!!)

Me: That's fine. I'll tell you what, I'll put your dinner in a Tupperware container and take it to Preeti's. You get the tube there and we'll pick you up at the station.

A: Great. Sorry about this.

Two minutes later, the phone rings:

A: Ma, there's a tube strike. I'm just leaving work. Can you check on the Internet and see if any stations are open.

Me: I thought it was ending at 6?

A: Everyone at work says it's still on till 9. Anyway, ring me. OK?

I checked on the Internet – everything was down!

Me: Angel – get the overground and I'll meet you at the station. Ring me from your end because it'll take me a good 10 minutes to get there.

Phoned Louise and told her not to come round to me for a lift: I'd pick her up when I'd got Alice – whenever that was. Tried to ring Una but the answer phone was on. Left a message to the same effect.

A: Ma, I'm getting the high-speed link. It takes 7 minutes and I'm leaving now.

Eeeek! Stuffed my dinner down my throat and threw Alice's into a container with a fork, kissed Sam goodbye and got into the car. But, just as I was leaving Sam said he'd felt really ill all day. Great – now he tells me! Then he realised he'd forgotten to take ANY tablets at all today! Jesus wept! Told him to take them now and rest. Leapt into the car and sped off to collect Alice.

Got there just as Alice was walking towards me. Drove back with her eating her dinner in the passenger seat. Got to Una's at 7.30 to be told she'd already left for my house – she hadn't heard the message. (What's the point of an answer phone if you don't listen to it?) So drove round to ours to try and catch her before she got Sam out of bed or off the settee - but failed. She was chatting to Sam on the doorstep. Just had time to drop off Alice's dish, her to dash to the loo, me kiss Sam (again) grab Una and off to pick up Louise. Mad!

Still got to Preeti's by 8.10 and had a lovely evening. It is so important for me to have evenings like this with all my girlfriends and talking about things other than hospitals and doctors. Gave Preeti her box of sweet meats for Diwali and she gave me some divas to light in the window for Lachmi to come and bless us for another year – didn't do it last Diwali, so that explains why it's been such a crap year! Dropped the others back and got home about 11. Alice and I had a glass of wine and catch up, then went up at about 12.30. Lovely!

Thursday November 4th

Chemo +7

Only managed 4 hours sleep. Knackered! Made Alice breakfast and we looked at some of her wedding photos and had a chat. She was saying that Sam is a legend after the way he helped out at their wedding and it must be very hard for him to know that he can't contribute in the same way at Tom's. I hadn't really thought of that.

When she'd gone to work, I took Sam's breakfast up. He was struggling to get out of bed. I keep telling him to take time off but he won't. He could hardly put one foot in front of the other.

I sat by the lake and reflected on last night and how fortunate I am to have so many good friends. I truly do believe I have been blessed in this life: my family, my friends, Sam, my home, the charity grant, the Macmillan grant, the NHS, the welfare state... And on and on goes the list. I shed a little tear of gratitude. It was so lovely and mild and the sun was shining on the glorious trees. It really is a wonderful way to start the day.

Friday November 5th

Chemo +8

I set up some arts and craft things in the sitting room and then left at 8 to collect Lily from the station. She ran down the platform towards me with arms outstretched. I could gobble her up, I love her so much.

Had a fabulous day. We did sticking leaves and making collages with bark and twigs. It was wonderful. We raked up all the leaves from the lawn and she helped me put them in the recycling bag – although she fell in it - twice!

Saturday November 6th

Chemo +9

There was a letter from the Carers' Allowance people and I thought: Yay! I'm going to get my Carers' Allowance and then I can get a cleaner. But when I opened it, they said they needed more information about my self-employment. My heart sank – more form-filling! And more delay.

We went shopping and Sam was clearly in a lot of pain in both hands. He kept wincing and doubling up clutching them to his chest. He couldn't push the trolley or lift things on to the conveyor. He's also got these weird lines on his hands. Lord knows what they are.

When we got home, I made dinner but I was very emotional again. Feel so cross with myself. I kept bursting into tears. Sam's the one with cancer and yet he's the one supporting me half the time, instead of it being the other way round. Sam was very sweet saying, in the New Year, when he's off the chemo, I should go away for a couple of days just to have some rest and time for myself - but that made me feel even more guilty. He says, we're a team: we help each other out in times of hardship – but he's the one who's ill and I'm the one who's whinging.

Sunday November 7th

Chemo +10

What is the matter with me? Today I started to make lunch but dropped the kitchen roll and collapsed into tears again. Sam told me to go and have a wander up to the farmers' market. He said it might cheer me up. It was nice but it was full of people I know. Which is fine - most of the time. But today I really didn't want to be filling people in on how Sam is, or telling those who didn't know the saga of the last 6 months. I know I must sound a real grump at the moment – nothing's right. I went to get some cash out and realised I didn't have my bank card and came so close to dissolving into tears again - in the middle of the High Street.

Sam told me to go away next weekend – take a couple of days to myself but I'd prefer it if we went together. I do want a holiday, but I keep thinking: what if he does die? I'll have years of being on my own. I want to make the most of the time we have together – and if it turns out that we've got another 30 years, all well and good! But we might not have.

We went out for a drive in the afternoon and Sam said he wanted to drive. But he misjudged a turning and tried to turn before a bollard which would have taken us straight into a wall. I shouted, "No!" and he braked just in time – and there was a car coming towards us. It's things like that that make me question his ability to drive at the moment but he's adamant he's OK.

On the way back we could see lots of fireworks going off, so Sam drove us to the top of the road and we sat in the car and watched the display at the rugby club. Magnificent! It was lovely and reminded me of our first bonfire night together when we walked up to the footbridge and stood on there watching all the fireworks going off for miles around. Very romantic!

Monday November 8th

Chemo +11

Sam had his blood test and was then called in by The Leprechaun. It was all a bit weird and I'm not sure why Sam even had to go because The Leprechaun said exactly what had been said before: except that he clearly hadn't read Sam's notes - again! He kept saying Sam had CLL which we'd already established that he hasn't and then said, "Well the diagnosis isn't straight forward but what we do know is that you're getting better much more quickly than we'd thought." Then, when I asked about the thrombosis, he referred to it being in Sam's lungs and had to be reminded that it was in his right jugular. He said it was impossible to tell if it was dispersing from the CT scan – which is odd, because it was first spotted on a CT scan! But, at the end of the day, he said that all being well Sam should be OK without any medication once he's in remission. Which is good news. Then, when Sam showed him the lines on his hands, he said he'd never known anything like them, nor the amount of pain he's in. He said he couldn't give any indication whether or not it would go once the chemo's stopped. But, Sam said, he'd rather be in pain for the rest of his life and know that the cancer has gone. If that's the price he has to pay for a clean bill of health, then so be it.

I then asked about the para-protein levels in Sam's blood but he said they haven't been checked since August! So, he sent him back for a second blood test.

Tuesday November 9th

Chemo +12

TEN HOURS SLEEP LAST NIGHT! TEN HOURS! Fabulous!

Sam's talking about doing a Lands End to John O'Groats bike ride to raise money for Cancer Research next year. We'll see how that one goes. And he wants to do a marathon for them as well. I do hope he does get fit enough to do all these things – it would mean so much to him. At the moment he can barely get off the settee, so there's a long way to go. Not that I'm going to step on anyone's dreams.

It was so cold, I tried to light a fire but didn't have any wood and the firelighters wouldn't take. And I don't have the car to go to the garage or DIY place to buy some. Checked the bank account and we were overdrawn – AGAIN! God knows where the money goes. But, walked up the High Street to get some peas for tonight's supper and, hey presto, there was a skip full of wood off-cuts. And then came home and saw that I'd got a tax rebate of £1500! THANK YOU UNIVERSE! How amazing is that: two prayers answered in the space of an hour!

Wednesday November 10th

Chemo +13

Started to do the Carers' Allowance form but all the dates were all over the place – it said they wanted it back by 18th October 2010 – i.e. 3 weeks ago! And 2 weeks before I even sent it off. And they wanted my figures from 6th April 2010 to 5th April 2010!! So they want my business accounts for minus one day? Bonkers! I rang them up and a man said, "Someone's not been doing their job properly." (You think?) Anyway, he said he'll put a note of our call on the computer and speak to the people dealing with my case because it sounds as though I've sent them everything they need. We'll see! I have about as much confidence in these government departments to deal with things as I would a chimp with a chainsaw to take out a splinter.

4.40 pm

Had such a fantastic day: I wrote! All afternoon! A packager has asked me to submit a partial for a commission. I've finished the prologue of the writing sample. 800 words. Hardly War and Peace but it's the first writing I've done for 6 months. I feel like me again. *[A packager is a company that is subcontracted by a publishing house to commission authors to write books. They often supply the synopsis and characters for a book and authors flesh it out into an entire novel. I've tried packaged books before and found it quite difficult to get the right tone the company's looking for.]*

Thursday November 11th

Chemo +14

Walked over to the lake this morning as it was so wet and blustery. Sat in the rain and watched the wind whip up little waves on the lake – not exactly a surfing venue, but they must have been a good 3 or 4 inches – which is significantly bigger than the usual mill pond ripples.

A woman from the Carers' Allowance people rang today – the bloke I spoke to yesterday had given me totally duff information! I do have to fill in the form and I have to fill it in for the LAST financial year! I said, "But I wasn't a carer then, and I earned more last year than I've been earning since my husband's been ill." Anyway, she said it had to be done – and I can't just send in a copy of my tax return, I have to fill the whole thing in again on their form!

Sam got home and, when I went into the kitchen, he'd put all the fairy lights on and he swept me up in his arms and started to smooch round the sitting room singing `Moon River.' It was so lovely and romantic. I just revelled in the moment.

Then suddenly, he was freezing again. Every part of his skin was cold to the touch. He wrapped himself in a blanket on the settee and fell asleep at 7.30.

Friday November 12th - 4 am

Chemo +15

After a lovely cuddle in bed this morning, I said I'd like to drive Sam to work so that I can have the car to go to the lake and yoga as my knee's not up to fast cycling yet. But, as he was getting into the car, the wind caught the door and whipped it back, twisting his hand with it. He screamed with pain and sat doubled up in the passenger seat clutching it to his chest. I could weep when things like that happen. I feel so impotent. I dropped him off at work but got held up in traffic coming back – had barely 15 minutes by the lake, then couldn't find a parking spot at yoga and had to park miles away. Then, the bulk of the session was on our knees! Just the body part I was hoping to protect, but I did it gently and didn't over stretch myself, so it didn't hurt.

I then spent the afternoon filling in the CA form for self-employment. Which bears very little resemblance to the Inland Revenue Tax Return, so it's not just a case of transferring figures from one form to another – they separate out half the categories! Plus - last year's income was about 3 times more than this year's so far!

Later

Went to pick up Sam then went to do the shopping. It was pouring with rain and the Friday night traffic was awful, but as we drove into the car park, he realised he'd left his tablets at work! So Sam drove back to work again and joined me later. He insisted on pushing the trolley and then lifting the bags of shopping but he was then in excruciating pain in both hands, doubling up and crying out. I've told him if he doesn't stop trying to be all macho and actually start to take care of himself,

I'll have to strap up his hands and make him wear a sling just so that he doesn't use them. He wasn't impressed. He went up to do his Clexane and came down, bent double and holding out his sweatshirt so that it didn't touch him. It's so awful to watch him like this and not be able to do anything to make it better. I was very emotional again this evening and then I feel guilty because I'm supposed to be being strong and supportive for him and I'm just a useless wimp much of the time.

Sunday November 14th

Chemo +17

This morning Sam was sitting in the bath. He said, "It's been a good year this year, hasn't it?"

I wondered what planet he'd been living on!

Me: In what way?

Sam: In lots of ways. I mean I've conquered cancer for one thing.

Bless – what an amazing outlook.

When he came down, he was hoovering and dusting again with Nina Simone blaring out, he whisked me up and we were slow dancing round the sitting room. So lovely and romantic when he's like this. I started tidying up the kitchen and study but, at about 1pm I came over very nauseous. I made some toasted cheese sandwiches for lunch but then fell asleep and slept for 3 hours on the settee. I must have been exhausted.

Monday November 15th

Chemo +18

It was the Macmillan Support Group today and we were discussing `Fatigue.' It amazes me that no one warns you about this. Both the cancer patients and carers who go there are always exhausted: the patients because of the treatments and the carers because of the emotional and physical demands on them. Didn't feel quite so bad about being tired all the time.

Came out at 4pm and there was the most magnificent sunset – a massive crimson sun going down over the station. Phenomenal! I kept dodging from one side of the road to the other to try and see it in all its glory. What I really needed to do was walk down the middle of the main road, backwards, but thought that might be slightly lethal, so had to make do with turning round every few yards. It was truly breath-taking.

Sam got home absolutely frozen. I brought down his big jumper and he put it on, along with his anorak and woolly hunter's hat and boots. He looked as though he was going into the wilds of Alaska rather than sitting watching TV in a centrally heated house. Then, of course, he suddenly became so hot he thought he was going to pass out. He had to strip it all off again. The concept of a happy medium is one that seems to have escaped his body.

He showed me some black spots that have started all over his legs, which is worrying. And his legs were twitching again as he sat with them up. I wish they'd get this sorted out. I said I'd like to go to the doctor with him on Tuesday and ask if he even needed the 6th chemo if he's done so well. What's the point of pumping him full of more toxins? He says he can actually feel it in his body eating away at things, especially round his liver area and the top of his chest near where the large lymphoma was. Can't even begin to imagine it!

Tuesday November 16th

Chemo +19

Woke up at 1.30 and was awake for nearly 4 hours! A couple of decent nights' sleep, now back to this. It drives me nuts.

I was at the NHS counsellor again today – Mrs Frosty. My appointment was 10 am and I got there at 9.50. She walked through the door at 10.06 and came to collect me at 10.10.

Me: Can I ask if you have a problem with me, because this is twice I've seen you and both times you've been late. If I was 10 minutes late to my appointment you would be within your rights to cancel my therapy, but you've been late twice without so much as an explanation or apology.

Counsellor: No, I don't have a problem with you. Does that answer your question? (Oh yes. It answers it very well, thank you!)

We then went on to talk about my writing and she couldn't see any reason why I shouldn't be able to write 2500 words by 30th.

Counsellor: If this was paid employment, you'd have to knuckle down and get on with it. You wouldn't be able to have coffee with a friend, so you need to treat it as a proper job.

I then said that I was worried that, even if I did get the commission, I wouldn't be able to meet the deadlines with what's going on at the moment.

Counsellor: Do you actually want this commission?

Me: Of course I want it!

Counsellor: Well then stop living your life in `what ifs.'

FFS! I came out feeling utterly exasperated. It was not constructive. She seems to have no understanding of depression or exhaustion and caring for someone - or the effect that has on the creative process.

When Sam came home, I just started sobbing on his chest as he walked through the door. He was really sweet and said (again) that I should go away and have a few days to myself. When I said that wasn't possible he told me to go to a spa and get pampered. Tempting as that is, we've got a lot of expenditure coming up with the wedding so I couldn't really justify it. If I get accepted to do this commission, I might go.

He then told me that when he'd gone out of the house this morning, he couldn't turn the key in the lock because of his hands and had spent almost 10 minutes trying. He'd screamed out in pain and the woman over the road had come across to see if he was all right. How could I go away and leave him like that? It's dreadful watching him so helpless and dependent and that stupid counsellor has no understanding or appreciation of the toll it takes.

Friday November 19th

Chemo +22

Foggy today. Cycled over to the lake and it was eerily misty and spooky. The herons were about, flapping through the fog like prehistoric beings – wonderful and so majestic.

Did the corrections to the writing sample and sent it off – fingers crossed.

Saturday November 20th

Chemo +23

I had my nails done for Tilly's hen party tonight. I was very excited and took a long time to do my hair and make-up and have a bath. At one point Sam came upstairs and said that he and Myles were frozen. I told him to put on either the heating or the fire but he said he'd forgotten how! But when I went down he'd put on both the fire and the heating and it was like a furnace in the sitting room, yet he was wearing his coat and was wrapped in a blanket. He has no way of moderating his body temperature at all.

I got the tube and got chatted up on the train! Ok, so he was drunk, but it was still a nice little ego boost. The restaurant looked lovely and the hen-do was great and took my mind off everything. My girls were there, of course, and Tilly's mum. Fabulous! And then Sam and Myles came to pick me up from the station which was very sweet.

Tuesday November 23rd

Chemo +25

Sam was at the hospital to have his pre-chemo blood tests today and I went up to the West End to get something to wear for the wedding. Eventually, I found a dress that fitted and looked really lovely - thank goodness. It's less than 3 weeks to go.

I felt really happy and relaxed but when I got home there was a message on the answer phone from my agent. I didn't get the commission. They'd liked my writing and said they'd like to work with me in the future (they probably say that to every writer) but they'd had another submission that was better. I just dissolved. I really don't know how much longer I can keep kidding myself that I'm a writer. I've had nothing published for over 2 years. I feel so desolate. When I was writing I felt alive. I just love writing and creating stories - but I also need the money. I really don't know what to do.

Sam was very understanding when he got home. He always is when I'm upset and feeling vulnerable – he rises to the `big strong protector' role very well. Not that I need protecting! He said he'd asked The Leprechaun if he could have therapy as he was feeling very low and he said he'd look into why it hadn't happened before. Homer Simpson was nowhere to be seen apparently. He wasn't told the results of his blood test, but he said he'd ask on Thursday.

Wednesday November 24th

Chemo +26

Feeling very happy and relaxed having made a decision to carry on writing in the New Year but have a rest for now. But, when I got home there was a letter from the Carer's Allowance people. It said that I'd been refused Carers' Allowance BECAUSE I EARNED TOO MUCH!

I rang them up straight away and said: But I earn nothing! Nothing!

Woman: It's based on your last year's earnings. (What sort of lunacy is that?)

Me: But I wasn't a carer last year. My husband wasn't ill last year and I could work last year. He is ill now and I haven't been able to work since May.

Woman: Yes but you earn royalties.

Me: I received £143 in September! For the period from December to June: £143 for six months!

Woman: Yes but the money you earned last year is for this year. (What???)

Me: No, it isn't.

Woman: If you got paid weekly, you'd get paid at the end of the week and it would last you for the following week.

Me: But with self-employment it doesn't work that way. I don't get paid at the end of the year – I get paid throughout the year. I don't get paid in one lump and save up all my bills then say, I'll pay them next year!

I burst into tears and rang off. I then did some calculations and rang back. I spoke to another woman who said she knew about my case.

Me: This is bonkers! Since April this year I've earned £1400 – that's £41 per week and I was told that the limit was £100 per week.

Woman: You said you earned £6000 since April.

Me: No that was last year: I earned £6000 in total last financial year. So far this year I've earned £2000 and had £600 expenses.

Woman: Well, that's probably where the confusion is. You told us you earned £6000 since April.

Me: No, it isn't, because you've had all the figures in writing – several times.

Woman: There's no need to shout.

Me: I'm not shouting – I'm crying. I'm very upset about this. It's bad enough my husband has cancer and all the stress that that brings let alone all the added expense of travelling to and from appointments and the increased heating bills because he's so cold all the time. Plus, I can't work at all because I'm in a creative profession and I can't get creative when I'm under so much stress and can't go to schools for visits. And then I have all this added stress because someone thinks I earn too much at £41 per week!

I was sobbing and sobbing. In the end she said, "It's not our intention to cause people distress (but you managed it all the same!) so I'll go back to the assessor who assessed you and tell her your situation and ask her to look at the figures again."

I thanked her but still feel so upset about it. What sort of a stupid system is it when my income last year – which averaged out at only £115 per week anyway, is supposed to still be paying the bills? It's mad that I could have earned £99 a week and been awarded Carer's Allowance on top of that but if I'd earned £101 (or £115 in my case) I don't get anything. And how do they think that royalties earned 19 months ago are going to last till now?

Have wept on and off all day. I seem to be so fragile at the moment. Niamh popped round to see the dress and she loved it. She's so much more positive and upbeat than I am – and she's the one with cancer!

I did muster some energy to clean the sitting room – it's so dusty – as is everywhere else. I was counting on that money to get a cleaner once a fortnight, just so that I wasn't getting upset about the housework – I can't even kneel down at the moment with my knee as it is. Feel completely overwhelmed. And the ironing basket's like K2 - again!

Sam rang on his way home – he said, "Hon, I think I'm losing my mind. I went to do a home assessment today and when I got there, I'd lost the form. I don't know what I'd done with it. I looked everywhere." He loses things all the time: keys, wallet, phone, gloves, hat, scarf, chemo book. I despair.

Thursday November 25th

Round 6 of Chemo - hopefully last session

Oh my days! Chemo day today and we overslept. Finally left at just turned 10. Sam forgot his coat and it's -2o at the moment. Then he forgot his chemo book. Dear Lord!

No word from the Carer's Allowance people again. I don't know whether to write a formal appeal letter or if that's going to aggravate them more. Amy's sent me the link to find out who my MP is and get him/her on my side.

Sam was told that his para-protein level is down to 22 – not as low as I'd have liked after 6 months of chemo. Below 20 is the magic number apparently. It was 48 at the beginning.

He said he felt a strange anti-climax leaving the unit for (hopefully) the last time. Just wondering where we go from here? The doctor said it was a case of 'watch and wait' now. Not sure what that means: watch for the signs and wait for it to come back? Anyway, if it does come back, let's hope he's treated at Perry's and not here. If I never see Raphe's again, it'll be too soon!

But, for now, I can give my full attention to Tom and Tilly's wedding. Yay!

Part 3

Waiting

November 2010 – October 2018

For reasons that are probably obvious – i.e. the eight year time span - the section while Sam and I were watching and waiting for his cancer to come back will be greatly reduced in terms of diary entries. It will begin with excerpts from my journal because the problems Sam had with his health didn't end the second the chemo finished. But, as our journey progressed and his bouts of illness decreased, there were some profoundly uplifting moments in our lives and our relationship – as well as the inevitable dips that come with any marriage let alone a marriage with cancer constantly hovering in the background.

Friday November 26th

It's -3° this morning. Magnificent colours - burnished bronzes and golds and rusts reflected on a solid pond.

I feel quite low this morning and I don't know why. It's a fabulous morning and Sam's getting better – or at least his cancer is: the neuropathy in his hands is still very bad. We've got the wedding in 2 weeks, which I'm so looking forward to and we're spending Christmas with Amy, Chris and Lily. So many good things coming up!

It's so cold at the moment we've got the heating on 24hrs, plus the fire in the evenings and on top of that, Sam sits with his big woolly hat, his thermal gloves and his huge fluffy slippers, all wrapped up in a blanket. And, even then, I have to keep taking his temperature to check that he's not going into hypothermia. He was in such pain with his hands that he went to bed at 8.30. I've bought him some thermal socks and gloves to keep for bed and he put those on. He was really depressed about it again.

Wednesday December 8th

Tom and Tilly's `paper' wedding day!

Chemo +13

Big Wedding – 3 days

Today was Tom and Tilly's registry office wedding: a low key affair compared to Saturday's Big Barn Bonanza!

Sam's hands were so painful this morning that he couldn't get out of bed. He had to roll out and then crash back in again because he couldn't lower himself gently. And his hands got so hot in the sleeping gloves last night that they were really painful and woke him up several times. The socks are a success though. I've cut the elastic on the socks and gloves – we don't want him ending up with thrombosis.

We went to Tom' and Tilly's on the tube and met the others in the pub before walking up to the Register Office. Everyone was in good spirits and it was nice to see Tilly wearing my Monsoon top – something borrowed AND blue! She had a huge orange daisy sticking out of her jeans back pocket: her token bouquet! The service was very short and to the point, yet I still felt extremely emotional. It seems just the blink of an eye since I was hugely pregnant with Tom, then pushing him out into the world and there he was: all grown-up and handsome and getting married! My last baby to tie the knot: they're all settled now.

Thursday December 9th

Big Wedding – 2 days

I went over to the lake early this morning and got there just as the sun was coming up: the sky looked like an enormous cosmic rasher of streaky bacon – all pink and yellow, and it was reflected on the trees across the lake. Absolutely breath-taking!

Sunday December 12th

Chemo +19

Wow! On Saturday we got to the barn and were blown away by how fantastic it looked. Like something out of a Disney fantasy: all fairy lights and tinsel and fake snow. So proud of my children: the attention to detail and impeccability were second to none. They'd all worked so hard – I'm always impressed at how hard my children work and how well they work together to create these events. The main barn had an enormous twelve foot Christmas tree in the corner. Tilly looked stunning, like a 1920s flapper with her simple headdress and beautiful dress with its little shrug and Tom looked so handsome and happy – I just sobbed through most of the service. It was so emotional. Then we all tossed fake snow as confetti as they walked down the aisle.

They'd placed us near one of the heaters in the warmest spot, so that Sam didn't get cold. Unfortunately, he's got a nasty ulcer that's really painful and so sore that it's hard for him to eat. He had to wear his gloves all the time but other than that, he managed to stay pretty warm. It was a truly amazing day – I danced like a loony all evening and Sam managed a couple of slow dances too. At one point I saw my children all hugging each other and dancing together and felt such a powerful surge of love and admiration and pride, I was just sitting there, weeping at the table.

We finally got a cab back to the hotel at midnight and, although the room was stiflingly hot, Sam was shivering. When I woke at 3.30, he was freezing and I couldn't see or feel him breathing. I felt sick. I thought he'd overdone it and died in the night. I went cold and was prodding him to wake him up. In the end he shouted at me to stop hitting him and I've never felt so relieved!

Wednesday December 15th

Sam's bottom lip is now so swollen he looks as though he's done a couple of rounds with Joe Calzaghe. He was so shocked at how it looks that he's going to go to the day unit and get checked out.

I rang the Carers' Allowance people again today. Waited for the interminable recorded message, listened to Handel's Water Music for God knows how long, then a voice told me that, 'all their agents were busy and would I ring back later.' Aaaaggghhh! When I did get through to someone, she told me that my case had been sent off on 2nd December to seek advice as to whether or not I can be treated as a special case. Fingers crossed - but I was in floods again with the frustration of it all.

Of course, when Sam got to the day unit it was closed! We'd both forgotten it shuts on Wednesdays. Anyway, he'd knocked and knocked until a nurse came and she took his blood and BP and sent for the doctor to come across. Apparently his `blood count is low' but he can't remember whether it's haemoglobin or white cells. He's been taking less and less of his black treacle lately, so it wouldn't surprise me if it's his haemoglobin. *[One of the Macmillan nurses was also a nutritionist and told me that 1 tablespoon of black treacle contains as much iron as 9 egg yolks, so I'd been giving it to Sam every day. His Hb had risen from 6.4 – 14. Normal is about 13.]* Homer Simpson and The Leprechaun came over and said he'd picked up a mouth infection (didn't need a medical degree to work that out) which is not uncommon as people come off chemo – it's a sort of withdrawal thing. They've given him 2 lots of antibiotics and some mouth wash but told him not to take Paracetamol, which he has been doing, as it could mask other symptoms and/or a temperature.

Later

Sam looked awful when he got home. He was coughing and shivering and his temperature was 38.4! Oh god - here we go again! Later it rose to 39.7! I took it every 15 minutes for the next hour and it ranged from 39.7 – 39.4. I rang Raphe's – God, what a dire place that is!

Me: (after ringing and ringing and ringing.) My husband is a cancer patient of Head Honcho can you put me through to the haematology on-call doctor please. (As it tells you to do in the blue book.)

171

Switchboard: Haematology? Is that blood?

Me: Yes, can you put me through to the on-call haematologist please.

Switchboard: I don't know who that is. Is it the blood doctor?

Me: Yes. Can you put me through please?

Switchboard: I've got two numbers here. One's for haematology and the other's for the doctor on call.

Me: That's what I asked for – the on-call haematologist. This is urgent, can you put me through please?

Voice: Haematology.

Me: My husband is a patient of Head Honcho, he came in yesterday and saw Homer Simpson and the Leprechaun and now he's got a temperature of 39.6.

Voice: This is haematology.

Me: Yes, can I speak to the on-call doctor please.

Voice: This is the lab. I can't do that but I can put you back to switchboard.

Me: Yes please, do that. I really need to speak to the on-call doctor.

Drrrrrrrrrrrrrrrrrrrrrrrrrrrrrrrrrrrrrrrrrrrrrrrrrrrrrrrrrrrrrrrrrrrrrrrrrr

(Line goes dead!)

Attempt no 2:

Me: My husband is a cancer patient of Head Honcho can you put me through to the on-call haematologist please? This is urgent.

Switchboard: Hold on. (Several minutes of muzak.) Sorry he's not answering his bleep. I'll put you through to A&E.

A&E: Hello Majors.

Me: My husband is a cancer patient of HH, can I speak to the on-call haematologist please?

A&E: This is A&E majors. We can't help you. You need to speak to the on-call haematologist.

Me: I know – that's who I'm trying to get hold of but they put me through to you.

A&E: But we're A&E majors. We don't have anything to do with what you're asking.

Me: So why was I put through to you? (Getting a tad frustrated by this time)

A&E: Well, I don't know what you expect me to do. You should have been put through to the on-call haematologist.

Me: Well, if you had a switchboard that was run by anything other than prancing ponies I might get somewhere!

Attempt no 3:

Me: OK – now I will say this very slowly. I NEED TO SPEAK TO THE ON-CALL HAEMATOLOGIST. MY HUSBAND HAS CANCER AND HE HAS A TEMPERATURE OF 39.6. THIS IS URGENT!

Switchboard: I've already tried to get him for you but if he doesn't answer his bleep - what am I supposed to do?

Me: I don't know – keep trying?

Switchboard: That's what I was doing. Hold on...

Different Voice: Do you want to speak to the haematology reg?

Me: Yes please.

Voice: Hold on.

And then, hallelujah - The Leprechaun came on the line. I told him about Sam and that he didn't want to go into A&E and he said, "Well if he doesn't want to come in, there's nothing we can do." I burst into tears. (AGAIN!)

Me: But his temperature is so high, Doctor. Did you listen to his chest yesterday? He's coughing really badly.

Leprechaun: No it was my colleague Homer Simpson who saw your husband.

Me: But his temperature is 39.6 and he's got a dreadful cough.

Leprechaun: It sounds as though his mouth infection has gone to his chest but if he refuses to come in there's nothing we can do. Is he taking his antibiotics?

Me: Yes.

Leprechaun: It sounds as though he needs some different ones but the unit's closed and we have no wards open. You can give him some Paracetamol tonight to bring his temperature down and he can come into the unit tomorrow if he won't come in tonight.

Me: (Sobbing) I'm sorry doctor. I've tried to reason with him but he can be very stubborn.

Leprechaun: Yes, I know. He was very difficult yesterday. (Hallelujah! At least they're seeing it too now.)

My heart sank. I came off the phone and told Sam that he needed different antibiotics. He said he'd go along to A&E but wouldn't stay in hospital because it was so stressful when he was admitted in the summer.

Me: OK but, Hon, they kept you alive. Whatever you or I think about them, they saved your life in the summer.

Sam: All right I'll go. Give me a minute.

I went downstairs and waited and waited. At 10 to 8 I went up and he was still in bed.

Me: Are we going to A&E or not?

Sam: No.

FOR FUCK'S SAKE! I poured myself a large glass of wine. Sod it!

Friday December 17th

Sam's temperature went up and up till it reached 40.1o - which it still is. His cough is dreadful and his breathing very shallow and panty.

When he went for his bath he walked straight into the wall, then he slipped getting into the bath – he's really not stable on

175

his feet but he keeps saying, "I'm fine, I'm OK, there's nothing wrong with me." He's also saying that he remembers nothing of last night – so perhaps it was delirium? Or selective memory syndrome?

6.45 pm

I took Sam to the Day Unit but the staff there were less than happy to see him, in fact the sister was visibly annoyed, saying, "We can't cope with you Sam: there are only 2 of us on today. You should've gone to A&E last night. I mean you came in here on Wednesday when we were shut. You can't just come up here and expect to be seen like that. (Which, actually, isn't what the Macmillan team told us!) Why didn't you go to A&E last night?"

Sam: I was too tired. I couldn't make it down the stairs to the car.

Sister: Well, why didn't you ring 999 for an ambulance? (Glaring at me!)

I sooooo wanted to say Fuck you! But I restrained myself.

So off we went to A&E. The whole triage business is very frustrating and there was no one at the window, so we went to reception who told us to go back to the window and wait till someone came. I said, "My husband is a cancer patient with a temperature of over 40, he needs to be seen urgently." To which he replied, "Triage will be the judge of that."

After a while someone came to the window but sent us back to the receptionist, who then wanted everything bar his inside leg measurement – despite the fact that they'd already got it in his records - then they sent us to follow the red line to `Majors.' Sam was called in to the assessment room, but the little male nurse refused to let me in (even though every other time I've been allowed in) and I sat and sat and sat until he called someone else into the same room.

Me: Excuse me – but where's my husband? He was in that room.

Him: Wait a minute I'm dealing with this patient.

Me: Excuse me but you were dealing with my husband, now where is he?

He pointed through the door and I went in and found Sam in the cubicle. A doctor came fairly quickly – within about half an hour anyway – and sent him for a chest X-ray. The Leprechaun and another haematologist came in and said he'd got sepsis again, but they were very happy with the treatment he was being given. The Leprechaun was very sweet actually and said he'd been at home when I called and he'd said to his wife that he wished there was something he could have done to help and any time I needed to talk, to ring and ask for him to be bleeped. So, I take back all my thoughts about his ability in the past.

Sam's temperature had gone down slightly to 39.7 by this time. He was put onto IV antibiotics and it came down fairly quickly to 38.3 then 37.6.

He went for his X-ray, then another doctor came in and went through all the same stuff as the previous one – asking the same questions – twice! He said Sam would probably be kept in for about 3 days observation to make sure everything was OK and to try and find out where the infection was that was causing the temperature. (His mouth ulcers?)

Sam was very low and quite despondent when we were waiting. His right hand is excruciating again and the cannula was very painful. He said, "I'm sick of all this. If this is what the rest of my life's going to be like, I think it's just not worth it. What's the point? I'm so angry that this has happened to me. I've always prided myself on my physical strength and now I can't even take the top off a yoghurt or fasten my own clothes. I'd rather it just ended now if it's not going to get any better. I mean what's the point of getting rid of the cancer if I'm going to spend the rest of my life in and out of this place with these things in my arms and my hands cramping up all the time?"

I was sitting there crying my eyes out. What can I say? I can't say it's not going to be like this forever because I don't know. It might be. When he's being positive he goes on about all the things he's going to do 'when he's well again' but is he ever going to be well again? It all seems so hopeless sometimes. They took Sam to the emergency ward and put him in a side ward with infection control notices on the door.

I feel very strange this evening. My asthma is quite bad, probably stress related. I might have to go to the GP in the morning, but I won't tell Sam: he'll worry. I feel sad and lonely and flat – I feel as though I need to cry and yet I'm sick to death of crying. I'm tired and numb. I worry all the time about Sam – he is his own worst enemy where his health is concerned. I also worry for myself because if Sam does die, I'm right up the creek without a paddle. Since my royalties dried up, he's been our only bread winner. Although I suppose I could go on the dole and get housing benefit and everything else I can get from the state, but it's something that I do worry about - not to mention possibly losing him. Because, although he can be a difficult bugger at times, I love him to pieces and I know he loves me. I've never laughed as much as I have since I've been with Sam - although I've never cried as much either of late! We've been to such wonderful places and done so many amazing things together and I've learned so much while I've been with him. And I can be totally myself with him – doing funny dances or telling jokes or farting: he accepts me as a whole human being. He just says, "I love you for who you are and you're a very beautiful, sexy woman." I can't bear to think of what life would be like without him. Now I am bawling again – but I probably need to.

Saturday December 18th

Still crying! I went up to bed at 9 but couldn't sleep. I rang Sam a couple of times. He said he'd been dozing on and off but his temperature had spiked again – 39+ again, so they put the fan on him. Sam rang at 1.20 am to say that they were moving him to a different ward – at that time in the morning! They said a bed had just become available. I'm thinking, why does a bed become available in the middle of the night? That's not a normal discharge time. Probably means the patient died! I didn't say that to him though. Woke up at 6.15. Coughing and wheezing like an 80 year old on 60 a day!

Sam's in a side room because of his infectious state. A nurse came in with nutritional information saying that he should be on a special diet. (First we've heard of this!) He's not allowed any cold food – no salad, no bread unless it's less than 24 hrs old or toasted, no cold fish or meat, no eggs unless very well done, nothing microwaved, no takeaways, everything should be freshly cooked and not reheated! Why have we not been told this before? Plus – that rules out his staple diet of sandwiches and/or omelettes! What on earth am I going to feed him now? I was going to take him up the fruit salad I'd made but I'm not so sure now – it's cold, fruit and more than 24 hours old! [The condition was Neutropenia which is an abnormally low level of neutrophils - a type of white blood cell. It's usually caused by chemotherapy and/or blood cancers. The diet she talked about was called a neutropenic diet.]

I zapped myself up with steroids and inhalers and my chest is much better. I really want to talk to someone but who? It's the week before Christmas – who wants to listen to a wailing woman? I want someone to put their arms round me and hold me and let me cry and comfort me and make it all alright again – but of course they can't.

It started to snow at about 11 am and was blizzard conditions by 12. Our road was about 5"deep and utterly impassable, so I decided there was no way I was taking the car out – I'd walk to Raphe's. I loaded up a backpack with long-life fruit juice, fruit, slippers and all sorts of other stuff, donned my arctic parka, ski gloves, hat and snow chains and set off at 1.30. The problem with snow chains is that, although they stop you from slipping, they get clogged up with snow so, even by the end of the road, my feet were so heavy that my thighs were beginning to ache. I kept plodding on and when I got there the nurse said, "Visiting isn't till 2.30!"

Me: I don't know what time it is.

Nurse: Two thirty to seven thirty!

Me: No, the time now. I don't wear a watch.

Nurse: It's 2.20.

I was all of 10 minutes early – slap my wrists and put me in detention!

Sam was very low. He's been told he's likely to be in till Monday or Tuesday – yet he's still talking about doing his charity toy delivery on Wednesday. I get so frustrated with the man. What part of 'you're very ill' does he not get? *[Sam has done a toy delivery to the children's ward at Raphe's every Christmas since 2004 in memory of Frasier and also because he was in hospital himself every Christmas for the first six years of his life.]*

He's in solitary confinement and can't even leave the room to go to the loo. All his water has to be boiled and visitors monitored. I put some money on his TV but he says he's not even interested in that and he's not hungry or thirsty. He says he's anaemic and might have to have a blood transfusion. He was crying on and off and then I started. He was talking as though he was dying saying things like, "Well, we had a lovely dance on Saturday didn't we? If nothing else, we can go out on a high." I tried so hard to keep him positive, but it was very difficult.

6.30 Sam just rang to say a guy who shouts all the time had just tried to get into his room and had been kicking at the door. It took 3 nurses to remove him. Sam says he feels very frightened and daren't go to sleep now in case he tries again. He says he does not feel safe in there at all.

8.15 He's just rung again to say that the room is so hot he can hardly breathe, yet they can't turn the heating down and his temperature has gone up again. He's had to open the window, so now he's in a draught. They put the fan on but it's doing nothing because it's just pumping hot air at him. I still have a headache from being in there this afternoon.

Sunday December 19th

Several more calls to and from Sam – I've never heard him as low, ever! Again, he's talking about what's the point? I woke up at 5am hardly able to breathe. I coughed and coughed until I was sick – twice. Even after my inhalers, my peak/flow was only 340, whereas it's usually 460 – 470. I rang the out of hours doctor but he told me to go to Raphe's drop-in centre.

Me: I can't do that.

Dr: Why not?

Me: Because it's -5o, we've got 6" of snow, our road is impassable and I can hardly breathe.

Dr: Can't someone drive you?

Me: No, my husband has cancer and he's already in Raphe's.

Dr: Well get a cab! (Is he going to pay???)

Me: Why can't a doctor come out to me?

Dr: Because we have only one doctor on-call to cover the entire area and you're not a priority. Priority is given to people who are bed-bound or those, like your husband, who are terminally ill. (My husband is NOT terminally ill, thank you very much!!!)

Me: I've paid National Insurance all my life and I can't even get a doctor to come and see me when I'm ill!

Dr: If you go to St Raphael's they'll be expecting you.

So I got up, scraped the snow and ice off the car in the pitch dark and shovelled a sort of path down the road. Then I drove, very carefully, to A&E – two minor skids but nothing too bad.

The doctor said I'd got a chest infection and prescribed antibiotics. He said there was no significant wheeze. So why can't I breathe? Not visiting Sam today in case I give him whatever I've got.

When I got home I rang him, then staff nurse phoned me and said they were moving Sam a private room with its own bathroom and toilet. Hopefully he'll be able to get some proper rest.

7.30pm

Very little crying today: sob rating 2/10 - which has got to be an improvement! I wrapped all the Christmas presents, then wrapped myself up in blankets with a hot water bottle on the settee and slept. I've spoken to Sam a couple of times very briefly – he said this new room is quiet and much cooler, so hopefully he'll get some sleep. Although no private toilet as they'd said. He's on three different drips. The Leprechaun came to see him and said he might be able to come home tomorrow, which would be lovely.

Monday December 20th

Slept on the settee last night all snuggled up in a duvet. Not hugely comfortable but warm at least. I spoke to Sam several times last night.

Woke at 6.30 and I could breathe again – still coughing but at least I can get air into my lungs. It was -10°C last night and I discovered that our boiler is leaking! Great! Was very pleased with myself in that I didn't cry (yet!). Am currently trying to phone the engineer and also Perry's to cancel Sam's PET scan this morning. The Leprechaun said he'd do it on Friday, but I have no confidence in them at Raphe's, so am double checking – otherwise Perry's say they'll discharge him!

OK – crying factor rising again. I was on hold to the boiler engineers for 9 minutes when it told me to press 2, which I did and it cut me off! Repeat – only this time it was only 4 minutes on hold! And Perry's aren't answering. Sam's also asked me to take a whole load of his stuff into work for him and I've got to get to the GPs to get a repeat prescription for myself. Feel very close to breaking point again – but am NOT crying yet.

9.10am

Finally got through to Sam who says the room they put him in has NO heating at all and has water dripping through the ceiling onto his bed and on to the floor! One of the nurses said to him, "I don't know why they put you in this room. It's freezing." He says he's discharging himself because if he stays in there, he'll die. The nurse told him to wait for the doctor, but I told him I would support him if that's what he wanted to do and we would write a letter of complaint. But I'm worried if he does come home, I'm not a doctor or a nurse and I'd be worried sick all the time.

I then got through to Perry's who told me, the number on the top of the letter was incorrect and gave me a totally different one to ring! Jesus – what is wrong with everyone? I left a message.

I finally got through to the boiler people after going through to `anything else' – but the guy said there was nothing he could do as he was just admin and I had to keep trying the faults number.

Me: What is the point of that when I am on hold for 10 minutes and then told to replace the handset?

Man: Well, there's nothing else I can do.

Me: That's not an acceptable answer. My husband has cancer and we have a boiler that's only 2 years old yet is dripping water all over the place. I want you to either put me through to faults or let me speak to your superior.

In the end a man called Scott came on who was the supervisor and he took my number and said he'd email it across to faults but he was offering no guarantees.

Still not crying.

12 noon

Had been trying to ring Sam all morning but he's not picking up, so I rang the ward sister who said she was very sorry, but she'd told 'them' that the room wasn't suitable for a patient! She wanted to transfer Sam to another ward but he said he wanted to discharge himself because he had no confidence in them to get him well.

Then I started phoning around – I spoke to Head Honcho's secretary who listened and said she'd get on to it; then to PALS [Patient Advice and Liaison Service] – who were not a lot of use and just gave me the address of the complaints manager; then to Claire, the Macmillan nurse who said she'd go over to see him because his bloods were quite low and his temperature kept spiking and he really shouldn't be discharged until he was well enough. She also said that she was very cross that Sam had not been referred to the psychological services – she'd pressed and pressed and didn't know why the referral hadn't gone through. I also told her that they were refusing to give him his Amitriptyline because it hadn't been prescribed by the ward doctor. She said she'd get on to that. Also tried to get through to the Chief Nursing Officer but no joy.

Then Sam rang and there was such loud drilling overhead that I could hardly hear him, he was ranting and swearing – which is unusual for him. *[I'm the one who swears when I lose it.]* He said that a doctor had seen him this morning, a female doctor, and she said that a nurse could come to him at home and administer his antibiotics, which I'd feel much, much happier about.

Later

Sam rang again: the banging from the roof was even louder and he was having to shout just for me to hear him. While I was on the phone two people came into the room and I could hear one of them saying something about there was just one little leak. Sam said to me, "Lying cow! There are 3 leaks including one on my bed right next to my pillow. I've taken photos on my phone and shown Claire." Then another nurse came in and asked him what dosage of Amitriptyline he was on, so Claire's handled that. Good on her.

In the meantime, I'd lost my glasses, so I was walking round the house in my prescription sunglasses - in the middle of December! Thought I might have left them in the car but then couldn't find my car keys! God give me strength! Eventually found the spare set and my glasses were on the dashboard! Still haven't got through to the boiler engineers about the bloody boiler. I can see where the leak is – it looks like the overflow pipe has come away from the boiler, so I've propped it up with a piece of kindling which at least has minimised the amount of water leaking out. Have had a couple of bottom lip wobbles but no tears yet – very pleased with myself.

FINALLY got through to boiler people at 1.40! Spoke to a very nice man who told me that, from my description, it sounded as though the leak was from the condenser pipe which wasn't part of the boiler and the repair would have to be paid for. Now there's a surprise! We have a condensing boiler which, by definition, requires a condensing pipe - so why is it not part of the boiler? It comes out of the boiler and we would not have a condensing pipe if we didn't have condensing boiler. I was too tired to argue, so they're coming on Thursday to mend it. Meanwhile my kindling repair isn't quite as good as I'd initially thought. So much for my plumbing skills!

6.30pm

Claire rang to say that Sam would be moved to another ward – he was no. 1 priority and, once he'd left that ward, it would be condemned! They can find no cause for his sepsis other than the mouth ulcers. She also said that The Leprechaun had told the multidisciplinary team that he'd told me to take Sam to A&E on Friday morning! I said, "Claire, that's not true. I spoke to The Leprechaun myself and he said, `If he won't go to A&E tonight, give him 2 Paracetamol and take him to the Unit in the morning. I'll see him there.' And if he's telling people otherwise, then that's not the truth." I felt very cross – everyone's out to save their own backs but it just makes me out to look like a liar.

I drove up to see Sam in the afternoon and just had to follow the noise of the builders to his ward. The drilling overhead was appalling: it jarred my whole body – and he's had that since 9 o'clock this morning. Also, the room was freezing. I was wearing a thermal vest and a big woolly jumper and I was chilled to the bone. There was an old fashioned thermometer on the windowsill and it said 54°F. *[That's about 12°C!]*

I gave him a big cuddle when I first arrived, but it was downhill from then on. Everything I said or did was wrong and everything I'd brought was wrong. I stuck it out for 3 hours but, to be honest, and I feel very guilty writing this, it was a relief to leave. He was in such a foul mood. And I can understand why, but none of it is my fault. There were a couple of occasions when I could feel myself welling up – but I was strong and held the tears in. I WILL NOT CRY. I WILL NOT CRY.

Sam rang later and he apologised for how he'd been. We had a lovely chat and he said he'd be better tomorrow but he'd missed seeing me yesterday and felt so annoyed about everything and he needed to get it off his chest. He said he had his big woolly slippers on, his thermal gloves and his hunting hat – in bed! I'm still chilled to the bone and I've been home an hour now.

10pm

Sam phoned at 9.15 he said he'd been moved but it was hotter than the first ward and the window was wide open again. I told him that there was no happy medium at Raphe's – it was either full heating or no heating.

Still no tears today but I feel as though they're just under the surface ready to flood out. My asthma's been quite bad again tonight and I'm sure it's all stress – plus all the muscles round my rib cage are aching from carrying that heavy backpack on Saturday.

Sob factor: 0. Depression factor: 8

Tuesday December 21st

First lunar eclipse to coincide with the winter solstice for 372 years and I missed it because of cloud cover! Must have some astronomical significance – maybe a new positive universal energy?

I went to the hospital later and it was a case of another visiting time: another foul mood. I put up with it and put up with it but that was it. I let rip. "Fuck you!" And I picked up my stuff and walked out, then burst into tears in the corridor. A nurse scooped me up and spent 15 minutes of her break listening to me, then went back into the room and told Sam that, although everyone knew how hard it was for him, it was difficult for me too. I sat down again and it was stilted for a while but then Sam apologised and it was OK. At one point he told me that he'd fallen asleep last night and when he'd woken up, he'd messed the bed! He said the nurse had left the soiled sheet screwed up on the floor until the laundry came in the morning and it stank. I tried to reassure him that it was probably the antibiotics, but things like that must be really distressing for him. Feel so helpless.

Wednesday December 22nd

Sam rang to say that they weren't going to let him out today – although his temperature was down, his white blood cell count was very low and the growth factor injections hadn't really kicked in. He's terrified of having to stay in over Christmas. He said he spent the first 6 Christmases of his life in Great Ormond Street and says he has no intention of spending another in hospital.

Thursday December 23rd

Sam's just rung, spitting nails. (Just for a change!) Apparently the SHO said that he can't come out today. He's furious. He said 2 doctors came round this morning and told him that his temperature was down and although his white cell count was still low he should be able to come out today with oral antibiotics. But the woman doctor has said no – they need to see if he reacts to the new antibiotics because his white cells are so low. All of which makes sense to me, although I can see that it's disappointing for Sam, but he just doesn't seem to grasp that his life is in danger. He was shouting, "It's a joke! This whole thing is a joke!" If it is, it's a bloody crap one.

The boiler man came. Yay! Apparently I am a good plumber because he mended the leak with my piece of kindling! He says it's because the idiots who installed it had done it wrongly – grrr! Sam rang up to say that the psychiatrist had been to see him. She'd spent 20 minutes with him, asked if he was suicidal, then said he seemed OK to her and didn't need any further treatment! Jesus Christ! What sort of Mickey Mouse psychiatry is that? Any GCSE student could do better than that. And is suicide the only reason a patient needs emotional support?

Later

Sam rang. He sounded bright and breezy and said that he could come out and they were just getting his medicines together. He told me that Claire was appalled that the cannula had been in his arm for a whole week as it's supposed to be changed every 2 days. I went up to collect him and he was standing with his little boy lost eyes, unshaven, crumpled clothes. He put his arms round me. "I'm sorry. Please forgive me."

If, to err is human: to forgive divine, I think I'm being fast-tracked for goddess-hood!

Then a doctor came in asking why he needed Clexane as he wasn't written up for it (here we go again!) Sam told her it was because of a thrombosis in his neck and she said that it wasn't in his hospital notes. Yes it is! FFS!

Friday December 24th – Christmas Eve

I went over to the lake and sat on my fisherman's stool overlooking the frozen pond. It was beautiful. The first time I've been for over a week. I've missed all the snow – except for when I was trudging through it. All that's left now is the snowman's graveyard – great mounds of dirty ice all over the place. I wept, trying to get a grip on Christmas. I so want to feel happy and festive and yet I don't.

This evening, when Sam went to do his `growth factor' injection he came down, saying that no one had shown him how to do it and there were 2 needles and a vial of something which he didn't understand. He said he'd just injected himself with whatever was in the syringe – which was saline! I told him not to worry; it wouldn't have done him any harm and we'd read the instructions together tomorrow and work out how to do it, but I could see that he was agitated.

Saturday December 25th – Christmas Day.

Yay! We went to Amy's. Sam sat in a corner of the settee all day, except when we were eating, but it was lovely. Lily was gorgeous. It was a joy to watch her opening their presents.

Chris cooked the lunch, which was like a feast and absolutely delicious but we left before pudding – Sam was exhausted.

We did the growth factor injection together as best we could; the directions were very unclear and we couldn't find how much to give him anywhere. I put on surgical gloves and did as well as I could, but we decided to go up to Raphe's in the morning and get someone to show us – it's appalling that no one showed him how to do it before he left! He rang up but they said to go to the ward tomorrow as they couldn't tell him over the phone.

Sunday December 26th – Boxing Day

When I got back from the lake, I drove Sam up to Raphe's. We went to the ward and spoke to a nurse who didn't know Sam and questioned whether or not he'd been on the ward at all! Do they not keep records? Anyway, she just said, "You have to use all of it." And that was it. I dropped Sam back at home and he went straight up to bed and I went over to Tom and Tilly's to discuss all things wedding and honeymoon. They'd been to Iceland and it looked absolutely magical. They didn't actually see the Northern Lights but they swam in the Blue Lagoon and then went on to New York. Fabulous!

When I got home Sam was still in bed, but he came down at about 4 and I made us a little Christmas dinner of our own. My cough is still bad, even though I've finished a week of antibiotics and I'm absolutely exhausted. I slept for a little while on the settee and we went up to bed at 9 and I crashed out straight away.

Monday December 27th

Was woken at 4.30 by Sam having a nosebleed! There were a couple of clots and he had to stuff cotton wool up it but it did stop by about 5 am. Very worrying.

I went over to the lake and was crying. What's the point of getting over the lymphoma when it nukes your bone marrow and even a sneeze could kill you? There was a homeless man by a bonfire at the lake – fancy being homeless in this weather! Even though it's milder today, it's still cold. I was in no mood for meditation this morning, so just sat and stared at the trees. Haven't even got the mental capacity to clear my brain of thought.

When I got home Sam was crying. He says he's sick of being ill and being weak – he's tired of the injections and the nose bleeds and the flaking, itchy skin. He just wants it all to end and, although he loves me and loves his children, he doesn't know how much more he can take. He said he wouldn't do anything silly, but he'd had enough. We both sat on the settee and wept.

Tuesday December 28th

It's one of those grey `mizzle' days where everything's muted and misty but nevertheless it's quite stunning. I just sat and stared out across the lake and wondered what's going to happen? How long will this go on? Who knows? I know everything in life is an unknown but how do we live with that? How do we give ourselves something like a holiday to look forward to when we don't know if he'll even be here in the summer? I know all about the theory of living in the moment, but how do you actually put that into practice? And he's so depressed all the time: it's like living with The Spirit of Doom. That sounds terrible but it's hard to be philosophical and upbeat when he's so low.

Friday December 31st – New Year's Eve

I have never felt so glad to see the back of a year!

2011

Saturday January 1st – New Year's Day!

The bloody boiler has broken down again. Great start to 2011!

Tuesday January 4th

Sam has his scan today at Perry's so mustn't eat or drink anything after 7 am. When we got there they said I wasn't allowed to wait because of the amount of radiation emitted. I was in the cafeteria, blissfully unaware of what Sam was going through. He had a cannula put in his arm and then was injected with radioactive dye and sent to sit in a chair for an hour. Then he was taken into the room with the giant tube. He had to lie with his arms above his head but he's so broad across his shoulders and so rigid that he was too big to go through the tube: they had to haul his arms into position and tape them to the bed! He said he was in intense pain for the duration of the scan and kept shouting out, "Hurry up! I'm in agony here!" But they just kept telling him to keep still. It took almost an hour of him going backwards and forwards through the tunnel with his arms over his head, strapped to the table.

Afterwards he looked dreadful. He wasn't allowed to go near children or pregnant women for 4 hours because of the radiation level, so I was a bit nervous about hugging him – I know I'm not a child - or pregnant - but it's still worrying.

Wednesday January 5th

I rang the woman from the local Carer's Support Group and left a message saying that I really needed some support – especially dealing with the Carers' Allowance people. Then I rang the Carer's Allowance people (again!) who said that they needed more information from me and photocopies of all my royalty statements. I told them that they'd already had photocopies of everything – royalty statements, tax return – everything. The man said he'd get on to the assessors and they'd ring me back this afternoon. They didn't! Sam rang the DLA *[Disability Living Allowance]* people and told them about being in hospital for a week – they'll dock a week's money no doubt! Even though I was having to pay for petrol and car park fees to visit him and taking him his own food. It really doesn't pay to be honest.

Friday January 7th

We called at the Day Unit to pick up some more Clexane. The Leprechaun said that they'd had the preliminary results for the PET scan and 'metabolically' it looked very good and suggested full remission. I went back to the car and told Sam and he cried. Then I cried. We just sat outside the Day Unit weeping, partly with relief but partly because I was worried about Sam again, he was burning up but wouldn't go in to see a doctor in case they admitted him again. He insisted on going home and he said he just wanted to go straight to bed. I took his temperature and it was 39.6. For crying out loud! This is relentless. Rang the Day Unit and it was straight back in the car - heigh bloody ho, off to A&E we go! Jesus wept – might as well have a bloody season ticket!

When we got to A&E he went to the registration desk (as he'd been told) but was sent back to reception. He said to the woman, "I'm a cancer patient and I've got high blood pressure."

Me: No Hon – you haven't got high blood pressure, you've got a high temperature.

Sam: Have I? Oh yes.

I told the receptionist, (a po faced woman who looked as though she could turn you to stone with one flare of her nostril - just what you need when you're not feeling well) that Sam was a patient of Head Honcho and the Day Unit had told him to come straight up. She gave him a red token and sent us back to the registration desk. The man went through all his details again then sent him to follow the red line down the corridor to Majors. A nurse booked him in then we sat and sat and sat. About 40 minutes later he was called in to Triage where he was given 2 Paracetamol and sent back to reception to see the on-call GP. Back we went along the long corridor: saw The Gorgon in reception who sent us back to registration where he had to give all his details – again – was then sent to sit in the waiting area. When we'd been waiting an hour, I went back to registration and asked how long it was likely to be – I could feel Sam's head burning up – and she said that, unless a baby came in, he'd be next.

Thank God for neo-natal medicine because all the babies were healthy and Sam was called next. (How convenient that as soon as I go and complain, his name comes up!) We went along to see the on-call GP who asked all the same questions (have they never heard of communication?) then asked why Sam had been sent back up as he had to have blood tests so needed to go BACK to A&E! But, first, he had to go via reception and registration – AGAIN! Jesus wept! What a waste of time! Finally, reception sent him to registration who sent him back to A&E where we had to sit in a cramped cubicle with 8 other people – so much for infection control – before a nurse came and took his bloods – about 5 lots including cultures. Then we sat and sat and sat, while an old woman in a cubicle opposite shouted, "Help me! Please help me someone! I'm disabled. I need to see a doctor. Help me!" Over and over and over again on continuous loop – for 2 hours! Eventually Sam was taken into another cubicle and seen by a doctor who sent him for a chest X-ray and urine samples, then said that he needed to be admitted on IV antibiotics. We both wept: exhaustion, frustration, despair, anxiety – you name it!

Finally, at 9.10 pm – 6½ hours after we arrived - he was admitted to a side ward in the Emergency Assessment Unit. I bought him a day's TV and left at 9.20 feeling sad, depressed, angry and quite desolate. He looks so ill and so vulnerable.

Saturday January 8th

Sam's been transferred to another ward in the night and the sister said he was sleeping but his temperature's still high.

I packed a bag and went over there and they let me in to see him – he was burning up still but in better spirits than last time – he says he's learned his lesson and is going to accept whatever happens. We'll see!

Sunday January 9th

199

Sam rang and said his temperature is down to 36 – thank God! They took a blood test to see how his neutrophils are but, fingers crossed, he might be able to come out today – let's hope so.

I went over to the lake. It was cold, but clear and frosty. All the ice has gone now and it was beautiful. I always thought that my 50s would be a time for me – a time of abundance; kids off my hands, mortgage paid off, financially secure – but look at me: lurching from one crisis to another. I know, I know, this is all self-pity and I am very fortunate. I do my gratitude journal every night and I am genuinely grateful for what I have – I just thought there would be more in terms of peace and stability and contentment. Someone on TV this morning was talking about Quakers and their `peace at the core' and I thought: That's what I want! Peace at my core. More meditation; more gratitude; more forgiveness; more acceptance. I know the theory; it's the practice that's the problem!

Monday January 10th

Got off my pity pot today. Went over to the lake and the sunrise was glorious – a fabulous, apricot sky – breath-taking! I sat by the lake and did a good long meditation and sent distant healing to lots of people. It feels good to get back on track. Sam rang and said that the doctor had said that, although his temperature is down, his white blood count is still low and they need to monitor it for one or two days. He's very low again.

Tuesday January 11th AAAAAAAAAAGGGGGGHHH!

Am so pissed off! The woman from the Carers' Support group rang – it's a mere 8 days since I left a message asking her to call me! I told her what was going on with the Carers' Allowance people and she was very sympathetic and suggested I talk to The Carers' Advocate – she said, "He's a very nice man and very knowledgeable." She asked me why I didn't sign on the dole. I said, "How can I actively seek work when 3 out of 4 working days last week were consumed with taking Sam to doctors or hospitals?" She gave me another number to phone to see what other benefits I might be entitled to.

I rang this 'very nice and knowledgeable man' who sounded anything but 'nice.' He said, "I know you say you're self-employed and that's your choice and I make no judgement on that..." (Yeah, right, why say it then?) "..but why don't you get an ordinary job?"

Smug git! Oh, of course, that's a good idea: why didn't I think of that? Aged 57, been out of the workplace for 10 years, in a recession where there are millions of people looking for work AND, more importantly, I AM A FULL TIME CARER!!! Of course, I'll just pop out now and get myself a little job! Numpty!

He said he'd come and see me to go through my papers and give his opinion – which I might not like! So, going in there with an open mind then! He asked if Sam was on incapacity benefit and, when I said no, he said, "Why not?"

Me: Because, when he's not in hospital and is strong enough, he's still going to work

Advocate: Why?

Me: He needs to - psychologically. His boss has been very good and has allowed him to do as much or as little as he can but, even when he goes to work he needs care – I have to be here to open the door for him when he gets home because he can't turn his key in the lock and there are times when I have to take him to and from work. (AND – actually – this isn't about my husband: it's about me and my life and my job having gone down the pan!)

Advocate: I have every sympathy with carers (yes – it sounds like it!). I've done a lot of work with the support group so I'll come and look through everything and give you my opinion. But if I don't think there's any mileage in continuing, you might not like it but you'll just have to accept it.

And this is a man who's supposed to act as an advocate for people making appeals? By the end I felt like something he'd scraped off his shoe: or some benefit fraud who's on the scrounge. Does he really think that I want this role of carer? Feel so frustrated and exhausted with all this crap!

I rang the CA people again and spoke to a very nice woman who said my case was back from the Complex Decision Maker and had gone back up to the (ordinary?) Decision Maker to be reassessed, although she didn't think it would be done within a week. I gave her my mobile number and she said that she'd ask them to ring me when a decision had been made.

Sam rang me: the doctors came round this morning and told him that his PET scan was very good and showed that all the lymphomas had gone and there was no trace of cancer anywhere else in his body! Which is fantastic news, although they're still concerned that his bone marrow isn't working properly and said they'd take another look at his bone marrow in a couple of weeks but for now he could go home with the growth hormone injections. They told him he had to drink much, much more water than he is doing and he also needed to eat more protein and vegetables (all stuff I've been telling him for years but he's ignored – not that I'm one for I-told-you-so!). He said he cried when they went out of the room.

I got home and made myself some soup, then flopped down on the settee. I just wanted to sleep but was very aware that I needed to go and visit him this afternoon. I checked my emails and there was another rejection for my Young Adult novel and I just plummeted.

Wednesday January 12th

The Carers' Allowance people rang me and asked a few questions about 'What are ALCS?' *[Author's Licensing and Collecting Society – where authors are paid for photocopying rights etc.]* and 'Who is ***** Ltd?' *[My agent - and I'd already told them that at least twice!]* I explained everything and the woman said that she was sorry it had taken so long but she couldn't see a problem with my application and they'd back date it to November 1st! Yay! Truly a good day!

Then Sam rang at about 3 to say that his white cells were up to 1 so he could come home. Blessed relief.

Friday January 14th

I helped Sam with his growth hormone injection – which, hopefully, will be the last. Yay! Then he got up and I could hear him banging and crashing about – he was trying to put away my massage couch from the Reiki sharing group last night but his hands were too bad. I called him Mr Stubborn-Git, like some Bond villain. "Come, come now, Mr Stubborn-Git!" We were rolling up laughing. It's so good to laugh again after so many tears.

I went out to do some shopping, but when I rang Sam to check he was OK, he said he'd been sitting on the settee for nearly 2 hours just looking at his orange juice because he couldn't get the top off. Oh dear God! I'd forgotten to open it for him. What an idiot!

Saturday January 15th

Woke at 6.20 and did our meditation. Not particularly good today as my mind was all over the place. Had a lovely hour in bed laughing and joking – so wonderful to get back to this. "Whom do you seek, Mrs Bond?"

"I seek the one called Stubborn-Git!"

Monday January 17th

Had to go to Raphe's today. Got there at 10.15 for a 10.20 appointment, but they couldn't find his notes - again! They sent up to the ward, then over to the day unit while we sat and sat and sat. Eventually, at 11.15 Head Honcho came out and said that he'd see Sam regardless of the fact that he had no notes.

Then he dropped the bombshell: it appears that, although the PET scan showed that all the lymphomas had gone from Sam's body, he still has malignancy in his bone marrow. His Kapa para-proteins were at 23 – down from 48 but still very high and his neutrophils were still low. I asked if this meant that he did, after all, have two different cancers and Head Honcho said, "Yes, that's what it looks like and the lymphoma is probably a result of the malignancy in the bone marrow."

Apparently Sam's case will be discussed tomorrow with the Perry's team and he'll probably be transferred there for treatment – hallelujah!

Came home feeling very low and utterly bewildered. Sat in the car outside the house and cried together. How can they tell someone one minute that they're in complete remission and, a week later say: oh, by the way, you're not in remission after all: you've still got fairly advanced cancer in your bone marrow? It fucking sucks!

Tuesday January 18th

Sam went to see the Buddhist monks this morning. He's agreed to go once a week for instruction to find peace within. One of the monks said that in Thailand they have a herb that cures cancer and he'll get Sam some for Sunday. He said cancer can be cured with a strong mind, healthy eating and this herb. Am terrified of getting up too much hope in case it's dashed again but it's worth a try. Of course, if there is such a herb, it will have been suppressed in the west by Big Pharma – perish the thought that anything should deny them their mega bucks.

This afternoon tried to do some revisions on the YA novel but my brain just wasn't functioning. It was a lovely day, so I said to Sam that it would be nice to go for a walk round the block –

you'd have thought I'd suggested swallowing cyanide. In the end I said, "This is for you, you know. I can walk, no problem: I'm doing this to try and build up your strength." In the end he stopped grumbling and we had a very pleasant stroll, although he said he felt knackered when we got back.

Thursday January 20th

We had a long chat in bed this morning, wondering what this is all about – this life, illness, adversity? We're so much more fortunate than many people around the globe and yet even with our material wealth, life isn't easy or straight forward. And when I talk about our material wealth, I certainly don't mean we're rolling in it, but we get by and we have a house and food and running water and clothes and a car and so many belongings. I know all the theory about yin and yang - and the Dalai Lama says the purpose of life is to achieve happiness and even that is only fleeting, but why? Why is happiness fleeting? Why can't we be happy and contented all the time? Why can't we be healthy? Why can't the wealth be distributed equally around the world? Why are there earthquakes and floods and eruptions and plagues and pestilence? Why is there cruelty and lying and crime? I know, theologians will say I'm not meant to understand; I'm just supposed to 'be' with it. But I want answers. Of course, Sam immediately went into fix-it mode saying such things as, "It'll be all right." And I wanted to say: You don't know that. You are not Mystic Meg and I am not five years old, so don't tell me things will be OK when neither you nor I knows that. Things are not OK now, and that's all we can deal with – the here and now. But I didn't. I know he's a man and he's been programmed to protect the female of the species and he's finding it hard now that he can't. But I'd rather he said something like: I don't know what's going to happen and that's hard for me too. That I would find reassuring, because I'd know that he was dealing with reality and not some make-believe, childlike fantasy.

Sunday January 23rd

This afternoon Sam had his appointment with the monks and he came home with a bag of Bei Yanang leaves that the monks had shown him how to make into an infusion. They said he could add honey too, so I'll get him some Manuka to go in it. It costs the earth but is supposed to cure all sorts of ills.

Sunday January 30th

Sam was coughing a lot again and said his throat had been sore all day. When we went to bed I took his temperature and it was 38.1. Don't ya just love it when your cup runneth over?

Thursday February 3rd

Sam's temperature has teetered around the 37.5 – 37.8 mark most of the week and his right hand was quite swollen on Tuesday evening. He'd bumped into an old friend in the High Street who'd said, "Why are you walking around like an 80 year old – I hardly recognised you!" It hit Sam hard. He said to me, "Is that what I look like: an eighty year old?" I tried to reassure him but the reality is, he does shuffle around, hunched over, clutching his hands to his chest, very Fagin-like. Not at all the fit, upright, bouncy Sam that people used to know.

When Sam has his bath, I exfoliate his back and his head, then massage emulsifying ointment into him because his skin is so dry and flaky. Apparently it's all part of the chemo withdrawal effects. He's now developed dark mottling too, like some sort of reptilian skin, which is very unsightly. This morning he called me back to the bathroom and said, "Look at my leg. What's happening to it?" The skin on his shin was going the same way as his back and head and he hadn't realised what it looked like. I could see him deflating again.

I went off to pick up Lily for the day but, at 12.15 there was a phone call from the secretary at Sam's work to say that his boss had just sent him off to Raphe's because his hand was so swollen and needed attention. I kept trying to ring him but he was obviously driving. He rang me at 12.30 to say he'd just arrived at A&E. I then didn't hear anything else for three and a half hours. I was frantic. I couldn't even get up to Raphe's as he had the car and, even if I walked Lily there in the buggy, I couldn't get her home without a car seat. I didn't know if he'd got an infection, or a thrombosis, or whether he was going to be admitted again - or what was going on.

Lily and I did some baking but as I went to get the cake out of the tin, it fell into pieces! I was so close to tears, but I knew Lily would be upset if Granny started crying, so I put on a brave face. Lily was hardly eating anything and then, at 2 pm she went right down and became very floppy and flushed. I tried to get her to sleep on the settee but she wouldn't and then she shouted, "Gwanny – I done a big stinky poo in my knickers!" Perfect!

At about 4 pm I got a couple of texts from Sam to say he'd been on the merry-go-round again: Majors, then back to the GP and sitting in the waiting room full of people coughing and sneezing for 2 hours before going in to see the doctor. The doctor said he'd got an infection in his hand. He gave him very strong antibiotics and said that the FCR chemo that Sam had been on was very strong and caused all sorts of side effects, including infections in the hands! Why? How? And why did no one warn us?

Tuesday February 8th

Sam called in at the day unit. He said that Homer Simpson had spent about 20 minutes with him and said he hadn't got an infection: he'd got frost bite! He said he's given him tablets that open his blood vessels so that he gets more blood to his extremities, but his condition means that he can't feel when he's cold. I told him that we knew that by the fact that, when he wasn't running a high temperature, we struggled to keep him above 35o. He was also told that he mustn't go out for longer than ½ hour at a time and needed to wear 2 pairs of gloves. He said he had to take the tablets at night and not get out of bed as they would make him very dizzy.

Homer Simpson also said that he's also put him on Aspirin to prevent further heart attack or stroke. Further? I didn't even know he'd had one – when did that happen?

Wednesday February 9th

Today, as I exfoliated and moisturised Sam's back and head, I noticed that the reptilian scabs were all gone, although he's got small pimples covering his upper arms and shoulders now and they're very itchy. I'm assuming that must be the chemo coming out of his body too.

As we were watching TV, he suddenly cried out and clutched the right side of his neck and ear – he said he'd had a shooting pain right down that side of his neck and into his arm. I went cold – that was where he had the thrombosis in his jugular vein. He said he could feel and hear strange things in his right ear. Dear God! Was he having a stroke? His ankle is also swollen and sore but he won't let me either see it or give him Reiki.

Saturday February 12th

When I took Sam's breakfast up he was lying in bed in the dark watching TV. He said, "Ssh! I'm watching this programme: it's about a man who wants to be allowed to commit suicide legally because he's dying anyway." Jesus wept!

Monday February 14th – Valentine's Day.

OP at Raphe's

We were early today but, guess what? They couldn't find his notes - again. It's like a broken bloody record. Then the clinic was running 90 minutes late – and some! It was The Leprechaun and he couldn't tell us any more than last time but he was surprised that Homer Simpson didn't appear to have referred Sam to Perry's yet. (Deep bloody breaths, Kate!). He said that the para-protein levels took a week to come back so they hadn't got those results yet. And then he kept saying that Sam's Kappa Para-Protein levels in November were 15 - but that was not his para-proteins: it was his bone marrow percentage!

Then he said they were 12 – when in fact, according to the numbers on the screen, they were 17.7 and according to Head Honcho last month, they were 23! So, God knows what his actual levels are! It was as though he was just throwing out random numbers. It hardly instils confidence.

One thing he did say was that Sam's case was not straight forward and hadn't been from the beginning and that his plasma cells were changing but were somewhere between Lymphoma and Myeloma so, contrary to what Head Honcho had said last time, he didn't think Sam had two different conditions. He thought it was one condition: Lymphoplasmacytic Lymphoma – aka Waldenstrom's Macroglobulinemia! Distinct feeling of déjà vu. Weren't we here 8 months ago?

He also said that very few patients get the peripheral neuropathy that Sam's got, and very few get the cryoglobulinemia that Sam's developed. *[Cryoglobulins are abnormal proteins in the blood. The proteins can clump together at temperatures below 37°C and the clumps can impede blood circulation, damaging skin, joints, nerves and organs — especially your kidneys and liver].* Sam's is now presenting as 4 or 5 large red/brown blistery swellings on the joints of his fingers, as well as the reptilian skin patterns on his head, back and legs. Poor old Sam's managed to get both very rare side effects. That must be similar odds to winning the Lotto – but do you think my dear husband can pick six numbers?

Friday February 18th

This morning we talked about what's been going on for Sam and he said he'd been thinking about his hand and wondering if it'll ever get better. It is virtually useless and he's right handed, so it's having a huge impact on his life. He said all his reports at work need to be filled in manually and he can't hold the pen, so his writing looks like a 3 year old has written it – even his boss commented on it. He also said that people stare at his head sometimes because it goes white with the flaky skin. His left hand has slight problems and his foot is still painful and weak, but nothing compared to his right hand. I didn't know what to say, so I didn't say anything.

And he's quite poorly with a cold that just won't go away - despite having him on Echinacea, zinc, Life-Mel honey, Udo's oil, Aloe Vera, Bei Yanang Thai herbs and Old Uncle Tom Cobbley's magic elixir and all! But he insisted on going in to work because they're on a course this week. I didn't argue. It is his life and he clearly needs to work to feel valuable, so I just let him get on with it. And his temperature is still down, so no panic on that account.

I've noticed he's getting his words muddled up. The other day he was talking about, 'Aaron's sandwich' when he meant, 'Aaron's tattoo' and he said, 'Lily's sleeping coat' instead of her dressing gown. Similar things happen all the time: 'Let's cross the river' instead of let's cross the road.

Monday February 28th

I'm going to take a long hard look at my life and how to make money and sustain myself: be it downsizing, or getting some sort of employment, or what. I do need to be working and I do need to be earning. This limbo land of faffing around pottering in the house and garden and doing sweet FA is driving me nuts. I want to be writing again, but my brain isn't functioning on a creative level at all, so I need to think outside the box.

Sam's ankle is still very swollen and painful but he won't go to the doctor in case they say he's got to go back into hospital – it might just be a sprain or torn ligaments or something simple, but it concerns me that it might be DVT. I have voiced my concern a few times, but I now recognise that it's his life and his body and all I can do is listen, offer my opinion and not get upset if he chooses not to listen to it. Such a liberating way of being.

Wednesday March 2nd

Sam's got another blister on his knuckle and one of the earlier ones has now gone black. It worries me in case it's gangrene. Both Mum and Max had gangrene and ended up losing limbs. [My mother and brother were both Type 1 diabetics and had to have their legs amputated.] If he loses a finger, God knows how he'll be.

Thursday March 3rd

A recorded letter came this morning from Perry's. Finally managed to get hold of Sam and when I opened the letter, his appointment was only this morning at 10.20 - before the letter was even delivered! Sam rang them immediately and they apologised but the earliest they can see him now is NEXT Thursday! Another bloody week!

Disaster! My hands were slippery with hand cream and, as I pressed down my inhaler, it slipped and the plastic tube whacked into my bottom lip. I could feel it swelling up and there was blood all over my hands.

Me: Oh my God! I'm going into a school tomorrow and I've got a fat lip as though I've just gone ten rounds with Anthony Joshua!

Sam: I'll go and get you some frozen peas.

Five minutes later he came back with a frozen Quorn fillet!

Saturday March 5th

Great visit yesterday. Really enjoyed it. Did the shopping this morning and, as we were standing at the checkout, Sam and I were pulling silly faces at each other across the trolley and giggling. But, suddenly, I was overcome with a huge sense of panic at the thought of losing him. His face looked so drawn and ill and yet he was trying so hard to be upbeat and happy. An enormous wave of love and grief and fear overwhelmed me and I had to look away and try really hard to control my tears. When we got outside, I just put my arms round him and we just stood there in the car park hugging each other. A very poignant moment.

Monday March 7th

Sam woke me up: he'd found a lump in his scrotum. It's like a small third testicle – dear Lord! Can't take much more of this. I tried to reassure him that if it was cancerous, it would have been picked up on the PET scan two months ago – but I don't know if that's true or not. I said that he could go to the GP today or wait till Thursday when he goes to Perry's and tell them there. He said he'd wait till Thursday. He's obviously worried though.

Tuesday March 8th

When Sam got out of bed, I noticed that his left leg is very swollen. I suggested that he see someone about it but won't: he says he's sick of medics.

A social worker from the local Carer's Support Service came to reassess me and stayed about an hour. But, like most of these people, she talked all about herself and when she'd been caring for her elderly parents. She was nice enough, but I really don't want to hear all these people's problems. I've got enough of my own right now. The good thing was she asked me loads of questions and said my rating had come down from 32/35 to 21/35, which is excellent. She said that my initial score of 32 put me in the `danger' category (in danger of what?) and I really should have been referred back to my GP for emotional and physical support. Anyway, I'm within the 'moderate' band now. Good to know I'm mediocre!

Thursday March 10th

Perry's appointment day

Sam was called in to see a consultant who looked like Dawn French. She was very nice and, immediately, I felt so much better in her hands – she really listened and spent 50 minutes with Sam. We both felt confident enough to ask questions and she examined Sam. He showed her his swollen ankle and the lump in his scrotum but she said, although she didn't know exactly what they were, she thought they were probably all connected with his condition. She said that the neuropathy was probably nothing to do with the chemo but was more than likely the para proteins that had attacked the myelin sheath (which means it's unlikely to get better) but she did say that Sam's IMg level [para proteins] was down to 12 – which is good news. It would have been nice if Raphe's had told him, but hey ho! They hadn't sent half his notes over either, but what do you expect?

Sam was then sent off to get a full blood test and a specialist nurse took us up to the 3rd floor where she did the bloods herself – seven vials of the stuff – but none of the 'take a ticket and wait half a lifetime till your number comes up' nonsense. Then off for a chest X Ray – again, in and out in no time at all. So efficient.

He's got another bone marrow biopsy on Monday – under sedation, thank goodness - and then back in 3 weeks when they should have all his test results and they can take it from there. Apparently it's by no means certain that he'll have a stem cell transplant – it might still be 'watch and wait.'

Sunday March 13th

Sam was coughing all night and woke me up several times. Don't know what that's about. And also, that thing on his scrotum is bigger and blacker and more painful. His whole testicle area is enlarged and tender. He's very worried about it. And he's also developed a similar lesion on his top lip. I think it's probably to do with his depleted immune system because I know people with AIDS get lesions but I wish he'd get it checked out again.

Monday March 14th

Bone marrow biopsy day

Sam showed me the lesion on his goolie: it's even bigger and has started to chafe. It looks horrible – and really sore. I do wish he'd show someone but he won't: he says Dr Dawn French had seen it on Thursday (when it was half the size and not weeping) and said it was probably all connected to his condition so he was going with that. His whole body is now white with dry, flaking skin – not just his back and head as it used to be. Although his left leg looks slightly less swollen than it did last week.

Later

Sam was eventually called 2 hours after we'd arrived. When the car parking is £4 per hour, time costs money! A doctor came and gave Sam a couple of tablets to put under his tongue as a sedative, which sent him quite doolally. He was giggling at everything as though he was stoned off his head! Very funny!

Finally, she and the nurse then came and did the bone marrow biopsy. I was allowed to sit next to him and hold his hand as it was being done. She put enough LA in him to floor a horse – about 5 vials! Yet it still hurt him like hell, although he said it wasn't as bad as Raphe's. The whole process took about 25-30 mins and then he showed the doctor the lesion on his goolies. She said she wanted him to have an ultrasound scan of it and off she went.

Tuesday March 15th

Sam was in so much pain with his goolies and the site of the biopsy. He showed me the lesion on his scrotum. It's very sore and has been bleeding in the night, so I said I really thought he ought to see a doctor about it. And, thank God, he had an attack of common sense and rang the GP. She told him to go up there this afternoon. Hallelujah! She took one look at Sam's scrotum and was visibly shocked. She said, "Oh my goodness – that doesn't look right." She said it was an ulcer and took a swab and gave him some antibiotics. She also gave him stronger pain killers for the neuropathy, but he says he won't take it. So, Mr Stubborn Git – you prefer the pain eh?

When we got home he tried to ring the Perry's Day Unit but the line was busy, so he rang the Day Unit at Raphe's and spoke to The Leprechaun. He said that the antibiotics were the right way to go and to wear underpants that were neither too tight nor too loose. Sam then rang the specialist nurse at Perry's and she went and spoke to the doctor who'd seen Sam yesterday. She said that he was to have an ultrasound scan next Monday and, possibly a biopsy of the lesion/ulcer. Sam's heart sank. He feels as though his whole body is disintegrating and out of control. We got some gauze at the chemist and I put a light dressing on the ulcerated bit of his balls but it kept slipping off and I was reluctant to put any tape on to such a delicate area.

Afterwards we sat down and he dictated a list of 22 things he wants to achieve in life, which was a very positive thing. It was NOT called, things to do before I die – quite the opposite!

As we watched TV, I was doing my usual Hula-type dance sitting on the settee when Sam just burst into tears.

Sam: I love you so much. I can't tell you how much I love you. I've never met anyone like you in my life.

Of course, that set me off!

Me: I love you too. I don't want you to leave me.

Sam: I don't want to leave you. I don't want to die yet. I want another 40 years. I want to be able to watch you dancing and being silly till I'm very old.

Me: I want that too.

We just held each other, crying till Sam told me to go back and dance for him again. I tried but I was too sad. The rest of the evening was very quiet until we went up at 9.

Wednesday March 16th

Once Sam had left for work, I just broke down. I tried to ring Preeti but, of course, she was at work. I didn't have the energy to go to the lake so I just walked down to the park. I sat there, watching all the birds and ducks and geese. It was beautiful but I was so, so sad I couldn't focus my mind on anything. When I got home Preeti rang in her lunch break and I just started sobbing and sobbing. I couldn't stop. I told her how terrified I was that Sam was going to die and how frustrating it was that no one seemed to be able to put a name to his condition and how much I love him and how I'd never been loved the way he loves me and it all tumbled out in a mess of sobs and snot. For ages! She just listened: there was nothing she could say or do.

There's nothing anyone can do or say. At the end of the day, I'm the only one who can solve my problems – although not this one it seems!

Thursday March 17th

Yesterday was a `black hole' day. Total implosion. Just lay on the settee weeping and sleeping until Sam got home at 5 o'clock. He was so sweet – especially as he's the one who's supposed to be being supported.

Sam: What can I do to make this better for you?

Me: Get over cancer.

Sam: OK but apart from that? Right now – what would make you better?

Me: If you made dinner.

In the end, he made me some tomato soup for dinner. Bless him, he couldn't open the can though and had to bring it to me, but it was so lovely to have my meal brought on a tray so that I didn't have to get up or do anything – and he even cleared up afterwards (sort of! Best he could with his hands, anyway!) It's all the things like that that have gone since he's been ill – the sharing of the cooking and the cleaning and gardening – it makes my workload double and when I haven't had a full night's sleep for ages and haven't got anything to take my mind off what's going on, everything seems magnified.

Friday March 18th

The gauze had stuck to Sam's wound so it took ages to gently tease it off and then it looked OK – still red and sore but much less swollen. I bathed it in salty boiled water and dressed it with some of the non-adhesive hospital dressings we've got left over from when he had his biopsy wound – although it's very difficult attaching anything down there – the skin is so loose and delicate. Honestly, if it wasn't so tragic, it would be funny – wrapping his genitals in a bit of crepe bandage. He was walking like John Wayne as he went off to work.

Sunday March 20th

I look at Sam when he's asleep and he looks so calm and handsome and still young - despite a lesion coming up under his eye and the skin flaking off his head - then I see him walk and he looks a hundred. I find the whole thing very sad and very scary – and those words don't go a zillionth of the way to describing the actual feelings inside my head and my body.

Monday March 21st

Scan day at Perry's

Yet again, he was called 'Edward Samuels.' Why on God's green earth do people find it so difficult to get his name the right way round? Does George Michael get called Michael George? Is Fred Perry known as Perry Fred? Or Ray Charles, Charles Ray? It's not so hard, is it? It drives me nuts.

Anyway, the radiographer said that she couldn't see anything untoward on the scan, which was a relief but she did say that he should go to the day unit and get a nurse to dress the sore in order to keep it clean. She also said she thought they should do a biopsy of it but it wouldn't be a painful one like the bone marrow. So, off we went to the Day Unit on the third floor. The receptionists there are not the most friendly and, after Sam had explained the problem, one woman (who could've curdled custard) said, "What's your name?"

Sam: Samuel Edwards.

Woman: Edward Samuels? Go and sit down and I'll get a nurse to see you.

Sam: Samuel Edwards!

Then the nurse came through: Edward Samuels

Aaagh! She took him through to a side bay and said that it really wasn't her field of expertise to dress wounds (she's a nurse, isn't she?) and so she just slapped a piece of non-adhesive plaster on it (much the same as I've been doing) and told him to go to the practise nurse at his GPs and she'd be much better able to do it. Dear Lord! This is a teaching hospital and that's it? Stick this down your pants and come back in 10 days?

Sam rang the GP surgery but it was a case of make an appointment for the second Thursday of the next month without an R in it or phone up first thing in the morning and join the lottery for places. "You-are-being-held-in-a-queue. You-are-currently-number ... Seven-hundred-and -fifty-three! Please-hold-or-call-back-later-when-the-surgery-is-less-busy." Ridiculous!

Sam went off to work and I went to the MacMillan Support Group this afternoon. I'm not sure why I go. There's a little Glaswegian woman who's like a harbinger of doom: "Och, ah've seen off five o' ma friends this last month: Ah've bin ti three crematoria and two burials – all fra cancer." Way to cheer up a cancer support group!

Friday March 25th

Sam's skin is really getting to him – all across his shoulders and upper arms he's got spots and small lesions and, because he's black, they are even darker and quite noticeable. I told him they weren't noticeable to other people so that he didn't feel too self-conscious about them. The good news is: his lesion/ulcer is clearing up. I say to him, "Show us yer balls, chuck!" And he drops his pants for me to examine it.

Thursday March 31st

Perry's hospital day

Sam was called in and Dr Dawn (French) was very brief this time. She examined Sam and said that, although she could feel a small lump in his neck where he had the biopsy (and where his first large lymphoma was) nothing had shown up on the PET scan, so she thought it was probably scar tissue or a fatty lump. She said that Sam was in remission and that, although he had cancer in his bone marrow and para-proteins in his blood, they were at a minimal level and therefore she was going to suggest that nothing was done at the moment. I said, "What does that mean in reality? If we want to go on holiday can I tell the insurance company that Sam is in remission from cancer?" And she said, "Yes, absolutely." She didn't look at the lesion on his scrotum again but has referred him to the neurologist again for his hands. She also sent him off for more blood tests to see if it was the para proteins causing the neuropathy.

We were both in a bit of shock and I think she expected more of a joyful reaction from us but we've been here before in January and, five days later, Head Honcho said that the cancer in his bone marrow meant that he wasn't in remission so, considering that nothing's changed since then: no more chemo, no stem cell transplant – how come he's in remission now? We were both trying very hard to be pleased and excited. We held each other and said things like, "Thank God!" and, "What a relief!" but we both felt devoid of emotion. Very strange.

Friday April 1st

Remission is a strange thing – it's not `cured' and there's every chance the bloody thing will come back at some point, so it's really hard to feel excited because it's more like a stay of execution. I am trying very hard to feel pleased and joyful and ecstatic and yet I don't: I just feel flat.

Tuesday April 5th

Went over to the lake but it was very wild this morning; wet, windy and cold. Even in the dreary weather, the colours over there are all fresh and green and promising. Every shade from the bright lime of the alder catkins to the emerald of the newly opening leaves of the beeches. Of course, the oaks are the tardiest – as usual – not a leaf in sight yet. The gorse is in full bloom with its wonderful coconutty smell. A few flag irises are peeking out of the water, although no flowers yet, but everything's waking up. Beautiful!

Monday April 11th

Sam's boss rang to find out how he is and asked him to send his certificate in. I was at the computer when I heard manic screams from upstairs: Sam couldn't fill in his certificate. He kept putting his first name where his surname should be and vice versa, then he put his address as the wrong road. He can hardly hold the pen anyway but was so frustrated at the mental confusion. I tried to make light of it but he was clearly distressed. So, I Tippex-ed it all out and wrote it for him.

Tuesday April 19th

OP Appointment at Raphe's

It was a different doctor — one we hadn't seen before — very nice and friendly but, again, a totally different opinion. He said Sam wasn't in remission but had plateaued — which actually made more sense to us. He also said that he can't understand why Perry's have said not to do a stem cell transplant, although he did show us all the blood test results and Sam's lymphocytes and platelets are still low, so he thinks Perry's might be waiting until they've picked up even more before they do one, making sure that Sam has the best possible chance of making a full recovery. He said that Sam's bone marrow is clearly starting to kick in again, which is good but, unless he has a stem cell transplant, there is no hope of a cure and he'll just keep getting lymphoma and having to have more chemo for the rest of his life. He was obviously baffled by the neuropathy, as is everyone else it seems, and said, "But this is really disabling." You think?

Actually, he was really very nice and he did say, "These notes are like an encyclopaedia; I need to take them away and really get to grips with this case." Which I found reassuring.

Wednesday April 20th

Sam was in the bath when I heard the dreaded words, "Hon, come and look at this." Oh God! My heart sank. He's got 2 more lesions one on each knee – plus I'd noticed a couple on the backs of his legs yesterday but hadn't wanted to tell him as he was already very low. The other weird thing is, although his chest hair, eyebrows and underarm hair are all very thin, he's grown thick curly hair on the inside of both wrists. It's most odd.

Wednesday April 27th

Wow – what a lovely few days! Last Sunday we packed our cases and set off to Aldeburgh, in Suffolk. It was fabulous. It was gloriously sunny and warm and we sat on the beach and read. Sam still can't walk far – certainly not the length of the sea front and certainly not without a significant rest before going back. We were throwing stones into the sea and having a lovely time, but it's clear that Sam is very weak – he used to love skimming stones but now he can't sustain it for long.

I sat on the beach to do my meditation which I find so lovely and restorative with the sound of the waves – although I got back to the hotel looking as though I'd been pulled through a bed of seaweed backwards: my hair was all over the place.

After breakfast we went up to the room and shared the enormous bath together. It was lovely - and ages since we've done anything like that. I said I didn't want to go home. I don't usually feel that way but this time I really didn't want to go back. There's so much sadness and angst and stress at home, I just wanted to stay in the hotel forever. Not realistic, I know, but it had been so lovely and relaxing I never wanted it to end.

Thursday April 28th

Perry's appointment

Well, we got answers to most of our questions: Sam is in partial remission and the amount of cancer in his bone marrow is too small to be measurable (so that's a relief), Dr Dawn French said low grade is an obsolete term but because they haven't been able to actually categorise Sam's cancer, that's what they're using. And he doesn't need a stem cell transplant at this stage and might not ever. She did say that she doesn't want to see him again for 3 months and then he can decide whether he stays at Perry's for management or stays at Raphe's. He said he will stay at Perry's as he has more confidence in them – hallelujah!

Tuesday May 10th

My agent rang this morning and a publisher is interested in re-issuing some of my books and, possibly, the YA novel! Very exciting. We've got a meeting on Monday to discuss. Please let there be some money in it so that I can stop being beholden to the DWP! Even though Sam still can't undo bottles or take the top off yoghurts or walk very far, I feel guilty about drawing benefits.

Wednesday May 11th

[Sam had been complaining about blurred vision for about a week. I'd told him it was probably just getting old - most people go long sighted in their 40s. He was very unsettled about it – he's already got hardly any vision in his right eye, so to think that his left one was deteriorating was worrying. Then, over the weekend, it became bloodshot. I bought him some eye drops, thinking he might have a mild infection picked up from one of the kids at work.]

Oh my God! How stupid was I for thinking we were coming out of the tunnel? At 5.45pm yesterday, just as I was getting ready to go out for a drink, he staggered through the door, holding his eye and shouting, "Get me the drops! Get me the drops!"

I ran and got them out of the fridge and put 4 drops in, but he said he couldn't bear the light and it felt as though someone was squeezing the back of his eye. I felt sick! His sister, grandfather and 2 uncles have all had glaucoma and, because Max *[my brother]* also had it, I know the symptoms, one of which is pressure in the eyeball. I told him he needed to go to Moorfield's A&E but he wouldn't. He went straight to bed and drew the curtains.

I wasn't happy leaving him but he insisted I went out saying I needed it. Which is true, but his health comes first. I met a friend in town and rang Sam from the pub but he was crying on the phone and sounded very frightened, so I downed my drink and came straight home.

This morning he said his eye felt better but I told him he couldn't mess around with eyes and he must go to Moorfield's - or Raphe's have a specialist eye department. He opted for Raphe's.

We were the first ones when it opened. He saw a very gruff young doctor who said that Sam's eyeball was inflamed and the pressure was raised which can be caused by arthritis, sarcoidosis or lymphoma – but not the sort of lymphoma Sam has! Great – he has neuropathy which is NOT caused by his type of chemo and now glaucoma which is NOT caused by his type of lymphoma. So, what the bloody hell is causing them then? The bloke wasn't exactly friendly and Sam doesn't ask questions at the best of times. He did say that Sam would be sent another appointment in about 3 – 4 weeks' time. So what happen in the meantime?

I drove him to work and then popped in to see Niamh – she gave me some plants, then I cycled up to the chemist to get Sam's prescription. The pharmacist said that one of his drops was a steroid but the other was a beta-blocker. When I looked it up on the internet it said that it was specifically for glaucoma and some types of glaucoma are caused by lymphoma metastasising in the eye. I tried to phone Claire because I'm freaking myself out reading things on the Internet but she wasn't in. I left a message.

Thursday May 12th

Sam's eye is looking much better. Phew! Had a long chat this morning and he's very despondent about everything: his body with all the lesions and spots and neuropathy; living with cancer and knowing that it will return at some point; his job which he doesn't find fulfilling and which is all going to change in terms of sick pay and doctors' appointments. And now his eyesight! I don't know what to say when he's so low.

Claire rang: she's talked to the team and they say the info about glaucoma and lymphoma is archaic and it's no longer considered to be linked. Which is a relief in one way but it also means that his condition must be something else completely. She was very sweet and said she'd try and find out which doctor we saw and try to get a bit more information.

Friday May 20th

Off to the Neurological Hospital today. Saw a very nice man who spent a good 45 minutes with us and seems to think that Sam's neuropathy was caused by one of his chemo drugs: Fludarabine (despite everyone at Raphe's saying it wasn't!) and it would probably go away totally within about a year. He's got to have an MRI on the hand and arm but he feels very sure that it's not the paraproteins that have destroyed the myelin sheath. Thank goodness! He did say though that he also thought Sam had a type of glaucoma when he examined his eyes – but at least that's manageable.

Got home and there was a letter from Raphe's saying that the George Clooney look-alike neurologist had NOT referred Sam to the neurological hospital but did think he ought to be referred to a different one! Sam was furious and gave me permission to speak to the secretary on his behalf. I told her that the letter was a load of poppycock and I had been there when he'd said that Sam should go to the specialist hospital and, in fact, he had already been! She said she'd get him to phone me back but he didn't. What a load of tosspots!

Wednesday June 1st

In the afternoon, I cycled to the town hall to get a parking permit – free now that Sam has a blue badge. I checked the letter and double checked that I'd got all the relevant info. Oh my days! What a load of incompetent nincompoops! They wouldn't accept all my papers because the car is registered to me and the blue badge is in Sam's name – never mind that I had proof that he lived with me and was my husband. They said I had to come back tomorrow with the insurance documents as proof that he drives the car! I burst into tears on the spot. I was exhausted with all the crap that's going on but the woman kept saying, "Well, if you'd brought the correct papers." I thrust the letter at her and said, "I have brought the correct papers. You show me where on that letter it says that I have to bring an insurance document to prove that my husband drives the car. Where? Show me!" The man in the next booth leaned over and said, "This is not my colleague's fault. Stop having a go at her."

Me: You butt out! You've got your own client so mind your own business.

I was in a right state by the time I left – minus parking permit! And then I had to cycle home again.

Thursday June 2nd

Took Sam into work, then took the car into town with the insurance documents to get the parking permit. Did I get it? Of course not! The old permit is in my name and, as I'm not the blue badge holder, I can't have a free permit. Even though Sam is my husband, they've seen proof of residence AND proof that he's insured for the car. I have to go back and fill out another form in his name and provide his NI number and get him to sign it. Jesus bloody Christ! Do these people think I have nothing better to do than fanny back and forth because they are so stupid that they can't even put the correct information in the letter!

Monday June 6th

OP appointment at Raphe's

Saw The Leprechaun. Still quite a few low blood counts: white blood cells, lymphocytes and red blood cells – although interestingly, his haemoglobin is 13.2 – black treacle rules!

Tuesday June 7th

Set off at 7 am to go to the neurological hospital for his MRI. Got there at 8 and Sam was the first one in. By 10:45 I was getting worried and was thinking of sending out a search party. When he came out, they'd done his hand, arm and shoulder but had then injected him with dye and done his entire spine and head – hence the length of time. Just hope they didn't find anything sinister in there.

Wednesday June 8th

Went to a friend's funeral this afternoon. She died of NHL and it's really hit me very hard.

Later

One thing's for sure, when I go I want bright colours – none of this black rubbish (unless someone's a Goth!) and I want balloons and sparklers and none of this PC stuff about no flowers: I want lots of natural flowers – no formal wreaths – but lots of beautiful sprays and single stems and peonies and sweat peas and freesias – all the pretty, scented flowers. And I want a wicker box, like a big picnic hamper with flowers in it – or a cardboard coffin that people can write on or stick pictures on – something biodegradable. And I think I'll be buried in a woodland cemetery with no headstone – just a granite birdbath somewhere to be remembered by. And lots of happy music – maybe even fireworks. And, for a hearse, I want a VW campervan.

Thursday June 9th

I've got a publication date for the YA novel: OCTOBER 19TH! Yay! So happy and excited.

Wednesday July 6th

And Sam got a letter from the psychological services saying that he was on a waiting list for therapy and it would be 6 – 9 months! SIX TO NINE MONTHS! I wish we could get some money from somewhere and go private. He's in a lot of pain again in both hands and his legs and, at one point he doubled up holding his abdomen where his liver is. He's also got more brown spots on his hands and some weird red marks around the ball of his thumb. At least he's at Perry's on Thursday so he can get it all checked out then.

Monday July 18th

[I'd been paid an advance of £2K for my YA book, minus my agent's fee + VAT and, foolishly, I'd told the CA people so they'd stopped my payment.]

Rang the Carers' Allowance people – again - who want the ins and outs of a duck's arse – AGAIN! I told the guy that they'd had 2 lots of photocopies of all my stuff already: why were they asking for it again? And the letter wasn't even correct English: What was you getting paid £2000 for? Seriously?

Later

Sam's eye appointment was 3.10 but he wasn't seen by the doctor till 5pm. It was a young guy and he said that the pressure in Sam's eye was down and the condition he has isn't glaucoma but uveitis – where cells accumulate in the uvea, the central layer of the eye but, because of the lymphoma, his body can't clear them and they cause the eye to swell up and the pressure increases. He says it's likely to keep happening and all they can do is treat it when it happens.

Wednesday July 20th

Continuing saga of the DWP! The CA decision maker was supposed to ring me back at 11am today but she didn't so I rang them at 11.15. Apparently the bloke on Monday shouldn't have told me that someone would ring me in 48 hours, as it's a 5 day wait! She then went away and came back saying that the decision maker was in a meeting and would phone me tomorrow afternoon at 2.30.

Elaine came round to lunch and the woman from the CA rang at 2.30 today! I explained the whole business but she said that as a writer I wasn't allowed to claim any expenses at all. For fuck's sake! I pointed out that I have to pay 15% +VAT to my agent; I have to buy paper and ink; and pay for website hosting and travel to and from schools and meetings. Who is supposed to pay for all that? She just kept repeating that I was only allowed to claim for childcare and I had to take it up with my MP. I got really upset so Elaine took over, saying she was a social worker, but she didn't get anywhere with them either. It's like trying to get through to robots.

Thursday July 21st.

Perry's OP appointment

Sam saw another consultant and he was really nice. He said he'd never heard of uveitis being caused by lymphoma, so will contact Raphe's to find out what they said. Sam asked how ill he was as he hadn't a clue. The doctor said he had one of the more serious types of lymphoma and it would significantly affect his life expectancy. Having said that, he had known of some patients living for 10 years with what Sam's got. I think Sam has been in denial about it and, although I'd read up about it on the internet, it was a shock to hear it come out of the mouth of a consultant. But then, Sam said to me that the doctor had said that his wasn't the most serious type and he could live for 10 – 20 years. He'd totally misheard. It must be so hard for him.

Wednesday August 10th

A truly magical day. Six of us from book group went to Hever Castle for the day with a picnic. We laughed so much and it was gloriously sunny and we sat by the stream for our really quite magnificent picnic with wine and party poppers. We were the last ones out and had to be almost shown the gate at closing time – such a wonderful day. And I am so lucky to have this network of friends. I'll be eternally grateful for the support and genuine friendship they have shown me. They are all remarkable women in their own right – powerful, caring, generous and they give so much to society. There's no bitchiness amongst us - a rare occurrence amongst groups of women in my experience - and to be able to laugh like that is a wonderful gift. I am very much blessed.

Sunday August 7th

Several things are worrying me at the moment:

1) Sam's wheezing again – which was one of the signs that he had masses in his lungs. Almost every night I hear him, like an old man with chronic bronchitis.

2) He's also got bad breath again. He'd had it for about 2 years before he was diagnosed and, of course, it was the masses in his liver and/or stomach that were causing it. As soon as he started chemo, it went but now it's back.

3) The skin lesions are getting worse and more prolific.

4) And he's exhausted all the time again – after the chemo we had a period when he didn't fall asleep on

the settee but he's back to sleeping most evenings again and sometimes in the daytime too.

It goes round and round in my head - is it all starting up again? When Dr Dawn French said, "It could be years: it could be less," is this the less? It's like living in limbo. At least when he was having treatment, there was something to focus on. This 'watch and wait' policy is a living hell. The lesions in particular are coming up fast and furious – none on his face or head at the moment, thank goodness, but his hands, arms, legs, shoulders, back. And the worst one is on his balls. Horrible: the skin's all peeled off and trying to dress it is like trying to dress a blancmange. He hates it and feels repulsed by his own body.

Tried to get insurance to go on holiday in September but, for Sam, the quotes ranged from £400 - £500! More than a holiday would cost! So, a staycation it is then! In the end I booked a hotel in Bournemouth – not quite what I'd envisaged but Sam's happier because it's close to London. He doesn't want to travel too far in case he gets ill again.

Tuesday August 9th

Rioting all over London last night. Very, very sad. Rang The Sun this morning and offered to put up any families made homeless by the riots - need to do something.

Niamh called round on her way back from Perry's and we sat in the garden chatting. She told me that her cancer had invaded her liver now, but the new drugs she'd been on seem to have zapped it to the size of a pea. She said, "I didn't tell most people. I told my sister and she cried because we all know what cancer in the liver means, but I know you understand what it's like, so I don't mind telling you. I know this cancer is going to kill me and that's all right. I'm just going to make the most of every single day." After she'd gone, I cried.

Tuesday August 16th

I went to the doctor's and Dr K saw me. She was very understanding and gave me Temazepam to both help me sleep and to ease my anxiety.

Then a letter came with the results of Sam's MRI and it said that he had 'higher and anterior brachial plexus lesions.' I looked it up on the Internet and it's lesions on the nerves from the neck and upper spinal column to the arm, often caused by trauma such as motor-cycle accidents, shoulder wrenching or often seen in breast cancer! God knows what that means.

Wednesday August 24th

Did all my Carers' Allowance Appeal stuff today and, when I read the letter again, it says that the advance for the YA book works out at £100.01 per week – one penny over the £100 limit! So that's why they've cancelled my CA!! One penny! How petty can you get? So, I rang my MP and made an appointment to go and see him at his surgery on Friday. Don't know if he'll be able to do anything.

Friday August 26th

Yesterday was so fantastic. Niamh and I went to Broadstairs for the day. It was peeing down when we set off and I was really quite anxious about the weather, but it cleared up and, by the time we got there, it was red hot and glorious. We had lunch then went for a wander round the town – she loved it. We didn't go on the beach but went round all the charity shops and gifty type shops and she was really delighted. It was great to see her so happy.

Sunday August 28th

I had a meeting with my MP on Friday about my Carers Allowance, which turned out to be less than useless. He said he'd write to them on my behalf but, as he was in opposition, what could he do?

Saturday October 1st

Drove us down to Bournemouth last Saturday for a well-earned holiday. The weather was hot and glorious: an Indian summer, but the hotel was dire. Dirty; crap food; nothing for vegetarians other than beans and slimy half-cooked eggs. Gross! And as for the service! Basil Fawlty could teach them a thing or two.

Spent most of the time on the beach, meditating, reading and gathering shells. I went in the sea, which I love. I was jumping the huge waves and body surfing and generally playing like a child. Sam has never been a water person and now, with his cancer, he's even less likely to go in. He sat on the beach and read with his coat and gloves on. There was me splashing around in my cozzie and he's all wrapped up like Ranulph Fiennes heading for the Arctic.

October

Throughout October our situation plumbed new depths of misery. Sam and I were rowing almost constantly and, although my YA book was due for publication there were appalling problems with the publisher, the proofs, the book jacket and the blurb, all of which had me in tears most days.

I was frantic with worry about our financial situation, so I'd taken the plunge and updated my training as an educational assessor so that I could go back to work for a charity in central London that supports children with learning difficulties. This kept the DWP from our door but it was also added stress I could have done without. Plus, my 'chattering mind' as the Buddhists call it, was telling me that I'd let myself down for giving up on my dream of writing. I couldn't sleep. I didn't want to talk to my friends or my children because I didn't want to burden them with my problems. And, with Sam and me not talking, I'd never felt so alone.

One day I just took off in the car and drove to Broadstairs in Kent. I sat in the car looking at the cliffs at Kingsland Bay and contemplated putting my foot down and driving straight over them. Fortunately, my phone rang and broke my chain of thought. It was Niamh and I came home and made an appointment with the doctor who increased my Temazepam. It wasn't the lovely Dr K but another of the doctors in the practise. He sat and listened to all my woes and said that everyone at the surgery was aware of our situation (uh-oh!) but the problem was, when Sam went up there, he presented as though nothing was going on so they couldn't intervene. Where had I heard that before?

November

I continued taking my anti-depressant although they made me feel queasy. One of the side-effects was stated as being loss of appetite and weight loss (yay!) but another was: increase in appetite and weight gain. Guess which one I got? Sod's Law!

Sam continued to get the lesions on his arms, back, legs and even a couple of small ones on his face which he found particularly distressing but none as bad as the one on his scrotum.

I managed to persuade Perry's to do a brain scan to check out whether or not his mental confusion and forgetfulness was caused by mini strokes or another thrombosis? Nothing came up on the scan and I then started to worry that, if there was nothing there, perhaps it was permanent damage caused by chemo-brain. Chemo-brain is not something most doctors warn patients about but it's a well-recognised side effect of chemotherapy: word retrieval difficulties, short term memory problems, irritability, mood swings – not unlike the beginnings of dementia.

Sam finally began psychotherapy which followed on from counselling with the Helen Rollason Centre. They both helped enormously. My own counselling – not so much!

The other uplifting thing that happened was, as well as running his Gift a Gift Appeal for the children in hospital over Christmas, Sam also decided to expand his work and start a food drive for the poorest families in the borough. I don't know anyone else who gives as much to others as Sam, but I do sometimes wish he'd care for himself as much as he cares for other people.

Saturday December 3rd

Sam is being so loving and co-operative of late and says it's to do with the therapy – long may it continue. This Sam is adorable. He's the man I married.

Niamh rang, she's been very depressed of late. She says her hair's come back all bristly and grey and horrible, so she's still wearing a wig: she's lost 8" in height; got wonky boobs and no waist. None of her clothes fit her and she'd got the devil's own job trying to buy anything that does. And, of course, there's the uncertainty of having cancer and knowing it will, ultimately, kill her. And, God! Do we know about that one! Anyway, she's having counselling now too, also at the Helen Rollason Centre, and feels much better.

Saturday December 17th

Can't believe a week has passed and I haven't had time to write a word. And a blinding week it's been too! Nary a harsh word twixt Sam and myself: he's continuing to be loving and attentive and wonderful. Am revelling in the fact that I'm being treated like a queen at the moment.

So, highlights of the last week:

1) Sam has been selected to be an Olympic torch bearer! He's so overwhelmed with gratitude.

2) His para-proteins were down to 7.6 and all his other blood counts were within the normal range, so fingers crossed he keeps improving.

3) Have done all our Christmas shopping – all wrapped and under the tree and all our cards are made, written and posted! Woo hoo! How organised am I?

4) Had the McMillan Christmas party and Niamh went with me – very low key but really enjoyable.

5) Sam's done a couple of DJ gigs, one for charity but the other for £100 – so that will be nice for Christmas.

6) Sam's food drive is thriving and so many people – including my friends – have donated so that he can feed about 30 families over Christmas. Plus, the Give a Gift Appeal is also going really well again. Feel so proud of him.

7) Have had some magnificent sunrises but also some blustery winds and rain, plus sleety snowy stuff yesterday – sitting by the lake in my all-weather gear, freezing and wet but still utterly exhilarating.

Christmas

The week running up to Christmas was ram packed full of fantastic social events. It couldn't have been more different from the previous Christmas. There were parties and lunches and pantos with Lily. And Sam did his toy delivery to the Children's Ward at Raphe's, as well as taking food hampers and toys to some of the families he worked with.

On Christmas Day we worked at the Salvation Army, where another woman and I worked in the kitchen, cooking, serving and washing up for 30 guests while Sam ferried people in from B&B accommodation, then played games with the kids. We arrived about 11.15 and were all cleared up and hoovered by 4.30. Then we drove down to pick up Elaine and brought her back for Christmas dinner here – which I'd prepared the night before thankfully, so only had to stick it in the oven. Sam crashed out on the settee and I just kept waking him up to come and eat then he'd crash out again. Took Elaine home about 10.30 then collapsed into bed ourselves.

New Year's Eve

Sam was going to the Emirates with Dil and the boys *[Preeti's family]* to watch Arsenal while Amy, Chris and Lily were coming here for NY. In the morning, I only went and super-glued my fingers together! Doh! They were in permanent Namaste but with a Nemo fridge magnet in between! So, Sam's solution was to come at me with a kitchen knife saying he'd prise them apart! Oh my god! I thought I was going to end up in A&E - if not with glued hands, then with severed fingers. Anyway, after about half an hour of warm soapy water and nail varnish remover, I managed to get them apart – phew!

2012

2012 saw the first flickers of light at the end of the otoscope. It was a year of secrets and surprises: some beyond anything we could possibly have imagined – and I'm an author of fiction!

Throughout his adult life, Sam had devoted himself to voluntary work within the community alongside working full time. In 2007 he'd won the two national awards for his work and was runner up in another. It covered the whole spectrum of the community: tea clubs and memory cafes for the elderly; discos for adults and young people with learning difficulties; juggling and balancing classes for children; football training with teenagers, bringing an end to the postcode warfare between two local gangs; setting up a foodbank; running non-contact boxing for women and vulnerable adults; taking adults with mobility difficulties shopping; running anti-bullying events in schools and borough-wide and organising anti-racism football tournaments. It was what made him tick. And, for Sam, his inability to continue with his voluntary work was one of the most heart-breaking things about having cancer.

Tuesday January 31st

Woke up to the magic text from Tom, (plus photo) saying: Baby Caleb was born at 6.09am and weighed in at 7lbs 15 oz! What a poppet! Lots of phone calls and texts flying about. Such excitement. In the evening Sam and I opened a bottle of Prosecco to celebrate, but it was too dry for Sam so drank it all myself. Would've been rude not to!

Saturday February 11th

Oh my God! The YA book has arrived. Not happy. Much smaller than I'd imagined – it's a B format with tiny font and I do worry that teenagers won't be inclined to spend £7.99 on what looks like a very small book with microscopic print. And the jacket's more suited to 9-12 year olds rather than Young Adults. Gutted!

Thursday February 24th

Sam was up at Perry's today. He saw a different woman who had enormous earrings. She said that Sam was in 'total remission' and the cancer 'might not come back ever.' Relieved as we were to hear that, it flies in the face of everything else we've been told. Plus, his para proteins were at 9.2 in November, up from 7.6 in October but she said that didn't matter: 'It's the same thing.' Er, no – 9.2 is not the same as 7.6! It's a slight increase. Anyway, she said there was no sign of any disease anywhere in his body - other than the para proteins. But the para proteins are an indication of his cancer, so how does that work?

She also said that his brain scan was normal and, "Although we are not doubting what you say when you tell us all the side effects, there's no organic reason for them." Up yours darling!

Thursday March 1st

World Book Day.

I was in another school today and had to be there for 8 am, so set the alarm for 5.15. I was dressed in jogging bottoms and a hoodie, à la gangsta-style, to reflect my YA book. Found it interesting that, when I'm dressed in my usual clothes I frequently get someone offering to carry my very heavy bag up and down the steps but, when I was dressed `urban,' not a single offer. And then, when I was walking from the station, I tried to ask a woman for directions but, before I could even speak, she stuck her hand in my face and said, "I'm too busy!" What an effect our outer appearance has!

There was a beautiful moment as the train crossed the Thames and the sun was rising over the river. There was a light mist and all the skyscrapers and cranes and the power station were swathed in the hazy pink of the dawn – breath taking!

When I got to the school they were really welcoming and took me to the dance studio to wait for the first year group. One hundred and eighty Year 8s [12-13 year olds] and they were fantastic. They were followed by another entire year group of Year 10s: 180 inner-city 14 and 15 year olds, but they were brilliant. And, when I was reading, you could've heard a pin drop. I was sitting there in my gangsta attire with Gangsta's Paradise playing and they were brilliant. The Year 9s weren't so hot, but it was nothing I couldn't handle. And I signed about 20 copies, which is great. Felt like me again. And, I got paid! Yay!

Thursday March 22nd

Woke up at 5.30 and Sam wasn't there – he'd been downstairs since 2.30 again. He'd just discovered that his eyelashes have gone – 18 months after chemo finished. His eyebrows went months ago but he was very sad to lose his lashes. Women would have given their eye-teeth for them, so long and fluttery were they! In fact, they haven't fallen out completely: they're noticeably shorter and thinner, but still there - just about.

Monday April 16th

The DWP have written to say that Sam won't be getting mobility allowance anymore as he can walk 50-100 m without having to rest which is considered mobile! He can't even get to the station or the bus stop - and the doctors' is ten times that distance but, hey ho! They know best? That's a loss of, not only £200 per month, but also his blue badge, freedom pass and free congestion charge. There are apparently 22 millionaires in the cabinet, so how on earth can these people understand what it's like for Joe Bloggs?

Tuesday May 1st

Sam's ill again and has lots of pain in his abdomen. I'm concerned that it's the lymphoma come back in his liver. He was doubled up with the pain. I gave him a cuddle and felt, what seemed like, scratches on his back but when I looked, it was a rash – about the size of a saucer. My heart sank – I know lymphoma can also affect the skin but I didn't tell him that.

Thursday May 3rd

Sam's got shingles! It's like fucking whack-a-mole: as soon as we think one thing's sorted, another pops its head up! He's in such a state – and the rash has spread to his front and is all in his deep scars from childhood. He's in agony. I've been up and down all day with his tablets and ointment – it's all different times and doses so there's no way he could manage that himself.

Friday May 4th

I was doing *[educational]* screenings all day, so got up at 6 and made us both breakfast, plus made Sam some sandwiches for his lunch and wrote out a timetable for his tablets.

Got home knackered and Sam was in a dreadful state. Even walking hurts and he can't bear anything to touch his skin. His temperature was 38.2 again, which is the danger point but, it would have been pointless even suggesting he went to A&E, so I said we'd just monitor it.

Sunday May 6th

I made Sam get out of bed so that I could boil-wash the bedding. It's coated with all his greasy ointment and blood from his blisters, so I need to get that clean – the last thing we want is any cross infection. He was moaning and groaning so, in the end, I told him that my ex-mother-in-law had had Hodgkin's Lymphoma and she got shingles and she died! I don't think he realises that this is a serious illness.

Friday May 11th

I had to scrub and boil all Sam's bedding and white T-shirts again because they'd got blood on them from where his blisters have scabbed and dropped off. There has to be more to life than this.

Sitting watching TV tonight and I just imploded. I need to be earning more than I am. I know that makes me sound really materialistic but I am so sick of worrying about how we're going to manage. I keep thinking: what is it I'm doing or not doing? Is it that I don't work hard enough? That I fritter money away – I bought myself some more Asda jeans for £10 plus some socks for both of us. I go to yoga at £3.60 a time – I could quit that but it helps to keep me sane-ish. Sam was talking about getting another job but he doesn't realise that he wouldn't pass a medical with his cancer. The assessments have tailed off a bit too of late. We could sell the house and downsize but to where? It would mean moving away and all my friends and my support networks are here. Round and round I go – and never get anywhere.

Monday May 14th

Sam's in a pretty dreadful state again today. The pain in his liver area is excruciating again and, where the blisters have scabbed, some of the scabs have come off and he's left with large areas of open wound.

Thursday May 17th

I didn't get out to the lake until almost 10 and then just sat and contemplated the world. Didn't send Reiki – and I always feel a bit guilty when I don't send healing. When I got back, I just burst into tears and Sam was very sweet; just listening and not trying to fix it for me.

Saturday May 19th

Cycled to a new Zumba class that's FREE! It was great – really fantastic and then I cycled back and felt so good in myself.

Thursday May 31st

Grandbaby number 3 has arrived!!! Yay!

Got a phone call from Chris to say Gabriel – Gabe - had been born at 9.36am by C-Section and everything had gone well. Delighted!

Friday June 29th

Just heard that we've got an allotment!!! Woo hoo! Perhaps we can save some money on some home-grown veggies? Very excited!!! *[We'd applied for an allotment before Sam got ill and had been waiting about 2 years.]*

Sunday July 1st

Sam's gone off to the bike shop to get his bike sorted out because he says he's going to start cycling to work as from tomorrow – eeeeeeeeek! I am so not happy about it but what can I do? They've taken away his blue badge and his freedom pass and we can't afford to pay the extra petrol for him to drive every day, or the fares to go on public transport! He hasn't been on a bike in over 2 years and he's still got neuropathy in his hand, so doing the gears and brakes will be painful – but he's determined to do it!

Sunday July 22nd

Sam's Olympic torch relay – mega excitement.

We got up at 4am and I had to drive him to the sports centre for 5.15 – all a bit haphazard up there and no one seemed to know what anyone was supposed to be doing. I got back at about 6am and took Alice's dog for a walk on The Green.

Got everyone else up at 6.30 and did breakfast, then went off to catch the tube and meet Aaron. Engineering works, so all delayed (typical) and all a bit hectic trying to meet Aaron and steer my lot + babies + Lily + Myles on to the tube. Talk about Fred Carnot's Circus! Anyway, met loads of others on the train and had to leg it up the road from the station to the High Road where Sam was doing his bit. Just got there in time. Very proud. He came over and kissed me – bless him – then Aaron and I ran down the High Road while our neighbours kept an eye on Myles for me. Totally mad – people crowding round Sam and shouting his name. Very emotional. Then we all headed back to the park where, again, Sam was mobbed with people wanting photos taken with the torch.

We met Elaine and all headed back on the bus, then set to making the food. Elaine and Tilly were absolute angels and I couldn't have done it without them. They made sandwiches and cooked all morning until the people started arriving at 1.30 - bless them. And Lily was such a poppet, setting things out and fetching and carrying – wonderful. Aaron stayed too and met up with his cousins and aunts and uncles and all the neighbours came in. It was a really lovely day. Most people had left by about 7.30 and Sam and I collapsed with happy exhaustion but it was such a fabulous day – and the sun shone too!

September...

...was very up and down. Sam was anti-climaxed after the Torch Relay and I was doing assessments and screenings but was desperate to do some creative writing again. We'd noticed some cracks above the window in my office and also the front door had started to jam. A survey confirmed that the house was subsiding! I'd come off my anti-depressants but went back on them within a week!

Thursday October 18th

Sam was at Perry's and everything's still stable, although his para-proteins were up from 5.6 last time, to 8. The doctor said they weren't worried unless they got into double figures, but it's the first time for ages that they've been going in the wrong direction. It's a tad worrying, although we're not getting paranoid.

The previous 2 weeks we'd had structural engineers, bore hole diggers, arboriculturists, drain people and carpenters. And that was before the big work even began. I was dreading it.

Most of the work had to be done in my office – I didn't know how the hell was I going to work. Plus, of course, we had to pay an excess of £1100! So, thank God, I'd got some assessment work at the time.

Sunday October 21st

I went down big time on Thursday. Got myself into a right state because I knew I should be cleaning the house or digging the allotment or ironing or doing something constructive but I didn't want to. After the carpenter went (and we'd got a working front door – first time for about 3 months!) I just went under with the thought of all the work that has to be done. All the crap in the cellar and the stuff in my office that's got to be cleared – and our bedroom. In fact, the whole of the front of the house has to be put into storage.

Tuesday October 30th

Written in retrospect.

Life trundled on as normal for about a week and a half. Then, last Friday, I had a lovely day planned – yoga in the morning and the teacher had asked me to do the register, money, heating and lock up afterwards. Then I was going to dash home, quick change and head up to the city where I was meeting Tilly and Baby Caleb for lunch. But, on the way to yoga, Sam's boss rang and said that a woman from a TV production team wanted to speak to me about a surprise programme they're doing on Sam – one of those 'dreams come true' type programmes for Christmas and it all had to be strictly hush-hush. I was, "Yeah, right!"

I got to yoga, turned on the heating, put out the mats and the register and money box then, as soon as the replacement teacher arrived, I had to go out and spend ½ hour on the phone to this producer woman until my battery ran out! Apparently, it's not a prank and she needed to phone me back at 12. I knew my timing was going to be tight but then, Sod's Law: the class overran by 5 minutes, people were chatting away afterwards and wouldn't go home, some people hadn't paid or signed the register and I couldn't leave as I had the key to lock up. I was getting a tad anxious about getting home by 12 and in my haste, I locked 2 women in the loo! Naturally, I let them out when I realised, but that delayed everything. Then there were police in the park, so I couldn't cycle through there; my bag fell off my bike and, when I bent down to pick it up, my bike fell over and everything fell out! Oh! My! God! It was chaos.

When I eventually got home, I took the call from the production company – all very rushed. Did a quick-change act and, as I was going up the road to the station, I rang Tilly to say that I'd be about 30 – 40 minutes late, when – wallop! My foot hit a wonky bit of pavement and I went over on my ankle. I knew, as soon as it happened, it was broken. I heard it snap! I screamed and dropped my phone and all I could think was that I had to let Tilly know that I hadn't been mugged or raped - or worse!

So, there I was, in the rain, sobbing my eyes out on the pavement trying to reassure her that I was OK but would NOT be joining her for lunch. I rang an ambulance and told Sam to meet me at A&E but it was agony and I could hardly speak for crying so much. A man from up the road came over with his dressing gown to keep me warm, then another neighbour pulled up and got me a blanket, cushion and umbrella. Then Terry from next door turned up and said he'd stay with me. And all the time, kids from the High School were walking by and stepping over me, as though I was just some bag lady who happened to be in their way!

Sam arrived at Raphe's as they were wheeling me through to X-Ray. Bless him – he was in a state of high anxiety, as usual when there's anything wrong with me. And the long and the short of it is – I've broken a bone in my ankle and am in plaster from knee to toe! But, in between seeing doctors and having X-Rays and being discharged, I was trying to make subtle phone calls to the TV company about an interview next week, without letting on to Sam what was going on!

Yesterday I spent the morning on the phone to National Accident Helpline, trying to get some sort of compensation because I'll have to take cabs up to the city to do my assessments until my plaster comes off, but they said, "The damage to the pavement isn't significant enough to take on the case." Well, it was significant enough to break my ankle!

Then, this morning, a woman from the TV production company came to interview me about Sam and all his good works and then she's going off to interview him – pretending it's for a magazine article. It is going to be so hard not to let slip. But I must be absolutely stringent with myself. She asked if he'd like to go to Darussalam in India to meet the Dali Lama – which would be so wonderful for him. I daren't even start to believe that they could do that. They also made some suggestions of other, lesser treats for him like playing or refereeing at Wembley or the Emirates Stadium or going to Cirque du Soleil, but I will pray they do the Dali Lama thing – that really would be a life-time ambition.

Saturday November 3rd

What a bloody week I've had! Made fifty times more difficult by Sam, Mr Bloody Stubborn Git! I could brain him sometimes.

The phone calls, texts and emails to and from the production company have been relentless all week – mostly during the day but occasionally when Sam was sitting next to me on the settee. Anyway, after many, many conversations they've decided to send us to Las Vegas for 5 days to see Cirque du Soleil and/or Blue Man Group, BB King, Estelle and God knows what else. They've also set up a training session with Arsenal and a clown workshop for him. But, it needed for him to defer his jury service – without him knowing why he had to defer it. Piece of cake – NOT!

The producer rang the Old Bailey and set it all up with the bloke there, then she rang Sam's boss and OK-ed it with him for work and I came up with the story that I needed him near home in case I fell over when I was on crutches. But he absolutely refused to change it. He dug his heels in and said, categorically, no! I rang his boss and, in the end he came up with the idea that Fathers for Justice wanted to work with him so he agreed to defer for them – but not for me! Grrr! And, to top it all, he was going on and on about: how could I go behind his back and ring the Old Bailey? OMG! I DIDN'T! It was the producer. But, of course, I couldn't say that.

So, it was all set up for him to have the surprise on Tuesday evening when he does his football practice. They needed him to go to a different sports ground from usual – one which was open enough to do the filming. But he was refusing. FFS! He makes life so difficult. In the end I had to sneak his phone and get the number for the guy from the sports organisation. I told him to phone Sam and tell him to say it's for a group of disabled kids - and double pay. Honest to God – and I was having to do all this on crutches – which takes 50 times longer and is a million times harder work.

Meanwhile, I've done 2 assessments (by cab at £30 each way – that's £120 of my hard earned money); sorted out his medical stuff for the insurance; got the washing and ironing ready to pack. I've been back to the fracture clinic but they said I couldn't put my foot down for another 3 weeks – so I've had to hire a wheelchair for when we're in Vegas and buy a waterproof casing for my cast in case there's a pool – plus some new clothes over the internet and hope they fit – because I can't get to any shops on my own. It's been a bloody nightmare. On Friday, I asked Sam to carry the washing basket down for me so that I could put the washing on:

F: I'll do it over the weekend.

Me: Actually hon, I'd like it done now so that I can put the washing in before I go to work.

F: There's no hurry. It doesn't need doing just yet. (Yes it does because we're going away next week!!!)

Oh my God! The battle of the washing went on for 40 minutes!!!! FORTY BLOODY MINUTES!

Sunday November 4th

I still don't know if Sam's going to go to the new ground on Tuesday – he hasn't said anything and I can't keep asking him or it'll look suspicious. It's bad enough I've had to keep surreptitiously probing things like, "If you could meet anyone in the world, who would it be?" "If you had a choice, would you prefer to go to a concert or a magic show?" So that I can feed back his answers to the production team.

Tuesday November 6th

Vegas baby!

Oh my days – what a bloody nightmare! Sam refused to go to the new ground tonight! I was backwards and forwards on the phone to the world and his wife. Anyway, the production team went to Plan B and got all set up for his usual ground. BUT! He bloody well cried off going there too. He says he's got a cold and it's raining! He never misses football training. Ever! Even when he was having chemo. Talk about inadvertently stuffing it all up! Anyway, they're all going to come here now - in about an hour's time! So excited.

Colin Jackson, the athlete, is going to turn up at the door with some cough medicine for Sam's 'cold,' then a stretch limo is going to arrive with five of his friends and colleagues wearing t-shirts that spell out Vegas! I've got Amy and the children and a couple of others primed to stand round the corner and arrive just as the limo's pulling up. Anyway, fingers crossed it all goes to plan.

My wheelchair was delivered yesterday and the bloke stood in the road and shouted, "So who's going to Vegas then?" I was shushing him like mad. Luckily Sam wasn't home – but I'd had to tell the woman at the hire place where we were going for the flight insurance on the chair, never expecting the delivery man to blab it to the entire street.

Anyway, it's now 4.20pm and I'm waiting for Sam to pull up before I send a text to everyone to let them know. Feeling very nervous. Sam's coming home expecting to take me off to Tesco, so I need to keep him here until everyone can arrive. And I've been trying to phone him to find out where he is and how close to home but he's not picking up – an awkward bugger to the last!

Monday November 19th

Oh my God – what a whirlwind of a time we've had. Sam was stubborn right to the last. When he finally got home from work – at 5.20 (when everyone had been primed since 4pm) he put the wheelchair in the car and said, "Come on then, let's go shopping!" I was trying to stall him – but then HE got in the car too saying he was going to wait for me. I was doing everything in my power to get him back in. I was phoning the crew:

Me: He's outside in the car!'

Crew: Get him back in the house – get him back in the house!!!

This went on for about 10 minutes. His boss rang him on the landline and was asking for dates and all sorts of rubbish. Nightmare! Then the doorbell rang and he refused to open the door because he didn't know who it was!!!

Oh my days, I was going ballistic, yelling, "Open the door! Just open the door!"

In the end, he did open the door and Colin Jackson and the 7 man crew were on the doorstep with a huge light and boom mic. And Sam just looked blank and said, "What's all this about then? I was just going shopping."

"Cut! Can we do that again with a little more enthusiasm?"

They came in the house and were doing interviews. Sam's sister was here and then Amy and the children – all trying to keep quiet. Then the crew took Sam outside where a limo was waiting (they'd put a cone outside our house so that Sam wouldn't park there but, Sam being Sam, had just moved it and parked anyway! So, they'd had to get my car keys and move the car to let the limo pull up!) Then out of the limo jumped these 5 guys all wearing tee-shirts that spelled V-E-G-A-S. And Sam just nodded and said, "OK"' So again, it was, "Cut! Once more but try to look a bit more surprised this time."

Afterwards we had pizzas and fizz and had to do lots of paperwork with the crew - then Alice came over to stay the night, so I finally crashed out at about midnight after a bonkers few days.

Wednesday November 7th

Sam had to do 2 mad shopping trips to buy clothes to take before the car came to collect us at 11 am and take us to Heathrow. We were met by a lovely man called Michael, the PR Manager of British Airways, and whisked through our own personal check in desk - all being filmed. Then we were taken to the Business Class lounge for free food and drinks – where I started on the champagne! We flew Business Class – all filmed – eating, sleeping, chatting, everything. It was a 10½ hour flight with an 8 hour time difference, so quite bizarre.

Got to the MGM Grand Hotel, in Las Vegas, at about 9pm Pacific Time (5am GMT!) and crashed out in our room overlooking The Strip. All quite overwhelming.

The next day we were whisked off to meet John Legend, the R&B singer, at the Soul Train Awards dress rehearsal. Of course,

I was in my blooming wheelchair and on crutches for all this! Then John Legend invited us to the awards in the evening: Billy Crystal, Aretha Franklin, Neo and loads of others.

Before that, we went back to the hotel and had to be filmed going into a penthouse suite so that it looked as though we were staying there! I was interviewed about Sam before we went off to the Soul Train Awards – fast tracked because I was in a wheelchair – so there are some advantages. Sam was in his element watching all the stars of his youth. We left at about 10.30. It was only halfway through but we were exhausted and hadn't eaten since breakfast. *[Unbeknown to us, the headline act was Stevie Wonder – one of the people Sam had really wanted to meet. But he didn't come on stage until 2am and there was no way we could have stayed awake until then.]*

Back at the hotel, we ordered a pizza from room service and ate it sitting in the massive Jacuzzi bath (me with my plaster cast hanging over the side) in one of the 2 bathrooms in our suite. Then crashed out at about 1am!

The next day, they said they wanted to film Sam in front of the boxing ring in the foyer of the hotel. But who should walk up to him but Audley Harrison! They drove us to a gym where Audley trains when he's in Vegas – Pat Barry's Boxing Club – and they did lots of filming there, including Sam going in the ring and sparring with Audley Harrison. Honestly, they were chatting away about boxing as if they'd known each other for years.

From there we went back to the hotel for Sam to be interviewed, and they did some shooting in and around Vegas. In the evening we had some free time so we got a cab to drive us all round the Old Town and Fremont Street, then down The Strip. It cost $100 but the guy really knew his stuff and it was very interesting. He had no medical insurance so worked 7 days a week, 14 hours a day and he's 64 years old. Horrendous! We moan about the NHS but at least we've got it. God knows how much all Sam's treatment would've cost if we lived out there.

Saturday, they drove us out to the Las Vegas road sign to do some filming and, while we were there, Colin Jackson arrived again with some juggling balls and told Sam he was going to have a circus workshop with Cirque du Soleil! Sam got chatting to a local policeman, had his photo taken with the police car and the guy gave him a police badge! Then we all went off to The Mirage Hotel, had lunch, then made our way to the Cirque du Soleil Beatles Love show — backstage! Unfortunately, I wasn't allowed in because of my crutches, so the fixer, an English guy who lives in Vegas, was my babysitter for 2 hours while Sam, Colin and the camera crew went backstage for Sam's clown workshop.

When Sam came out, the crew said we had to stop off somewhere else - which was a warehouse on an industrial estate that just happened to be David Copperfield's rehearsal studio! So, in we went, and Sam took part in an illusion before being filmed with David Copperfield and then dashing back to the hotel and getting a cab back to The Mirage for the Cirque du Soleil show. We also managed to catch a glimpse of the volcano erupting at the entrance of The Mirage. All so over-the-top but mind blowing.

Cirque was amazing. Corrie, the Fool, was supposed to find Sam and engage him in the show but he couldn't find him because we had to sit right at the back at the top because of my wheelchair! Not that that mattered: it was still a phenomenal show.

And on Sunday, Sam and Colin Jackson took a red Mustang convertible on a road trip up to Red Rock Canyon. Fabulous! I was in the Range Rover bringing up the rear with the crew – and my wheelchair! It was the most fabulous scenery!

It was bitterly cold up there though: 41oF (5oC) and snow on the ground, but the most amazing azure sky: totally clear. And the silence - wow! The canyon has rattle snakes, scorpions, tortoises, eagles – and I saw one as we entered the 'loop.' It was reminiscent of the old cowboy films Dad used to watch. In fact, it was the home of a Native American tribe, the Paiute. The whole thing was breath-taking – and such a contrast to the artificial glitz and development of the city.

We went for lunch at the Red Rock Hotel diner – a real American diner with about a dozen screens all playing different ball games and most of the clientele were in their team's strip. I had a sandwich that cost $11 and came with a bowl of soup but Colin picked up the bill. Such a lovely bloke.

Then, that evening, we went to see David Copperfield's show – we had front row seats and, when we ordered drinks, we were told, "They're courtesy of David!" He was mind-boggling. We were right at the front and didn't see how a massive car just appeared right there in front of us. Phenomenal!

When we got back to the room, the producer said he wanted some night shots of us around Vegas but Sam put his foot down and said he wasn't going out again, he was exhausted. Anyway, the camera crew got delayed so I said, if it didn't happen by 10pm then it wasn't going to work and we'd just have to do it before we went to the airport on Monday.

On the Monday, we had to be out of the room by 11am and then had much of the day to ourselves – not that you can do much in 5 hours when you've got no money and are in a wheelchair. Anyway, a couple of days previously, I'd been sitting in the foyer when a woman came up to me and said, "Here you go, honey. There's $75 on it. Enjoy!" and handed me a credit card for a shopping mall called Crystals. So we headed off to Crystals, which was no mean feat in a wheelchair – Vegas is not made for pedestrians, let alone those with limited mobility - to find that it was full of designer shops so $75 wouldn't even buy a piece of loo paper! We did find a newsagent that had souvenir sweets and books so bought all our gifts courtesy of this lovely stranger who gave me her credit card. And the expiry date was my birthday – how serendipitous is that?

Went back to the MGM and had lunch in the Rainforest Café – which was fantastic - then met the crew to do our night shoot. We all had a go on the casino machines but couldn't work them – doh! I was saying, "Just press the buttons – any buttons. Just press anything!" Hey ho! We were not destined to win the jackpot!

We did the final around-town-night-shots as it went dark, then off to the airport and flew back business class again. Such luxury – lay-back beds, free food and drink, films and TV ad infinitum, wonderful. And not a film crew in sight this time.

A car picked us up and drove us home and we arrived back at about 5pm on Tuesday afternoon. Mad – totally mad! Felt as though we'd been in a parallel universe. What a fabulous – and mind-blowing experience! Talk about being blessed!

Tuesday November 27th

Yay! The plaster has come off my leg! But an air-boot went on! So I'm still restricted and can't drive or cycle yet – aaaaaagh!

Friday November 30th

Sam got home at 6 just in time for the producer to phone and tell him that there are 2 tickets waiting for him and his boss to go to the Emirates Stadium tomorrow – to be collected at 1pm! They're sending him to see Arsenal play, although it won't be filmed because they've got enough footage from Vegas!

Saturday December 1st

Sam set off to meet his boss and go to watch Arsenal. I rang Niamh but she told me that her last scan had found more lumps, so she's got another 2 week radiotherapy course and was feeling a very low again. I was gutted.

Afterwards I rang Preeti and she listened to me without trying to fix anything and I cried and cried. I told her about Niamh and that the hospital think Sam DOES have glaucoma and that since getting back from Vegas, Sam and I have been at loggerheads again; that I was really sad that I wasn't able to do any writing at the moment because all my attention was focused on earning money and doing assessments: I'd sacrificed so much to be an author and now I've had to switch off that side of my life which I saddens me hugely. I'm not actively writing and my last book, the YA novel, was a total flop. I'm hoping it's due to the awful jacket and format and not my writing!

At the end she said, "God, Kate – I don't know how you haven't hit the bottle with everything that's going on in your life – you really haven't had it easy have you!" Which, in a bizarre way, helped. Because sometimes I think I'm a bit of a drama queen who exaggerates things for the effect of a good story – but, actually, I'm not exaggerating – there really are lots and lots of things going on at the moment and I am handling it fairly well. I felt so much better for talking to her. Bless her; she's more like a sister than a friend.

Then Sam rang from the Emirates – they were given a guided tour of all the players' areas and now they've got their own box – indoors and outdoors! And afterwards they've been told to stay in the box, so he thinks they're probably going to meet some of the players! He was on such a high. Anyway, now I really need to get on with writing up my screening reports. Still – it pays the bills! And has paid for Christmas!! £800 this week and another £600 to come before Christmas. Phew!

Sunday December 2nd

I went over to the lake this morning – first time for 5 weeks. It was clear and crisp and part of the lake was frozen. Utterly magnificent! There was a police helicopter circling overhead for the whole time, so it was hardly conducive to meditation but I did see the kingfisher again! I was so delighted that I cried a little bit – with joy, that is. I thought they'd all been killed off in the two bitter winters but there it was, blue and orange and magical, skimming across the water – so beautiful. What an honour. And how good that the helicopter was there because if I'd been sitting there meditating, I might have missed it.

Tuesday December 11th

Sam broke down and said how terrified he was of going blind – the appointment has come through for 16th January – 6 weeks away and his eyes are really painful sometimes. We both wept and cuddled. Have increased my anti-depressants again.

Yesterday we were at Raphe's and his bloods are still OK, which was a relief but, Head Honcho said that the glaucoma was nothing to do with Lymphoma – it was a totally different condition. Somehow that makes it worse: at least if it was related, there'd be some link or explanation but if it's a totally different source, it makes Sam extremely unlucky health-wise.

Sunday December 16th – in retrospect

Thursday *[13th]* was absolutely bonkers. We had to get up early for Sam to be at Perry's at 9am. He was seen very quickly and everything's OK: para-proteins still at 5ish, so that's good, and we were home by 10.15.

Sky Filming Day

The limo was ½ hour late picking us up but we got to BBC TV Centre in time. We had to wait in the green room with occasional trips up to hair and make-up as well as getting changed. It was a great afternoon, with lots of laughter. There were 7 stories altogether: two little girls whose dad died in Afghanistan; two children whose dad died in a house fire; a family whose daughter was killed in a car crash; a couple whose house was flooded twice in two weeks; a young couple who got married because he'd been given 3 months to live; a young girl who cares for her grandmother - and Sam. We were last on and it went really quickly. We didn't actually finish till about 10.30 and then Morrison's provided 4 trolley-loads of food, all in bags for Sam's food bank campaign + an entire transit van-full to be delivered on Friday. We got home about midnight and sat up talking for ages. On such a high!

End of December...

Immediately after the TV filming, Sam and I prepped a Christmas meal for several of the families Sam worked with. My friend, Lou, and I cooked the meal for 35, including: turkey, halal chicken and vegan roasts with all the trimmings. Sam bought presents for all the children and his boss dressed up as Santa. Then Sam played games with the kids. Lou and I served the meal and afterwards one of the mums said, "Thank you so much. No one has ever treated me like this before: cooking me a meal and buying my children presents and giving me food. It's been wonderful"' It's what makes it all worthwhile. Sam also took toys to the children's ward at Raphe's again on 19th December.

Sadly, on the day of the toy delivery, I had 2 missed calls from him. When I did get hold of him, he sounded dreadful. His voice was flat and he sounded as though he'd been crying. He wouldn't tell me what was going on and I was freaking out big time – I thought he'd lost his job, or Perry's had rung up with bad news about his latest bloods. It transpired that his ex-wife had rung him and said that she and Myles were moving to the West Country before Christmas: she'd sold the house, got a new job and hadn't said a word. It knocked us both for six and we just sat and wept.

The TV programme was aired on the Sunday before Christmas and we had Sam's family round to watch it, then drove to mid-Wales on Christmas Eve to spend Christmas with my family in a cottage in the Brecon Beacons. It was wonderful to be with all my children and grandchildren and to watch them open their presents. A lovely Christmas with everyone mucking in with the cooking and washing up. Fabulous!

Friday December 28th

Wales in retrospect

Amy and her family left at about 12.30 yesterday and, shortly afterwards, the rest of us all started throwing up. Norovirus! Horrendous. Sam was the only one unaffected, thankfully. I moved into the family suite so that I would be near a loo and slept in the single bed while Sam took the double bed at the other side of the room.

At about 10.30pm I threw up and fainted, hitting my nose. It bled a little bit, but then, at about 12.30 I remember sitting up on the side of the bed and saying to Sam, "Oh no – it's happening again!" The next thing I knew, I was lying on the floor, throwing up and Sam was standing over me saying, "Don't move, there's blood everywhere." Not that I could move anyway. It turns out, I'd hit the door-frame as I went down, split my head open and fractured my collar bone in 3 places!

Sam drove us back to London so that I could go to Raphe's A&E rather than Swansea, but there's nothing they can do with a broken collar bone except put it in a sling – FOR 8 WEEKS! The bruise goes right along my shoulder and down to my boob, like a map of Africa. And they glued the gash on my eyebrow back together again.

So many plans for January and now all I can do is sit here like a lemon.

2013

Throughout January, if I wasn't at the Fracture Clinic for my ankle, I was there for my collar bone. It got to the point that we were on first name terms and, as soon as I hobbled in, the receptionist would say, "Hi, Kate – just take a seat and I'll book you in." I couldn't start physio on my ankle in case it jarred my shoulder, so I was caught in a loop of broken bones. Eventually, it became clear that my collar bone wasn't going to heal by itself, so I had to have an operation to have a titanium plate and eight screws inserted to hold it together. Bionic woman, I am not!

The tables were well and truly turned, with Sam having to be my carer for a change, although I continued with the educational assessments and screenings, travelling all over London, one-handed, shuffling and dragging a shopping trolley around with my materials in it, like some eccentric old bag-lady.

Friday February 15th

Yesterday, Sam woke up with a raging temperature and he's coughing up foul green stuff. I rang the doctor and asked for a home visit but they refused! His temperature was 38.4 and rose steadily during the day. One of the doctors rang at about 12.30 and I told him that Sam's temperature was now 39.1. He said that he should be in hospital for IV antibiotics but Sam took the phone and asked me to shut the door. Then the doctor rang back about 10 minutes later and said that Sam needed urgent blood tests and he had to be at the surgery asap and get to Raphe's by 1.30 to have them done. When we got to the surgery, I got out to pick up the blood test form but the doctor asked me to go through to his room. He said, "I think I should warn you that we're concerned that this could be the cancer starting up again, so your husband needs blood tests and a chest X-ray urgently." I know it had been lingering about at the back of my mind, but it was harsh to hear it from a doctor. I didn't say anything to Sam – he was already stressed out and snapping at me. Anyway, they did the blood test and then we went to Raphe's for his X Ray. But then, we didn't know what to do as his temperature was still high and he was as weak as a kitten, so we went into the walk in centre at A&E. The doctor there gave him a prescription for antibiotics but said that she didn't recommend that he took them because of the cancer? WTF! How does that work? There's one doctor saying he should be in hospital on IV antibiotics and another saying he shouldn't take them at all! So why give them to him?

When we got home, I gave him some more Paracetamol and his temperature started to come down slowly – it was 38.5 by the time I went to bed. Sam wanted to stay downstairs but, when I came down this morning he'd been sick all over the sitting room – disgusting black stuff. God knows what that is. And his temperature was still hovering around the mid 38s, but he's not drinking enough and won't go to hospital.

I had to go to the GP to get an appointment for myself but, when I got home, he'd thrown up all over the bed and rug in the bedroom too – and it's the disgusting black stuff again. Gross. And I am so not good with vomit.

12 noon

Sam's temperature spiked again this morning: 39. I gave him some Paracetamol and it's down to 38, which is a relief. I did some one-armed washing up and emptied the recycling bin – everything's so complicated trying to do it one-handed. It all takes so long: the recycling, the washing, taking the clean washing upstairs – scrubbing the carpets! I had to squirt the stains with Vanish, then carry a bucket with as much warm water as I could manage and scrub left-handed till it came off – or most of it did. I'll have to hire a carpet cleaner as soon as my shoulder's working again.

Monday February 18th

Ordered a cab and we went to the doctor's for our joint appointments. I was first and got the results of my blood tests – all OK, phew! Then it was Sam's turn – she brought up his blood results and there were all these red exclamation marks. She said it showed that he had bacterial infections and she thought he should go back to outpatients to be seen by his oncologists. She did give him antibiotics though and told him to take them immediately, so who knows?

He was still burning up and coughing and feeling sick, so he went straight to bed and I slept in the spare room.

Tuesday February 19th

I walked up to the physio. He massaged my ankle and I've now got much more movement in it but he said there was no point in doing more – I had to get my shoulder sorted, then come back for my ankle – I might as well buy a room up there!

The secretary from work rang: I'll be doing 5 screenings and 3 assessments in a week! Bloody hell! I'll be working every hour God sends and hopefully won't get too confused about which kid did what and how! Plus, I've got a creative writing workshop at the adult institute. But at least I might be able to pay off some of the credit cards! Yay!

The amazing Dr K phoned Sam this evening and said that Head Honcho doesn't think the pattern of blood results is related to lymphoma, which is a relief! It really is like living under a cloud all the time – is it/ isn't it? Plus, the anti-biotics seem to be working and his temperature is down again – only slightly above normal. Another crisis averted.

April

We had a few more scary episodes with Sam: we spent a wonderful few hours on the allotment one Saturday but in the evening he started shivering and burning up. His temperature went up to 38.8 – but would he go to the hospital as he's supposed to? Of course not! Then, on the Monday morning, I got up early to go off for my assessment and he'd been sick in the night – all over the bed and it was that disgusting black stuff again. His temperature kept spiking for a few days. His blood tests from Perry's were good – his para proteins were down to 4 which was the lowest they'd been, so clearly the temperature and vomiting wasn't as a result of the cancer coming back. Who knows what caused it?

Thursday May 2nd

Jesus wept! No sooner had I breathed again than there was a phone call. It was Dr Dawn from Perry's. My heart sank. They'd only rung on Tuesday to say Sam's bloods were looking good and then, 48 hours later they were ringing back. I could tell from Sam's face that it wasn't good news. Apparently his PSA *[prostate specific antigen]* blood test for prostate cancer has shown up positive. Dawn French said it was very unlikely and yet, hey presto, here we are again playing the waiting game. He's been referred to a urologist for an urgent 2 week cancer referral and more tests.

We were both in shock but I had to go straight out to have my eyes tested. I felt very 'other worldly': not really in touch with reality. Anyway, I've ordered new glasses including a proper fat-off pair of Victoria Beckham-type sunglasses with prescription lenses! I might not be knocking 'em dead on the beaches of St Tropez, but at least they might hide my puffy eyes from all the crying.

Saturday May 4th

Bugger me! On Thursday morning, I went out for a power walk with Una and only went and broke my bloody ankle – AGAIN!!!! I could not believe it! There I was right at the bottom of the slope near the lake, sprawled on the ground. Una helped me up and I was ringing Sam like mad but he'd gone back to sleep, so I had to phone Louise to ask her to come and pick me up. Una practically carried me to the car park where Lou was waiting and drove me home, by which time Sam was up.

Anyway, I'm in plaster up to my knee again and back at the fracture clinic on Thursday. I was only there on Tuesday for my collar bone – it's as though I'm getting withdrawal symptoms! When I walk in they're all, "Hi Kate!" I feel as though I should have my own chair in the waiting room with a plaque on it.

The problem is, of course, that my broken collar bone isn't strong enough for me to put all my weight on the crutches. So, I'm praying that they'll let me use an air-boot on Thursday. Ankles and crutches crossed!

Monday May 13th

Well, the good news is – I don't have a broken ankle! Yay! Apparently it's torn ligaments. They cut off my plaster and said I'd have to wear an air boot for 3 weeks so, hey presto, I produced one from my bag and said, "Here's one I wore earlier!" How's that for recycling?

Thursday May 16th

We were at City General for Sam's prostate consultation today. Got there at 10.15 for his 10.30 appointment and he was finally called at 1.15 for a 5 minute consultation. It's a brand new hospital that cost gazillions but has hardly any staff: 27 consulting rooms and only one doctor! Hence the 3 hour wait. And then he had to have a blood test which took another 30 minutes so all in all, it was almost 4 hours we were there. Talk about infuriating! So, the long and the short of it is that we know no more now than we did before we went.

Tuesday May 21st

Went for a bike ride this morning to the lake, air boot and all – fabulous! Mind you, it's bloody freezing. The calendar might say

May but the Universe seems to think it's March! Sat and meditated for almost an hour and it was so lovely: dull, dank but very peaceful. Several geese have goslings now – so cute and fluffy and trusting. A really fabulous start to the day – and my ankle didn't hurt at all. Yay!

Wednesday May 22nd

I did some work first thing, then went off to meet Amy and the children. We had a lovely day – bought Gabriel his first shoes. I feel so blessed.

When I got home, I was feeling really happy and full of the joys of life. And, of course, there's a big fat BUT coming! Sam had been to the doctor's and not said anything. Apparently, for the past 4 – 5 days his stools have been black and she thinks he's got internal bleeding! My heart sank. I've worried about that ever since he had those sessions with vomiting dark brown stuff and his food not going down properly but he wouldn't do anything about it or tell anyone and now he's obviously worried about this himself because it's the first time he's ever gone to the doctor without me on his case about it.

Now I feel as flat as a pancake and worried sick again. He's got a CT and ultrasound scan on June 11th at the City General, so maybe they'll be able to see what's going on with his gut as well as his prostate. Jesus, this is just never ending!

Thursday June 6th 2013

Another week passed by: another one of mixed emotions.

- I am now discharged from the fracture clinic with my ankle – yay!
- I forgot to go to physio for my shoulder – boo!
- I've had 2 Granny days this week– yay!
- Sam's developed tinnitus. It's now constant and driving him mad – boo!
- I had book group last night which was brilliant – yay!
- Sam's still coughing up green stuff and he's almost finished his 3rd lot of antibiotics – boo!
- My email account got hacked and has caused me masses of problems – boo! Boo! Boo!
- The weather's been glorious and I've been down to the lake a few times which is lovely and we went over to the allotment at the weekend and have got it a bit more sorted. So that should keep Adolf from the council off our backs.

Friday June 7th

Feel really low and quite depressed most of the time at the moment – can't seem to shift it. We were at Perry's again yesterday afternoon for Sam to have his CT scan for his prostate. He was in there an hour, which was quite stressful. We won't know the results for at least a week – so more waiting around!

I'm doing lots of sewing in the evenings which I really enjoy and is quite meditative: sitting doing my patchwork quilts by hand in front of the TV while Sam sleeps on the settee!

I said to Sam this morning – I just want to write and do the allotment and be with my family. I'm sick of struggling financially and doing stuff that my heart isn't into and schlepping up and down to hospitals – although that looks as though it's going to be the pattern of life as Sam and I both get older. On a positive note – I got my first free prescription yesterday: the pharmacist let me postdate it and gave me the medication for free! There has to some advantage of reaching the glorious 6-0 milestone.

Tuesday June 11th

We went off to the City General today. It was supposed to be for a rectal endoscopy and Sam was very anxious about it but, when we got there, they just did an ultrasound of his goolies. They told him they were fine and Sam was over the moon saying he was OK. But his prostate isn't in his ball bag! So how do we know? Jesus wept – is the NHS full of incompetent nincompoops?

Sunday June 16th

Had a little party today for my 60th birthday. I got up at about 6.30 and started by baking a cake, then got on with the prepping for the barbie. Tom and Tilly came over about 9.30 and I took them over to the allotment for a quick reccy – they both loved it. Feel very proud, although it's looking a tad overgrown again after all the rain and sunshine.

Amy et al arrived about 12.15 and then the others: all my friends from book group. Evan did the barbecues, while I cooked in the oven plus the veggie stuff and Sam did the drinks.

Aaron came over too, and I gave him a chocolate football boot from Thornton's to give to Sam for Fathers' Day. I was so pleased that he came. My abiding memory will be Lily, sitting on a chair with Liz and Louise chatting away like an adult! Such a sweetie. I am so proud of all my children and grandchildren – what an amazing family I have!

Sam did all the tidying up and washing up but then ended up with chest pains that got so bad I wanted to call 999 but, of course, he wouldn't let me. He stayed downstairs all night again and I woke up about 3 am, worried that he might have had a heart attack in the night. I came down and prodded him till his eyes opened, then went back to bed and left him on the settee.

Wednesday June 19th

Headed off to City General for Sam's endoscopy. Talk about déjà vu! When we got there, they didn't do the rectal one – surprise, surprise. They did a cystoscopy instead but said they couldn't do that because of a `blockage' and he'll have to have an operation. Why they haven't done a rectal endoscopy, I have no idea. Everything I read says it's a crucial part of the diagnostic procedure. What is wrong with these people?

Friday June 21st

Sometimes I just want to curl up and sleep for a thousand years – well, I don't really, unless all the rest of my family and friends also sleep for a thousand years, but I am so physically, mentally and emotionally exhausted! And I should really be scoring up an assessment but think it will have to wait till tomorrow. Am too tired.

Friday June 28th

I rang up and spoke to the secretary of the urology-oncologist. I pointed out that it's now 56 days since Sam was referred to him from Perry's and, according to NHS guidelines, for cancer patients, the time frame should be 35 days from referral to diagnosis but they hadn't even finished all the tests on Sam, so what was going on? She said that Sam was down as `routine' so I said, if Sam was down as `routine' then that suggested that he didn't have cancer, in which case, why had he not been told? I also said that, if Sam was found to have cancer I was going to take the matter higher. Sam then went on the phone and said he was going to go up there and 'kick up noise.' Hey presto – within 10 minutes a woman doctor rang him back.

She said that a prostate specialist nurse, Tim, would ring Sam. She said that there were 2 types of prostate cancers: one could be managed very successfully and the other was not so successful and could seriously impact his life. She said that Sam's CT scan was inconclusive and his PSA results were much higher than they should be for a man of his age. Therefore, he would have to have an MRI and a biopsy and a cystoscopy under anaesthetic and a stent fitted to keep the urethra open and he would have to be in hospital for about a week. She repeated that the nurse, Tim, would phone Sam tomorrow and explain everything.

Later

The builder and insurance guy came round about the subsidence and stayed about 2 hours. They argued the toss on the cracks at the back of the house saying they weren't part of the subsidence and they were down to us to sort out. They then said that we'd have to clear all the rooms ourselves. I said that wasn't going to happen as Sam has Stage 4 cancer and I have a persistent back problem and am recovering from shoulder surgery – so they agreed that Pickford's would do it. Result!

Sam was referred to Occupational Health for medical retirement on the grounds of Stage IV cancer, neuropathy, memory loss, glaucoma, stress, possible prostate cancer and fatigue. The nurse who assessed him said she'd never had a case with so much history of ill health and trauma in 10 years of doing the job and she couldn't see any reason why he shouldn't get early retirement, so that's something. Fingers crossed – for the umpteenth time.

I'm doing end-to-end assessments and am on my knees with exhaustion. Then today, the father of one little girl sent me a text saying: thank you for inspiring her. How lovely was that? Didn't think I could inspire anyone at that moment! A nice little ego-boost.

Sunday July 28th

Sam went back to Perry's on Thursday and his bloods are getting even better, which is great – although that doesn't explain why he's getting weaker and getting more pains in both arms so that he screams out at times. His biopsy is next Thursday and he's getting very stressed about it but it's in Outpatients so I think it must be a needle biopsy rather than under general anaesthetic.

I've been working like a bloody Trojan — assessments of course, but it's money, so must keep my eye on that fact and not get into resentment about them. I'm grateful that I've got this skill to fall back on.

Saturday August 3rd

Last Thursday Sam had his biopsy at Perry's. We got up there at about 9.20 for his 9.40 appointment and, while I was waiting for him to come out, Niamh and Aoife walked in! It was so lovely to see them. Bob the Bastard is in Ireland again — he seems to spend most of his time there at the moment and I think Niamh's really quite relieved.

Sam came out at about 11am and looked in a lot of pain. He was very shaky and dizzy so I went to the cafe and bought him a sandwich and some Lucozade and we sat in the waiting room for half an hour until he felt better. The doctor said that there was a `small fibrous mass' on his prostate and they took 6 samples for analysis. He said it was like having a staple gun shot up his bum. Poor man — he looked ashen as he was sitting there. And we won't know the results for 2 – 3 weeks! Which will take the whole time scale up to 4 months, when the government say it should be 61 days. It had better come back clear because, if it's cancerous, that is appalling and (if I can find the energy) I'll take them to the cleaners for the length of time this has taken.

Thursday August 22nd

It was Sam's results day and the good news is, he HASN'T got prostate cancer! Such a relief. Feel like one of the weights has been lifted from my shoulders. We both cried a bit.

I cycled over to the lake and had about an hour sitting there and meditating. And, I saw the kingfisher again! I always see that as a good omen – skimming across the water in a flash of orange and blue. I love it. My heart soars when I catch a glimpse of it and I haven't seen it for months so it brought a smile to my face this morning.

Tuesday August 27th

The day of Sam's investigative surgery at City General.

We got there at 6.50am but they were turning away everyone other than the patient, so I left.

It's 10am now and he's texted me to say that he's not on the list till this afternoon – so why he was told to be there at 7am God only knows. Left hand/right hand again. And then I started to worry that he might die under the anaesthetic and I got all tearful again. I know Sam can live up to his epithet of Mr Stubborn-Git, but I really shouldn't get cross: he's a good man with a huge heart. Not literally, thank God! Couldn't cope with any more illnesses. Have decided I should wear sackcloth and ashes and self-flagellate for a week to make amends for my crabbiness. Off to meet Una for coffee instead though!

Wednesday August 28th

They didn't keep Sam in overnight but, actually, the whole experience of City General has been appalling. He was texting me constantly throughout the morning saying how he was having to sit on uncomfortable chairs in the waiting room, he was cold, tired, hungry and thirsty – nil by mouth since midnight AND he has cancer! In the end, he complained (twice) and was eventually taken to a side room where he could at least rest. His operation was brought forward to 2.30 but, at 4.30 I got a text telling me to go and collect him as he'd been discharged. This was 2 hours after going down to theatre for an operation that took an hour under general anaesthetic.

By the time I got there it was about 5.30 and – apart from the fact that I was sent all round the houses to 2 different wards – Sam was standing up, bent over like an old man with 2 cannulas, one in each hand. There was dried blood down his left hand and wrist which hadn't been cleaned up and he had a catheter still inserted and a bag strapped to his leg. I got them to remove the cannulas but he had to go home with the catheter in place. He couldn't move his leg without painful chafing from it and it took us ages to walk to the front door of the hospital with Sam shuffling along like a geriatric snail. I called a cab but it took him forever to get into and out of it and then, there was no way he could even attempt the stairs at home so I had to make him up a bed on the settee. Apparently, they wouldn't do the stent operation because of his compromised immune system and yet they'll send him home into a non-sterile environment with a catheter in place!

He was told that a district nurse would come and remove it on Friday but, when we got back, there was a message on the answer phone saying that he should go back to the hospital on

Friday to have it out – no way! He stayed down all night but couldn't sleep because of the pain and also, the catheter kept leaking – really hygienic!

I have spent the whole morning on the phone trying to sort out the district nurse/hospital thing but got put through to about 5 different people, including a dental hygienist! Jesus wept! I rang the GP's surgery to try and get someone to come out and sort out the catheter because it's still leaking but she said that it's the domain of the hospital, not theirs – aaaaggh! I am not a nurse and yet why am I expected to be able to care for someone as though I were? No one seems to care. I am too tired to write any more – I just want to curl up somewhere and lapse into a coma.

Thursday August 29th

Finally, I got through to the urology secretary yesterday at about 1pm and she spoke to the doctor who came back with, "Direct your complaints through the proper channels: PALS!" Very helpful – not! So, I told the secretary that I was not happy and I wanted someone to come and sort out Sam's catheter and the doctor rang me back at about 3pm.

She said, if, when I had gone to collect Sam, I could see that my husband was not the man I had delivered to their care in the morning, I should not have allowed him to be discharged: I should have said something there and then. And Sam had been asked if he was OK to go home or if he wanted to stay in overnight and he said he was fine. (Which Sam denies totally.) I told her that she was passing the buck - I was not a doctor or a

287

nurse and it was not up to me to decide if a patient was fit to be discharged.

Dr: But if you could see that he was in pain and couldn't walk then you should have said something.

Me: But all your staff could also see that he could barely walk and no one seemed to care one iota – they still discharged him. Last time he had this operation he was kept in for a week. This time, when his immune system is compromised, you send him out within 2 hours of a general anaesthetic!

Dr: Things were different last time your husband had this operation – it was 5 years ago and there are more bugs in hospitals now, that's why we sent him home.

Me: He is lying on a fabric sofa where children, grandchildren and dogs have been. He's got a catheter in place – and it's leaking urine all over the sitting room – and you're telling me that's a more hygienic environment for a man with a compromised immune system?

Dr: A hospital is not a sterile environment.

Me: No but it's a damn site more hygienic than a fabric sofa in a family home.

Dr: Well, bring him back in then.

Me: How? How am I supposed to get him there? He can't walk for the pain and the catheter.

She was talking to me about my husband's 'pee-pee tube' like I was a 5 year old. I said, "Yes, doctor, I know my husband has a urethral stricture!" Stuff that up your stethoscope! Patronising cow!

And so it went on until she agreed that she would arrange for him to go up there on Friday to have it removed. So, we have to be up at 6am on Friday morning because the transport is coming for him at 7 for a 9am appointment. I'll go up by tube and meet him there but apparently it will take at least half a day.

Sam had hardly had any sleep because he had to keep emptying his catheter bag and mopping himself up due to the urine that's spilling everywhere. Apparently, they told him how to change the bags as soon as he'd come out of theatre, so he was still groggy from the anaesthetic and couldn't remember. This whole business is atrocious. I looked on the NHS website and City General has got mainly 1* and 2* ratings. There was one 5* and one 4* but most of the rest were slagging it off.

Anyway, it's glorious again today and I cycled over to the lake this morning. I just sat and breathed in the sunshine and the lake and the trees and the beauty of nature. Just took time for me before coming back. I really need to tidy my study and do my accounts but my brain just feels addled. I soooooooooo want a holiday.

Friday August 30th

Fuck! Fuck! Fuck! Fuck! Fuck! Aaaaaaagh!

Yesterday, Sam went to empty his catheter bag and there was not only urine leaking out, but also blood! He'd been given no discharge information so we didn't know if it was normal or not but it was going all over the loo and the floor as well as down his legs.

This morning I got up at 6 but Sam didn't want breakfast. The transport was supposed to be coming at 7am but, at 7.20 I rang up and was told that they were about 25 minutes away! Anyway, they arrived at about 8 o'clock and took Sam in the ambulance and I said I'd follow on later. The sitting room stinks of stale urine so I stripped off the settee covers and washed them but it had gone on to the actual cushions so I'll have to find a way of getting them cleaned.

I got up there at nearly 10am and Sam was sitting in a wheelchair in a corridor and had been told he'd be there until about 2pm. If he wasn't peeing properly by then, they might have to admit him. He was very difficult and we ended up having a row in the waiting room – in hushed tones, of course – so I came home.

And now I'm feeling a complete shit again! I know he's ill and I know he's scared and angry and I could really, really be sympathetic to all that if he didn't get so bloody arsy with me. I am so fed up. There's part of me hopes they keep him for a few days to give us both a break, but then the other part knows that (a) he hates hospitals and his mood is likely to be even worse and (b) there's so much MRSA and C-Diff in hospitals these days, the last thing either of us needs is another life threatening illness! Rock/hard place! Grrrr! Anyway, will finish washing the cushions and covers and then get back on to doing my accounts.

2.10

Sam got back by hospital transport at about 1pm. I was on the phone and he came up and put his arms round me and said how sorry he was and it was all his fault and he'd had time to reflect on what had happened!

Saturday September 7th

Unpleasant episode with the insurance people about the subsidence. I rang up and asked why my emails were not being answered and the guy said, "Because I haven't read them yet!"

OMG! That was so not the thing to say to me after everything that's been going on.

Me: It's 9 weeks since the loss adjuster said another engineer would come to look at it.

Case handler: We're in discussion with him on the matter.

Cue for me to totally lose it!

Me: It's been nine weeks! Nine weeks! How long does it take to say – you need to go and survey that house? And how, exactly, have they been 'discussing' it – one word a week? My husband has stage 4 cancer – we need this crap like a hole in the head. This was supposed to be sorted and ready to start the work – now it's going to go into the winter months and I have a husband with a compromised immune system who cannot regulate his body temperature and we're going to have builders in over the winter. This is not acceptable!

Hey presto! I got a phone call that afternoon to say that the surveyor would be round on Monday!

I then rang up and complained about the case handler but his superior had the same blasé attitude:

Supervisor: We've got a backlog of emails.

Me: How long is the backlog?

Supervisor: About a week.

Me: Well first of all, that's an unacceptable backlog for any company to admit to and, secondly, that does not excuse the fact that my email from 9 weeks ago hasn't been responded to!

Supervisor: Well, I can't do anything about the past – it's over with now – so what would you like me to do about it?

Me: For a start you can adopt a more apologetic tone of voice and actually express some sort of regret that your company has treated us like that and secondly, you can take *[case handler]* off our case – I don't want to deal with someone as incompetent as him anymore.

Supervisor: He's not incompetent...

Me: I can only speak from experience and, from where I'm sitting, he IS incompetent. And I want a new contractor...

He got a complete bollocking based on all the tension that's built up over the summer. Felt marginally better as a result!

Sam had been to Raphe's in the morning but, again, Head Honcho didn't even examine him. He said that one of his bloods was quite high and another was too low but Sam can't remember which was which or what it meant! But he told HH that he didn't want to be seen at Raphe's anymore and so he's been discharged. Hallelujah! It's only taken 3½ years.

Feeling very philosophical at the moment. I wonder if anyone ever discovers what life is really about – or for – or even if it has a purpose? Most of us go through this life believing that we're here to earn Brownie points before moving on to either hunker down with the sheep on the right hand side or learn our lessons from this life and progress up the incarnation levels to Nirvana. But what if that's not the case? What if when we're dead: we're dead? I do believe in some sort of hereafter but I also question it sometimes. And how do people face death? We all know we're going to die but to know how you're going to die and to have a time scale, however broad, how do you get your head round that? How does Sam deal with it? How does Niamh deal with it? I cannot imagine. It must be unbearable. No wonder Sam's so scared and angry all the time. So many questions and absolutely no answers. It's all so immense.

In September Sam celebrated his 50th birthday. I organised a big party for him – God bless credit cards! I wasn't even checking the total at this time – just paying off the minimum each month and then waking up at 3am in a cold sweat worrying about it. We'd anticipated that his early retirement would have come through by this stage but, due to some monumental cock-ups on the part of his boss, it hadn't even been agreed yet.

We put up bunting and tea-lights and fairy lights all around the garden; Sam DJ-ed, which he loved; people were dancing, Elaine and Tilly helped with the food, which was way too much, of course. Lily was entertaining everyone on the dance floor. The whole thing was brilliant and rounded off by the final record: Maggie May (for me) with everyone singing at the top of their voices.

Friday September 20th

Wow! Massive relief all round – Sam was not only paid his FULL salary today – but they also gave him nearly £200 more! Not sure what that's about and do hope they're not going to ask for it back at some point, but for the moment feel very, very relieved and grateful.

Tuesday September 24th – 2am!

Another humungous delay on the early retirement front. His boss has requested even MORE info from Perry's. They don't tell you all this when you get cancer - they only focus on the medical stuff, not all the financial crap and the chemo-brain and the mood swings and the emotional roller-coaster – the stress of `expectant management' just waiting for it come back, the lack of stability, the strain of it all. It's more than just a disease – it sucks the life out of you on every level of existence.

9am

At 3.30am I was wandering round Tesco in my pjs and jacket, buying ginger beer and natural yoghurt. And no, I'm not pregnant! Then I drove round for over an hour. I went to every house I've lived in and sat outside each one, reminiscing. I wept copiously outside each of them, then came home by about 5.20am and snuggled down next to Sam.

Friday September 27th

Alice had a ticket to the Globe but couldn't go, so gave it to me. I put on my dragonfly skirt, blue velvet DMs, grey jumper and a pashmina (Fabulous Fashionista!!) and headed off in the sunshine. I felt so free and at peace and truly happy. It's a long time since I've experienced that calm, serene, happiness that fills my soul. I wish to goodness I could bottle it. As I walked over the wibbly wobbly bridge at St Paul's, it was low tide and people were walking on the little tidal beaches. The waves were lapping on the wharfs. The sun was warm and wonderful and glistening off all the glass in the city. London looked magnificent. I wanted to breathe it all in. I bought myself lunch in the theatre cafe and a glass of wine, then sat in the sun waiting for the doors to open. It was amazing! I've never seen a production of Macbeth that managed to get so many laughs: the actors milked every nuance and facial expression out of the lines and it was brilliant. What an absolutely fantastic day! Came home feeling all dreamy and relaxed and we had a lovely evening together.

Monday September 30th

Wow! What a mind-blowing weekend! It was so beyond expectation, I can hardly find the words. Preeti took me to Kent for the weekend for my 60th birthday. The hotel was in the most idyllic location: perched looking out across Botany Bay, with its wild cliffs and stacks, rock pools and soft sand. And we just sat and talked and laughed and watched the waves. We drank Cava out of plastic tumblers and I haven't felt so relaxed for ages. It did me more good than a fortnight's holiday! Here's to Sisterhood!

Friday November 1st

Niamh rang up at lunch time and said that Bob had cleared out their joint savings account! What a bastard! He's been in Ireland now for months while his terminally ill wife contends with DVT and all manner of other complications; he sent her a letter expecting her to sign the house away as collateral for his business venture over there; sent her a £2.49 pair of gloves for her birthday and now he's used up all their money. Words fail me! How utterly, utterly selfish can anyone be?

Tuesday November 5th

Went over to the allotment. Wonderful! Super thrilled about the huge new manure heap all steaming and smelly. Piled on a few barrow-loads before it rained. Is it wrong that I get so excited about a pile of poo?

Thursday November 7th

Well, the builder started today – arrived at 8am without a schedule of work and didn't know what was to be done! Great start! Then he left at 2.40 without having done half the stuff in Myles' room. This does not bode well for the next 6 weeks!

Saturday November 10th

4pm – I am so near to cracking up! I have written 126 words – 126 measly words all day! That is less than a 1/10 of what would normally be considered a reasonable word count. And it's because of the aggro with the builders and the insurance company. Plus, I've got a new phone that's like the bloody Hadron Collider it's so complicated. The builders wanted photos of the work that hasn't been done and so I took pictures on the digital camera, then realised I'd sent the bloody USB lead off into storage. Am so screwed up I'd make Archimedes proud!

Wednesday December 11th

One of the worst days I can remember. It was the first frost of the winter with temperatures around − 3°. The painter was doing the front door, so that was wide open and the double-glazing men had the whole of the back of the house off - and back door − while I sat at my computer writing up assessments in: a jumper, fleece, padded jacket, fingerless gloves and a blanket wrapped round my legs. I was about 5 feet away from them as they hammered, drilled, sawed and crashed about. Shards of aluminium were flying across my face and landing on the keyboard as I typed and, generally, I just wanted to burst into tears. Sam was out trying to get presents for his toy appeal for kids in hospital over Christmas, so it was me and three builders in a house that was freezing, trying to work. The double-glazing guys asked what work I did that I had to carry on through these conditions. Indeed!

Monday December 16th

I had to be up at 6 for a double whammy of assessments but I was violently sick just before I set off − great! And my asthma was quite bad - I was coughing and coughing. I felt dreadful and, if I'd been in a salaried job, I'd have rung in sick. But I'm not. No work: no money. And Pickford's are bringing the furniture back today with Sam in charge. Hmmm!

Saturday December 21st

Had such an almighty row on Thursday! Sam's gone off to do the bloody food bank again and I'm supposed to be writing up my assessment reports. We have a tree with no decorations on it, presents that aren't wrapped, it's warm and wet outside and I feel about as Christmassy as an agnostic in August. Sod it! I have made a decision: the assessments can wait. I am putting some mulled wine on the stove, carols on the CD and lights on the tree. I will bloody well enjoy this Christmas if it kills me.

Monday December 23rd

Feeling so, so low again. All we seem to do is row. The person Sam has become has none of the features that I loved about him in the first place: his sense of humour, his spiritual side, his love of me, his sexiness: all gone – eaten up by the cancer. When you make your promises in front of the registrar you don't expect the part about 'worse and in sickness' to outweigh the 'better and in health' bit. Life's a bitch and then you die? Hey ho!

Sunday December 29th

Well, after all that, Christmas was fantastic! Sam woke up on Christmas morning and I could tell immediately that a switch had been flipped and he was back to being lovely Sam – such a relief. We went over to Amy's and got there about 11am. Her in-laws were there too and it was a madhouse with children and adults in every room, and champagne flowing and presents covering most of the floor – wonderful!

Tuesday December 31st

I cycled over to the lake again but the weather was the polar opposite of yesterday: wet, windy and dull. Nevertheless, I get such a surge of exhilaration when I sit there on my cushion with the wind blowing and the rain speckling my face. I feel so cosy in my Arctic Parka with the elements raging around me. Another lovely meditation: I need to find a way to maintain this even when I start assessing again.

2014

Sunday January 5th

Cycled over to the lake again – much calmer and drier today – the most magnificent sky: as though a huge fluffy candlewick bedspread had been thrown over a blue sheet. Beautiful.

Tuesday January 14th

I went round to Niamh's and we had a laugh and put the world to rights. Bless her, she wet herself. The indignity of this bloody disease! But at least we can laugh about it and she's not embarrassed in front of me.

Wednesday January 15th

OK, so my master plan of doing my tax return this morning has gone to pot – I've spent the whole morning doing Sam's DWP DLA *[Department of Work and Pensions Disability Living Allowance]* form and am now photocopying it. What a blooming palaver: 37 pages of repetitive and intimate details about every condition he has: lymphoma, glaucoma, urethral stricture, memory loss & neuropathy: how far can he walk in 1 minute? How long does it take him to walk 40 metres? Hold on, let me get a tape measure and a stopwatch and I'll time him. How long can he walk before he gets uncomfortably out of breath? How long does it take him to get upstairs? On some nights, he never does! How many minutes does it take to tie his shoelaces or do his catheter or get off the settee? Jesus! But what I did find was that, as I was writing it all down, it made such dreadfully depressing reading. And it was all true with no exaggerations but, my goodness, he does have such a lot going on for him.

Because we live with it daily, I don't realise quite how ill he actually is and how debilitating his conditions are. I suppose I've normalised it but seeing it down in black and white was tough reading.

Sunday February 23rd

We're at the end of the month almost and have I done any writing? Of course not! Although I have:

- Got my accounts in order,
- Had a structural engineer round and he pointed out lots of things on the front that the builders hadn't done – grrr!
- Had a lovely Valentine's Day with Sam,
- Been to Bournemouth for 4 days: walked, swam, Jacuzzi-ed, sauna-ed, steam roomed, slept - repeat. Bliss!
- Sorted out the allotment as far as possible with the waterlogged ground,
- And had my girlies and grandbabies over for the day on Friday, which was lovely.

On the downside: Sam's neuropathy seems to be spreading to his legs – he's had many bouts over the last week of excruciating pain that makes his leg seize up and, on a couple of occasions, he's toppled over and had to be supported to a chair till his leg can move again. (But he can't have any mobility allowance!) He did tell Dr Dawn French about it at his last appointment but she dismissed it as *'a touch of cramping'* – which it clearly isn't. Sam's a former sportsman; he knows what cramp feels like and this isn't it – he says it's short, agonising, electrical pain and the inability to move his leg – just like the pains in his hands. Let's hope his appointment with the neurologist comes through soon.

And on the upside - Alice is pregnant! So, so happy for them! Of course, it's all a bit anxious until she has a scan on Thursday to see that it's behaving itself and hasn't gone walkabout again. *[Alice had been having IVF and she'd had an ectopic pregnancy about a year previously.]* Soooo want to celebrate but need to keep a lid on things until it's more secure. But what joy if it's OK!

Monday February 24th

Niamh got locked in the house, bless her – the door has been sticking since last autumn but Bob didn't do anything about it when he paid a fleeting visit last month and she hasn't got the strength to pull it open sometimes. She rang me and I shot round there and did a shoulder barge like something off the Sweeney! Anyway, she's looking very well and I've told her she must not go to the hospital on her own – either Sam or I will go with her depending on whether or not I'm working and she agreed.

Thursday February 27th

I was doing my write-ups when Sam called me into the sitting room: he'd got a letter from one of his pensions and they needed more information so he wanted me to sit there and go through it with him. I get so frustrated! I need to get on with MY work and get it out of the way but he needs so much of my time and doesn't even realise it. I know he gets muddled and confused and, even as he was going through it with me, he was misreading things and missing bits out. It's really time consuming.

Then Niamh came round – she was locked out again. That front door needs planing down but useless lump Bob didn't do it and Patrick's *[her son]* made a hacking job of it and it still sticks. I gave it my shoulder again and let her in. Men! Honestly!

Wednesday March 5th

And, this morning, I woke up naturally at 6am and thought, *right! I'm going swimming!* So off I set at 6.30 to the Olympic pool. It took ages to get there but, once inside, it was amazing. Totally mind blowing! I swam in the 50m pool but there are 2 x 25m pools too - and hardly anyone in there. Most of the time, I had a whole lane to myself – fabulous.

Friday March 7th

Yesterday was World Book Day – and I had a booking! Yay! In fact, I had two bookings on one day. Whoop, whoop!

I woke at 5 and Sam drove me to Victoria for the 7am train to Surrey. A teacher was there to meet me and drive me to the school. Fabulous countryside – hills and heathland and woods with daffodils and snowdrops – beautiful!

The school was a small private school and my first group was Year 8, about 50 students, all in fancy dress. Then I had Year 7 followed by a book signing in the library at break. Then the librarian drove me to another school about a mile away; a state school this time to speak to the whole of Year 7 – 250 students. Again, they were great – more boys than girls but very engaged and asked really pertinent questions. Then I was in the library answering questions from students before I was driven back to the station and home!

It was a 10 hour full-on day and I was knackered. Slept for over 11 hours altogether! But it was the sleep of satisfaction. What a fabulous feeling!

Thursday April 3rd

Sam's been running every morning for a month now and his mood is certainly improved as a result. And he's sleeping in bed most nights, so all in all, things are a lot better on that front.

Been doing lots on the allotment but then, on Saturday, we went over in the afternoon only to find that the contractor who'd been dredging the ditch at the back of our allotment had demolished our shed and uprooted a whole load of mature shrubs from along the back. Gutted! Our beautiful plot is wrecked.

I've had a terrible sore throat for ages now, which is really bugging me – can't go swimming, or Zumba or cycling: feel so grotty. And can't eat much more than soup because it hurts to swallow. I know anything to do with the throat and the throat chakra is to do with communication and expression so it's no surprise that mine's playing up when I'm not expressing myself through my writing. I went to the doctor's on Tuesday but he was adamant that it was viral. I don't care! It's bright red and I can't swallow – just give me the antibiotics! Which he did, eventually – on condition I didn't take them?? But I did and it's much better.

Friday April 4th

Watched an interview with Jacqueline Wilson this morning as she's written her 100th book. Such an amazing woman and so gentle. She's got kidney problems and has to have dialysis 3 times a week, but still writes every single day, including Christmas Day. Thinks: this is where I'm going wrong. If I'm not assessing, I really ought to make the effort to write something every single day. Maybe not Christmas Day, though. E for effort Kate - really must try harder!

Tuesday April 8th

I've been not drinking for Lent although that went for a burton yesterday: I was knackered and very late home from work so I just thought: sod it! I've given my liver a break for a month and I'm not religious, so I bought a bottle of wine on my way home. Lovely!

Wednesday 21st May

- Wow! Can't believe it's been nearly 6 weeks since I wrote my diary. The reasons are threefold:
- Firstly, because I've been working flat out, am exhausted and mega stressed about work,
- Secondly because there's been masses of crap going on at the allotment with Adolf from the council and his numbskull workers who seem hell bent on ruining our lovely little plot,
- But thirdly – and best of all: we went away last week – yay! We had a week in Devon in Liz's cottage. Sooooo fabulous. Just sat and watched the boats in the harbour, went for

long walks along the breakwater, had a romantic picnic on a secluded cliff, swam in the sea – wonderful.

Tuesday July 1st – 3am!

Can't sleep. Am knackered most of the time – not helped by being awake at this ungodly hour and schlepping round Tesco's in my PJs on another ginger beer hunt!

Sam's been running and cycling most days and it's really helped his depression. Had his MOT blood tests last week: cholesterol and blood sugar are down slightly but not yet in the `healthy' range. BUT – the bad news is that his PSA is raised again, up to 5.6, suggesting that his prostate is flaring up. City General were supposed to be monitoring him but the doctor discharged him in February and now they won't see him again without a re-referral from his GP! So, the GP has referred him but it's back to playing the waiting game again.

On Sunday he got very emotional saying that he couldn't take any more – he'd had enough. He was sick of fighting and if he had to have chemo again, he didn't think he could face it. He just talked and talked for ages. I didn't say anything: I just listened and cried a bit. And Sam cried too.

I did 2 assessments yesterday: up at 6am, into work by 8.20: admin, filing and photocopying; first assessment 9.30 - 1.10pm. Had 20 minutes for a sandwich then 1.30 second assessment. Left the office at 5.40 and home at 6.30. So, a 9½ hour working day with a 20 minute break plus 2 hours' travelling. I am too old for this malarkey. When I was growing up women could retire with a State Pension at 60. Then they pulled that rug out from under our feet: it'll be another 4 years before I can retire. And even then I don't have a work pension, only the State one.

Anyway, it's now past 4am and I really should try and get some sleep – I have 2 reports to start writing up tomorrow and I'm brain dead. Dawn's breaking and the birds will be up soon.

Monday July 14th

Sam stayed at home – he's anxious about his PSA and the doctors have messed up again. He rang City General after 2 weeks of not hearing from them and they didn't have any referral from his GP! Rang the GP and the receptionist said the doctor had sent the referral letter to his oncologist at Perry's and not the urologist at City. Talk about a cock up! Anyway, they rang this morning and he's got an appointment on 31st July – another 2½ weeks away. That will have made it almost 6 weeks and the time frame is supposed to be 2 weeks! It's all so stressful.

And today would have been Max's 60th birthday. *[My brother who died aged 42.]* Happy birthday Max – wherever you are.

Thursday July 31st

Sam and I went to Perry's for him to see the urologist. He seemed really nice – much better than that twit at City. He said Sam's PSA is raised and needs to be investigated with another MRI and a biopsy under GA. Here we go round the mulberry bush...

Monday August 4th

Met up with Elaine and we walked down to the allotment. But, oh my days – she could hardly walk. She was huffing and puffing all the way there, then had to sit down for about an hour while I dug up some potatoes and picked some blackberries. I sat on the grass and we talked and talked then headed back up to the bus stop but she could hardly make it and was clinging on to the metal railings. I was utterly shocked. Hadn't realised quite how unfit she was.

Saturday August 9th

Horribly dizzy. *[I've suffered bouts of vertigo for many years since having both viral encephalitis and viral meningitis in my 30s]* Set off to Amy's birthday but Sam said that his leg was so painful that he didn't want to risk driving in case it went into spasm. Sam was walking with a stick, it was so bad. Despite feeling very wobbly, I said I'd drive. We'd no sooner got to the end of the road than Sam was screaming in pain saying he couldn't go and he needed to go to A&E. Ye gods! I said I'd take him but he was adamant that I should go to Amy's and he would get a cab. I knew it must be bad for him to offer to pay for a taxi! When I finally got there I burst into tears. Sam kept me posted with texts and until eventually he rang to say that it was DVT and he'd had to have another Clexane injection and go back the following day for another, and back on Monday for a scan. Aaagghh!

Sunday, I was still dizzy so slept in till about 11, then did some pottering about the house. I drove Sam to Raphe's at 2pm expecting him to just pop in and have his injection and come out again but, after about 10 minutes, I parked the car and went in. I was directed to the Ambulatory Clinic which was at the back of beyond but, when I got there, they were expecting Sam but hadn't seen him. So, I went all the way back but there was no sign of him in the waiting area and then I got a text saying he was in consulting rooms 7 – 10. I went through and told them that he should be in the Ambulatory Clinic and we walked all the way back again, with Sam refusing a wheelchair. When we got there, he was sent off to have an ultrasound scan, then back to the clinic and an examination by 2 doctors. His right thigh is slightly swollen on the outside and it does lock and collapse under him – even if he's lying on the settee or in bed - so something's going on. Anyway, the 2 doctors said they thought it was muscle strain and he should have physio. The scan showed no sign of DVT which Sam was over the moon about, but I'm not totally reassured. Anyway, I am exhausted and STILL dizzy and just want a bit of peace in my life. I've never liked roller coasters – much more of a sedate carousel type of person, myself.

Monday August 11th

I woke up at 8 am still feeling tired and still feeling dizzy – it is horrible. I hate it! I decided to ring the doctor but, by the time I got through, all the appointments were taken, so I'll have to go and queue up at 8am tomorrow to get an urgent one. Took some seasickness pills to calm it down.

Tuesday August 12th

I think one of my difficulties is that I don't know who I am at the moment – no wonder my head's spinning! I've made the decision to stop assessing and yet, I'm not actually writing or doing Reiki – so what is my role in life? I can't say I'm an author at the moment, or a Reiki healer, or 'retired' because I can't get my state pension. So, who, or what, am I? I know I need to knuckle down but, I am so unbelievably tired all the time and now the dizziness, I can't put my mind to any of it. I would LOVE to just go away somewhere and sleep for a month but that's not going to happen, so I'd better sort myself out pdq.

Wednesday August 13th

Took Niamh out to lunch today but she was really wobbly on her legs. I had to support her along the road and it was as if she was toppling forwards all the time. Five times between our house and the High Street she had to rest against a wall or a lamp post because she was in danger of falling over. She's so wizened and bent now, she looks about 80. We got to the new pub on the corner and found a table and then she realised she'd come out without her wig. She was devastated. I offered to phone Sam and ask him to go round to her house and get it for her *[we had her spare key]* but she said she'd be OK. I did notice people staring though, bless her.

We had a lovely lunch and caught up on the gossip but I had to phone Sam to come and pick us up because she would never have made it back otherwise. According to statistics, Niamh is a *'cancer survivor'* – it's been over 5 years since she was first diagnosed and yet, she hasn't survived at all – she's ravaged by it. Shuffling along, gripping on to my arm, only coming up to my shoulder when she used to be taller than me, bald – still! Sam finds it difficult to look at her because he thinks he'll go that way eventually - which I can understand.

Monday August 18th

Sam had his MRI on Thursday – he was in the machine for 45 minutes and came out very yellow and pale. He hates them and finds them so claustrophobic he can hardly breathe in there. When we got back, I couldn't speak – every time I opened my mouth to say anything, I just burst into tears. I've no idea what that was about – perhaps it just the stress of everything: Sam, Niamh, vertigo, money!

But on Saturday I had an *Earth Mother* day: I made my first ever batch of jam – blackberry from the allotment and it was delicious! Then I made a Danish apple cake with the apples I'd picked and then 2 loaves of bread: one olive bread and the other wholemeal fig and fennel made with seeds from the garden. We spent a good 2 hours on the allotment which is such bliss.

Thursday August 21st

Perry's day again today – Sam gets the results of his MRI from last week. Personally, I don't think they'll be able to tell us anything new: we know he has a mass on his prostate – it's just what that mass is that's the problem. So, I suspect they'll just send him for a biopsy under GA to find out more.

Monday August 25th - Bank Holiday

Well, I thought it was quite good news on Thursday – the mass on his prostate hasn't grown in a year (yay!) but he still has to have a biopsy under general anaesthetic which worries him sick and you'd have thought he'd been given a death sentence by the look on his face when we came out.

In the afternoon I took Niamh for a manicure. She insisted on walking because she said it's important that she gets some exercise every day, but it took us almost an hour to get there and we were 20 minutes late. They gave us an express service rather than a classic but it was Niamh's first ever manicure and she loved it. I gave her some jam and potatoes from the allotment and she was so grateful. Honestly, it's so little yet she seems so overwhelmed. Sam and I are on a rota of friends to take her to the hospital.

In the evening, Sam was ironing and playing music and I made some MORE jam – pear and ginger this time. It was such a lovely domestic scene and then Sam put on some 60s songs and we were dancing in the sitting room – until we did a smoochy one and our glasses got caught on each other's. Hysterical! Hooked together as though we were conjoined at the temple. That's what's so lovely at the moment – we're laughing so much. Sam's being lovely and funny and he looks very handsome now all his weird skin lesions have cleared up. I am truly blessed.

Monday September 15th

I took some cake round to Niamh but when she opened the door, she burst into tears. I just put my arms round her and gave her a massive hug and she sobbed and sobbed. She's feeling really rough and had run out of incontinence pads but didn't have the strength to go to the shops. What a blessing I went round there! Anyway, I cycled to the High St and got her two lots. But when I got back, I went to make her a cup of tea, but her electricity had gone! She was cooking on a little 2 ring

Primus camping stove and Patrick was working late so wouldn't
be home for ages. Oh my God – if there's such a thing as Karma,
I hope Bob gets his comeuppance for deserting her like this. The
man must have no conscience and no scruples whatsoever.

Thursday September 18th

I decided to have a cooking fest yesterday and took several
portions of food round to Niamh - and she was without
electricity again. She'd been up to the hospital for her blood
tests with a friend, then come home and slept for 2 hours, so I
thought she'd probably be too tired to cook anything. Then I
went down into the cellar and flipped the switch on her fuse
box although she said it would go again soon as the whole
house needs re-wiring. Honestly if I ever get my hands on that
shit of a husband of hers...!

Tuesday September 30th

Rang Niamh – first time for a week - and had the biggest shock
– on Tuesday night, Patrick had gone up to bed early. Niamh
went to bed but remembered she'd forgotten something so
went back down but then fell going up again. She had no phone
and couldn't move and Patrick couldn't hear her calling so she
laid there for over 8 hours getting colder and colder until
Patrick got up for work. I felt sick as she was telling me. The
ambulance came and took her to Raphe's. She hadn't broken
anything but couldn't even walk unaided and wasn't allowed to
leave until she could manage stairs. She's going to get one of
those alarms to wear round her neck and give them our
number as her contact so that, God forbid it should happen

again, she only has to press it and they'll ring us to go round. I just want to wrap her up in a big blanket and make it all better.

October

Thursday October 2nd

This morning Sam tried to phone the hospital to find out when his biopsy is but, after trying for half an hour to get through, no one has any record of it! Ye Gods! Why are these people so useless?

The urology secretary phoned Sam back and they've lost his referral! She's made an appointment for next week to have his pre-op and 23rd for his actual operation. That's 6 weeks they've been messing about. And if I hadn't pressed him to phone and keep phoning, they wouldn't have done anything at all. And this is supposed to be one of the top hospitals in the country – it beggars belief.

Wednesday October 15th

Sam went for his pre-op assessment on Tuesday but – again – they had no record of his procedure! He was up there for four hours trying to sort it out and kept phoning me for information that he'd forgotten. They said he had a chest infection, so needed antibiotics. But, if I'm at work, he forgets to take them. I suggested that he set his alarm on his watch for 8am, 2pm and 8pm to remind him but he still forgets, so what can I do?

Thursday October 16th

I rang Elaine but she wasn't well – which is so not Elaine. She says she's been feeling off colour for about a week, drinking lots and peeing a lot and very weak – sounds like Type 2 diabetes to me and she's a prime candidate.

Monday October 20th – 12.30am.

Oh my God! Just when things seem to be going OK, life takes a baseball bat to you.

I'd just finished yoga on Friday when my phone went and Elaine's number came up. But it wasn't Elaine, it was a woman telling me that Elaine had collapsed in the toilet. She'd rung me because mine was the last number on her phone. I told them to call an ambulance and I'd go to the hospital – in Harlow! I got there at about 12.45 but no one had any record of her being admitted. I went round to the main hospital but she wasn't in there either so I went back to A&E and asked them to check again. In the end I said, "I hope I'm being melodramatic here but, if she'd died at the scene, would you have a record of her here?" The woman went off and came back about 5 minutes later saying there was an unknown woman in resusc but she wasn't making any sense and they didn't know her name. Anyway, it was her and she was thrashing about, her eyes were rolling and she was shouting nonsense, so the doctors put me in the family room to wait. After a while they said I could see her and she recognised me but promptly had a seizure: shaking, eyes rolling, lolling to her left. They ushered me out again and took her off for a CT brain scan then the doctor came to talk to me and said that her BM *[Blood Glucose Monitor]* was 50+ *[it should be below 10]* and her BP *[Blood pressure]* was 260/157 (or thereabouts). I told him what I knew and they sent her off for a chest X-ray. Then an air-ambulance brought in car crash

315

victims so she was wheeled from resusc into A&E. She couldn't see, couldn't move her left side and her face was dropped at the left. I thought, more than once, that we were going to lose her. It's bad enough that Niamh is fading fast – I don't want to lose 2 friends! Finally got home at about 10pm totally knackered.

Drove back up to Harlow on Saturday. Elaine was much better: she was lucid, although she still can't remember her address (but she can remember mine!) she had some movement in her left leg, although none in her left arm yet and she still didn't have any vision. I'm going up to the hospital this afternoon to see her again.

When I was at school there were 2 career choices for girls: teacher or nurse. I never, ever, EVER wanted to be a nurse, yet here I am! I cared for mum and dad – even though they were 200 miles away - up and down to Yorkshire every couple of weeks for 3 years – and sometimes more frequently: I did my best to care for Max although he wasn't one to be cared for; I've brought up and nurtured my own children and Sam's to a degree. I'm currently caring for Sam, and Niamh quite a lot of the time, and now Elaine. I sometimes wonder who's caring for me? I just want to write my books.

I was talking to an ITU nurse telling her about all Sam's saga with his health and she said that, when he haemorrhaged after his biopsy on his neck and the haematoma afterwards, the blood supply to his brain will have been interrupted which could have caused some brain damage. The other day he swore blind that Alice had conceived naturally and, if she had had IVF,

I hadn't said anything to him! Two years we lived and breathed their IVF programme and yet he has absolutely no recollection.

And she's due to give birth any minute.

I want a quiet life filled with loveliness and gentle energies and grandbabies and happiness. I need to sleep but Sam's snoring like a brass band, so I might just crash on the settee for tonight.

Tuesday October 28th

Oh my days – the last week has been a whirlwind. I visited four different hospitals this week. Sam went into Perry's on Thursday for his biopsy under GA but was home in 12 hours. Then, on Friday he was peeing blood and, when I went upstairs, it was like the Texas Chainsaw Massacre in the bathroom! Horrible. Off to Raphe's A&E at midnight. But they think it was connected to the op. Anyway, it hasn't happened since which is a relief.

On Saturday, I went up to visit Elaine again. While I was sitting with her, I got a text to say Alice had gone into labour and was at the hospital. Finally got a message at noon to say that Wynter had been born and they were staying in hospital for 24 hours. Sam and I drove up to Ipswich for visiting time – fourth hospital in four days. Talk about an emotional roller coaster!

I cuddled Wynter for almost the whole time, and he is so adorable – and long! Almost 2 feet long. And so sweet. Alice was glowing – a picture of euphoria, bless her. Drank and entire bottle of Prosecco in the evening.

Yesterday I decided that I was having a rest day. I cycled over to the lake and was just about to head over to the allotment when my phone rang: it was Niamh. She'd gone for a walk with a friend but her legs had given way, could I go and pick her up? Feel so sad for her.

Anyway, I did get to the allotment and I made a bonfire and then just sat on our grotty garden chair in the late afternoon sunshine and did nothing. It was bliss. I watched the parakeets flying overhead and enjoyed the warmth of the sun on my face and did absolutely sod all until it started getting dark. What joy! No one was there, no sound, no phone calls, nothing but me and nature – wonderful.

Tuesday December 2nd

Saturday: At 4.50am, Tilly gave birth to grandbaby number 5 – Sebastian – 10lbs 3 oz!! Whoa! Poor Tilly! I went over on the train and Tom and Caleb met me at the station and we walked back to the flat. Tom is such a brilliant dad. I'm so proud of him and I had a lovely day with them all. And Sebastian is huge!

Wednesday December 17th

Oh good grief! Where does the time go? Bonkers few weeks - again! So, in a nutshell:

Tuesday, Niamh phoned to say would I walk her to the shops to buy some bread. I offered to go up myself as I had so much to do, but she was insistent that I walk her because she needed to get some exercise. But she's so weak now that she's tottering forward the whole time which puts a strain on me, trying to hold her upright. But then she got 4 bags of food which I had to carry in my left hand whilst holding her with my right and the whole round trip took 2 hours! Plus, I strained my back again!

Last Wednesday, book group Christmas dinner was at our house. Alice came over and laid the table – I felt so proud: it looked like something out of a magazine advert. It was all colour co-ordinated and I used my best crystal glasses and Mum's silver cutlery with candles everywhere and it was really pretty. We had the coal fire roaring and Christmas lights everywhere. Smashing!

Sunday, Sam and I went food shopping for the charity Christmas party in the morning and then wrapped presents in the afternoon for the toy appeal.

Last Monday was the day of Sam's charity Christmas party for families in crisis. Lou and Elaine came to help. We cooked turkey, Halal chicken and a Quorn roast for 32 people as well as roast potatoes, Yorkshire puddings, sprouts, peas, carrots, gravy, cranberry sauce, mince pies and custard. We laid the tables again to look really lovely and we had presents for 19 children and food hampers for 6 families. They all really enjoyed themselves and Sam was Santa, which he loved. We dropped Elaine off and then went to a local woman who's deaf and blind and who'd been mugged, leaving her with no money and no bus pass. Sam took her a bag of food and said she was very old and very vulnerable. There are so many vulnerable people, I wish we could support more of them.

One good thing is that Bob has decided to grace Niamh with his presence over Christmas, so I won't need to make her any meals again till January. And also, she'd asked me to take her to

Kate Edwards

Asda tomorrow, which I was worried about because of my back but now he's down, he can do it. We're still going to have a girlie manicure day on Monday but I don't need to worry about being her 'carer down the road' for a while.

End of Year Catch up:

- **Saturday December 20th** – Met up with Amy, Chris, Lily, Gabriel and their friend's family. We had a delicious lunch in the pub then we burst into a medley of Christmas songs including the entire 12 days of Christmas. Methinks the other diners were NOT overly impressed with our renditions but we had fun and it was very festive.
- **Sunday December 21st** we were wrapping presents for Sam's toy appeal at Raphe's on Monday and I was baking to take stuff away to Shropshire for Christmas. Some of Sam's family came over and I made mince pies as well as baked butternut squash and sweet potato, chestnut and cranberry burgers. They left at about 7 pm and it was lovely to see them all.
- **Monday December 22nd** I took Niamh for a manicure and she took me for a cup of tea afterwards. I'll miss her so much when she does, finally, go.
- Sam did his toy delivery at Raphe's then, in the evening, we ordered pizza and Sam suggested going to Shropshire a day early. Yay! I nearly bit his hand off.
- **Tuesday December 23rd** The car was packed to the rafters with food and presents and suitcases. Sam was pretty freaked out about how remote the house was but I thought it was magnificent. You had to drive across a field of

320

bullocks and then through a wood until you came to this gorgeous weather-boarded barn and cottage like something out of Little House on the Prairie. And miles and miles of nothingness.

- Christmas was utterly magical: massive inglenook fireplace with roaring log fires, beams, long dining table, comfy sofas, lovely farmhouse kitchen, utility room with extra fridge, Amazing! Slight downer was the bed! Sooo uncomfortable, which really didn't help my back. Also, the bathroom and loo were downstairs, which didn't really work for Sam with his 5-times-a-night peeing.

- We went for long walks in the country on Christmas Eve and Boxing Day, and I took Pixie out a couple of times on my own – I do miss having a dog but I know I couldn't cope with one at the moment with Sam's health as it is. The babies were adorable. And to be with all my children and all my grandchildren together in one place was wonderful. I thought my heart would explode with love.

- The food was fabulous, we played games in the evening, laughed a lot, drank a lot and, to top it all, it snowed on Boxing Day. Magnificent!

New Year was very quiet. In fact, Sam fell asleep in front of the TV from about 7pm. Then we went up to bed with a bottle of J2O each and toasted in the New Year in bed!

So long 2014 – not a bad year as years go. Bring on 2015!

2015

In January it had become obvious that we couldn't live on Sam's pension alone. I couldn't go back to assessing because I was faced with the prospect of having to re-train as my qualifications were so old. So I decided to apply for another job. The role of office manager had come up at the dyslexia charity where I'd worked, on and off, for over 20 years, so I applied and got it. It was part-time and, once I'd finished work, I could go home and switch off. Although the money wasn't particularly good, it was more than I'd get if I (attempted) to register for Carers' Allowance again!

And, FINALLY, the publisher of my YA novel agreed to revert the rights back to me so that I could move forwards with another publisher. I had to repay the advance I'd received but it was a huge relief and it felt like a ten tonne boulder had been lifted off me.

Tuesday February 17th

I feel as though I'm completely fragmented at the moment: doing the office job, trying to sort out the manuscript for the new publisher, preparing the manual for a Reiki course I'm teaching next week and writing a stage play - as well as trying to fit in cleaning the house, doing the allotment, tidying the garden, seeing the grandchildren plus, doing the washing, cooking, shopping etc. I don't feel as though I'm giving any one of those my full attention and I don't like it when I don't do a good job of something. I'm just over committed at the moment and am really regretting agreeing to do the Reiki course. Still, it's money!

Sam is planning a Land's End to John O'Groats bike ride to raise money for charity. The local press is getting very excited but he needs so much support with organising stuff, sometimes I could scream. His start date is set for May 10th and he'll be away for about a month, so perhaps I'll have some peace for a few weeks?

Thursday May 21st

As I write, Sam is 2 weeks into his Land's End to John O'Groats bike ride. But, am I getting the few weeks peace I'd hoped for? Absolutely not! I've ended up micromanaging the trip – even from hundreds of miles distance!

- We booked a hotel in Penzance and I drove us down there on May 7th. On the way down the A30 Sam said to me, "I'm not going to have to cycle on roads like this am I?" Quite what he was expecting, God only knows! But bearing in mind that his only practice had been to cycle the odd 30 mile trip on flat ground, I don't know why I was surprised. I said that, yes, if he wanted to get out of Cornwall, then he'd have to cycle on roads like that. He seemed shocked.
- In the hotel, Sam tried to set up the all-singing, all-dancing satnav that the bike shop had conned him into buying, but neither we, nor anyone else, could work it out. Instead, I bought him a GB road atlas and plotted his route for him.

- Saturday morning we drove to Land's End and he set off at 9.50am. I did not point out the memorial plaques on the wall for people who'd died doing LEJOG – including one guy who was on his 12th trek: so not a novice, by any means. I felt very tearful and more than a little anxious as I watched him head off up the road. I drove passed him about 10 minutes later and, as I watched him through my rear-view mirror, I wondered if that would be the last time I ever saw him. Hugely emotional.

- All the money he raises will be split between Cancer Research UK and a fund to get charitable status for his own charity work. He's aiming for about £10K. Over ambitious? We'll see!

- Sam did Land's End to Bodmin on the first day – 51 miles across Bodmin Moor, in the sweltering heat, then on to Okehampton, across Dartmoor and Exmoor in really, quite warm weather. He said the hills were unbelievable and he felt very low at times but also met some kind people who knocked money off his B&B bills, donated money and generally looked after him. His panier fell off – twice – as he was going up mega hills, so he had to go back down again and pick them up. He had to walk up loads of hills because his backpack was so heavy, it was pulling him backwards. He got a puncture, then someone directed him the wrong way and he didn't realise for about 3 miles.

- He's been drenched to the skin a couple of times and then, when he got to Shrewsbury last Friday, he was wandering about looking for somewhere to stay when a guy who used to work for Cancer Relief saw him and asked if he needed any help. They went round Shrewsbury together trying to find somewhere and, sadly, encountered a racist guy who was rude to Sam. Bless him, Sam walked away but the guy who was with him was furious and went home and tweeted about it. And it went viral! Sam did find somewhere to stay and he was inundated with money, someone paid his bill, he was interviewed on radio and for the local paper and greeted by a small crowd (about 30 people) outside his B&B. He was almost in tears. And the publicity followed him right up through Shropshire, Cheshire and Lancashire.

- He's now headed across the Lake District from Kendal to Carlisle and will be interviewed on Radio Cumbria tomorrow morning.

- He's had a few disasters: when he thought he'd lost his glasses and phone: he rang up in a right state, talking about going back to Bristol (from Gloucester), so I had to talk him through the steps: i) phone the hostel, ii) if they're there, get a train back, iii) if not, buy a pay as you go phone and some over-the-counter glasses but, first of all: double check all your bags and your room. Hey presto – there they were: he'd unpacked them and forgotten. But that whole episode took about an hour with Sam going to find a pay phone and ringing me every few minutes. Very stressful and exhausting – for me as well as him!

- The night before last, in Preston, he stepped on a screwdriver from his toolkit and pierced his foot. I told him to go to the hospital to get a tetanus injection and some antibiotics – did he? Of course not! And then he didn't phone me in the morning and his phone was turned off! I was beside myself – I even rang Preston A&E but when he did, finally, phone at 6.30pm from Kendal (having had another racist incident) he was all, "Why did you panic: if I was dead, the police would've been round by now." Jesus wept!

Friday May 29th

Sam has arrived in Wick – another hotel donated by a stranger – he's just itching to finish now. One day left of his marathon.

Monday June 8th

Last Monday, I got up at 6, packed up the car and set off to Scotland by 7am. I'd intended to stop at Berwick but I felt OK and the weather improved the further north I got, so I actually ended up driving for 9 hours and stopped at Aviemore. It was bitterly cold – snow on the mountains – and I stayed at a motel which didn't do breakfast, so I left at 7.45 and headed north, stopping for breakfast just north of Inverness.

The A9 road was appalling and I was shocked to see where Sam had cycled. I can understand why the cycling organisations tell cyclists not to use it. It's a death trap! Massive lorries thundering past and nowhere to overtake: all twisty-turny; uphill, down-dale – dreadful.

I finally arrived in Mey at about 1pm and Sam was in his room. We went over to Mey House, the 5* B&B where he'd been donated a room for the night on Saturday and I met the couple who ran it – lovely. We went round the Castle of Mey, which was owned by the Queen Mother. It was interesting enough and then we wandered down onto the beach, which was beautiful. Rocky, but lovely: not a sound other than the sea and the birds. You can see Orkney and the Old Man of Hoy and Stroma – fabulous.

On Tuesday morning we set off back going via John O'Groats, so that I could see where he actually finished. Then we meandered back, getting to Berwick by 6pm. I was knackered and the hotel was absolutely crap – possibly the worst hotel either of us has stayed in – ever!

Thursday June 18th

I feel like ME again! Yesterday, I cycled to the lake, then cycled to the allotment and watered it and spread some natural slug repellent and picked MORE strawberries – they are so delicious, nom, nom, nom! Then home to sort out the study and plan the rest of the day and, in the afternoon, I wrote! A thousand words, plus some authory FB and Twitter stuff. I didn't stop till almost 6pm and it makes such a difference to my whole being. I'm upbeat, happy, fulfilled, positive – FAB-U-LOUS dahling!

Thursday August 27th

Sam and I organised a coach trip to the seaside for low-income families. The rain that has plagued most of this summer actually stopped for a few hours, although it was quite chilly and cloudy – but no actual rain! Yay! Ten families turned up, which was great. We'd gone round Asda buying sandwiches, crisps, apples and water for them and I'd taken a bag full of buckets and spades that we keep for the grandchildren.

Sam and I sat on the beach and I went for a swim in the sea, then we mooched round the town. A lovely day and everyone said they'd enjoyed themselves. Several of the families were refugees and didn't speak much English but they did manage to express their gratitude.

October

Things were very difficult for us throughout the autumn of 2015. My job was becoming more and more stressful and less and less satisfying. I'd taken on the financial side of the charity as well as the bookings and general admin, and I didn't feel confident about it at all. As with most part-time jobs, although I was officially only working 12 hours a week, in reality, I was working double that.

And after the euphoria of completing his LEJOG bike ride, Sam had been largely drifting. He wasn't working, other that odd bits of charity work, and had nothing to focus on. He wouldn't go to the allotment without me because there'd been a couple of racist incidents, he wasn't interested in doing the garden or any DIY and had stopped doing his running and cycling. Sometimes he spent whole days under the duvet – on one occasion five days! And I was resentful. In my mind: I was working my socks off only to get home from work to find Sam either still in bed or lying on the settee watching football. I was so wrapped up in my own self-pity that I couldn't see how depressed Sam was.

His memory was dreadful and showed no sign of improving. He would put food on the grill and forget it – until the smoke-alarm went off. He left his keys in the door at least once a week – an open invitation to any passing thief. On one occasion, as I walked down the road, I could see our car door wide open across the pavement. The car radio was playing and the keys were in the ignition but there was no sign of Sam. The front door of the house was also open and, when I went in, Sam was lying on the sofa watching True Crime – oblivious to the fact we could have been the victims of true crime ourselves! Anyone could have stolen the car or walked into the house and robbed us of everything.

The neuropathy in his hands was also an ever present dampener on his spirits. It was (and still is) a constant background pain in both hands making it difficult to hold things or even move three of his fingers. There were – and still are – times when he gets excruciating shooting pains in his hands going right up to his elbow, causing him to scream out loud. He says it's as though an electric drill has pierced the nerves in his hands and arms. He's been seen by three different consultant neurologists: Raphe's, The Neurological Hospital and, most recently, Perry's.

Friday October 23rd

Dr K phoned Sam. Apparently, although everyone said that Sam's neuropathy is temporary and will go away eventually, Perry's neurology department think that it's permanent and he'll have it all his life - although they don't know why. Er, yes they do: it's the chemo: the same stuff that's affected his brain and his memory! Just in the past week, he's left the hot tap running downstairs when he came to bed – thank God I heard the boiler going and came down to check it; he's messed up his new phone; locked himself out of his iPad because he's forgotten his password more than 3 times, and got another parking ticket. He loses his keys and/or phone and/or wallet several times most weeks and forgets almost everything that's said to him so that I sometimes tell him things 5 or 6 times – even more sometimes. He starts the bath running and either doesn't put the plug in or turns on the cold tap rather than the hot, or he forgets it's running. And he's got another 2 PCNs for driving the wrong way down one-way streets. It's like living with someone with dementia!

Anyway, on the positive side, once he'd spoken to the doctor, his mood changed instantly and he was back to being `Super Sam' – hallelujah! It's as though now he's got a definitive answer, he can deal with it, rather than will it go away/won't it? How the human mind works.

Friday November 13th

My new working hours are Tuesday, Wednesday and Thursday 10 – 3, although I always get in early and usually work late. On Wednesday I was doing some of the financial stuff and just couldn't get my head round it. I came home and just cried and cried and cried.

Thursday: Sam was at Perry's so I went with him and went into work later. It was a new consultant and she said that Sam's bloods from 4 months ago were good – his Kappa Para proteins were at 3.6 - but his liver functions were raised, although they've fluctuated over the past 5 years, so she's not unduly worried at this stage. He's had a wheeze for about a month now, so I asked if he could have a chest X-ray just to be on the safe side. Anyway, she listened to his chest and said there was

330

no sign of an infections but sent him for an X-ray. But all looking good at the moment.

Friday November 27th

I think I've now got to grips with the financial side at work, which is a massive relief. On Wednesday evening I felt full of cold, sneezing and snuffling away, so I put slices of onions in some bed socks and left the rest of the raw onion on my bedside table and, hey presto, my cold was better the next day! It was amazing. At one point an advert came on TV with Status Quo music and Sam and I were bopping about in bed doing the rocker dance and I said, "Look at the pair of us: dancing in bed with me with onions in my socks! Who said romance was dead?" We were laughing so much, it was lovely. It's moments like that that I really cherish.

December

Sam's charity was finally set up – with the help of a company of accountants who'd been impressed by his bike ride. He'd raised just over £6K, so had given half to Cancer Research UK and used the rest to register his own voluntary work as a charity. It was the same things he'd been doing for decades but now it had an official charity number and he could apply for grants. It gave him a purpose again, for which I was truly grateful.

I gave up work at the dyslexia charity and on the way home I met a friend who said she hardly recognised me I looked so exhausted. I was, bizarrely, relieved: it was like affirmation that I was actually knackered and it wasn't all in my mind.

Sam did his usual toy delivery to children who were in hospital over Christmas at Raphe's and also added another local hospital and a children's hospice.

We'd arranged to help out at The Salvation Army again on Christmas Day but, on Christmas morning Sam had a voicemail from them saying they'd got a lot of helpers this year, so I wasn't needed but, if Sam could go and play games with the kids, they'd appreciate it. And he did!

Christmas Day – Friday December 25th

So Sam went off to the Sally Army at about 12.30 and isn't due back till 4pm - meaning that I'm on my own, on Christmas Day, watching reruns of Sherlock on Alibi and downing copious amounts of Merlot. It probably ranks as my worst Christmas ever.

2016

Sam got another chest infection which laid him very low with a temperature creeping up towards the 40o mark again. It was below freezing but we were sleeping with the window open and a fan on in the bedroom to try and keep him cool. He was in bed for a week but whenever I tried to get him out of bed to avoid DVT, he crashed out, exhausted. The GP sent him for blood tests to make sure it wasn't the lymphoma rearing it's God-awful malignant head again but, thank heavens, it wasn't and, eventually, he did recover.

Monday February 22nd

I went round to see Niamh. Her sister, Aoife, was visiting and I always like to catch up with her. Niamh was looking so small and frail. It's amazing she's still alive: 3 years ago her doctor gave her 12 – 18 months and she's not on any medication now – just palliative care. Bless her.

Saturday February 27th

Oh my days! What a week – again! Last Sunday we went out to a tiny village in Essex for Sam to be presented with his trophy for Completing LEJOG Through Adversity. The president of the LEJOG association presented him with it and there was an amazing spread. It was lovely. We left about 4pm and drove home but, when we got back, Sam wasn't feeling well again. His temperature was up and he went straight to bed.

He was in bed all week and his temperature spiking up to 38.6. He got the rigors twice and was sneezing but no sign of a chest infection this time. I was up and downstairs taking his temperature, administering his medication, making his meals. I rang the doctor and asked for a call back and Dr K rang me and asked me to take Sam up there. It was a glorious day and I drove him up there and we went straight in. There was no sign of infection – she listened to his chest and tested his urine, looked down his ears and throat but nothing. So she gave him a prescription for antibiotics and said only take them on Thursday if his temperature was still raised. If he was still ill on Friday, go for another blood test. I was worried sick as there wasn't any apparent reason for the temperature and I was concerned that it might be sepsis again. On Thursday, his temperature was still high, so we started the antibiotics but on Friday morning I asked if he thought he should go for the blood test but his temperature was down to 35.5 – so we decided against. I know he must feel like a pin cushion sometimes but I think I'd have felt better if he'd had it – just to try and find out what was going on.

Thursday March 1st

Sam was at back at Perry's today. It was yet another consultant but at least he seemed genuinely concerned about Sam's repeated infections and spiking temperature. He did say that he didn't think it was the lymphoma returning (phew!) and was probably because the chemo had compromised his immunity. He gave him MORE antibiotics – stronger ones - and recommended that he has another CT scan but Sam refused because he doesn't like going in the machine. Deep breaths, Kate!

Tuesday March 22nd

I'd agreed to take Niamh out for lunch and, when I got there at 11.30, Patrick opened the door and said that he was coming with us. Apparently, Niamh had been so weak on Monday that she'd been crying because she thought she'd have to cancel today, so he said that he'd come too.

It took Patrick and me 25 minutes to get her from the dining room to the car as she shuffled a centimetre at a time on her Zimmer frame. Between us, we manoeuvred her into the car and put her wheelchair in the boot and then we headed off. It was so lovely to have lunch with her but Patrick insisted on sitting at the table with us, despite the fact that she'd asked him to sit over at the other side because, "Sure, you don't want to be listening to us old ladies and our chat." But, apparently, he did. Niamh had also said that she wanted to treat me because I do so much for her and, although I've told her a million times, it's not necessary, she was insistent. But, when Patrick and I went up to the counter to order, the bill came to £32. He took out a £20 note and said, "I suppose Mum's and mine will come to more than that, won't it?" The bloody cheek! He'd heard her say, very clearly, several times that she was treating me. I said, "Yes, it will, it'll be £32 Patrick!"

I felt really narked about it. Last time I got stuff for her, he was like the bloody Spanish inquisition when I asked for the money – which came to over £20. He was all: What's it for? How much did this cost, how much did that cost? Have you got the receipt? There have been loads of times I've done shopping for her when I haven't even asked for the money. How dare he insinuate that I'm fleecing her? Like father like bloody son!

Anyway, Niamh and I were chatting and, bless her, she dozed off in the middle of lunch. She looked like a tiny, wizened child slumped in her wheelchair with her tufty wisps of hair sticking out of her hair band. So, so sad.

Niamh-gate! The next six week period was one of the saddest for me.

Saturday April 9th

I went to Zumba. While I was there Niamh rang and asked if I could do her a favour. I asked if it was urgent or if it could wait till I'd got home. She said that was fine and asked me to get her some ham on the way.

By the time I got round there it was almost midday. I rang the bell three times but no one answered so I used our emergency key but the door was double locked. I rang and rang and then Patrick came down in his pyjamas to let me in. I went through and Niamh was sitting with one arm in and one arm out of her dressing gown and she asked if I could help her on with it and make her a cup of tea as Patrick had only just got up and was then going to football! I must admit, I was taken aback. Not at Niamh but at Patrick. It was midday and he hadn't even got out of bed to help his mother get dressed and have some breakfast? And that also meant she hadn't had her morphine yet.

Then Niamh said that Patrick was worried about leaving her on her own all afternoon while he was out and would I be on call in case of any problems? Don't get me wrong, I would move heaven and earth for Niamh and I understand that, if Patrick was really caring for her full time, he deserved an afternoon off for himself and I'd be happy to cover - BUT – he's a lazy sod who's out for all he can get and I absolutely object to being used so that he can stay in bed till lunch time and then swan off without even making her breakfast or lunch – plus, he didn't pay me for the ham!

In the end, I made her some sandwiches and a cup of tea and popped in every hour till 5 o'clock to see that she was OK. Patrick hadn't even fed the cat before he went out so that it was screeching around the house until I fed it. Poor little mite.

Tuesday April 12th

Went up the High Street and I bumped into Patrick and asked if I could have a word about Saturday. But he denied everything and walked off.

Wednesday April 13th – 3.30am!

I can't sleep. The situation with Patrick got really unpleasant yesterday. When I got home, he sent a text saying that he hadn't had time to discuss `my accusations' but wanted to do so later. I replied that they weren't `accusations' and I did not want his mum involved or upset over this. He then said that he would not be asking me to go round to keep an eye on Niamh anymore and would be coming round to discuss the `key holder arrangement.' The whole tone of his texts was very rude and, if

337

I didn't care so much about Niamh, I'd stuff the bloody key up his arse and good riddance to him.

Anyway, I phoned Aoife and told her about the incident with Patrick. I told her that I would not be giving back the key until Niamh asks me to as I am a designated key holder for her emergency services and would honour that promise to her. Aoife also told me that Patrick has Niamh's bank cards and keeps all her money. She also said that she thinks he's on drugs again. She said she was going to contact social services and tell them that Niamh's needs were not being met – that she needs 24 hr care and Patrick doesn't give her her medication *[morphine]* until he gets up which is sometimes 2 o'clock in the afternoon and she's in pain in her head and neck. I told her that on Saturday she was still in her pyjamas and, when I took her out for lunch before Easter, she was dressed in stained jog bottoms and a stained top. What is he doing all day? Surely he can use the washing machine and make sure she has clean clothes? I feel so sad about it. To be abandoned by her family when she's at the end of her life is pitiful.

Thursday April 14th

I haven't heard any more form Patrick, and Aoife said she tried to contact Bob but he's not answering his phone or phoning her back.

Sunday April 24th – 2am!

Another night when I can't sleep. Yesterday I had another `do' with Patrick and I'm so sad about the whole business.

I haven't seen Niamh for a couple of weeks, partly because I didn't want to go round there and see Patrick. But yesterday afternoon I assumed he would be out at football. I rang Niamh's landline but no one answered – twice. I deduced that he was out at the match and Niamh had either misplaced the phone or couldn't get to it in time. So round I went! I rang the doorbell 3 times – as is the agreement – then waited. Nothing! So I used the key and, as I opened the door called out, "Hello! It's only me! It's Kate!"

To which, Patrick shouted, "Who's that?"

Shit! My heart sank.

Me: It's me. I rang the doorbell 3 times before I came in.

P: I know I heard you. I want the key back.

Me: It's not yours to have back. I phoned to let your mum know I was coming.

P: I know.

Me: But no one answered either the phone or the door.

P: This is our home and I demand the key back.

Me: It's your parent's home and I haven't got a key for your benefit: it's for your mum.

I went through to the sitting room and sat down on a stool in front of Niamh and Patrick sat down on the settee next to her and, despite having said that he would not involve his mum said, in front of her, "Can I have the key back?"

Me: (To Niamh) Patrick wants me to give the emergency key back, love. What do you want?

N: Oh, I think I'd rather you kept it.

Me: OK, that's fine. I'll hang on to it for emergencies.

P: This is our house and I want the key back otherwise I'll have the locks changed.

Me: Well you just heard your mum, she wants me to keep it.

N: I don't want you two falling out.

Me: We're not falling out. It's fine.

P: It's nothing for you to worry about mum – this is between me and Kate and we'll sort it out between us.

N: Why aren't you getting on?

Me: We are, love – it's fine.

P: We'll sort it out later.

Anyway, he sat there the whole time so it was difficult to talk to Niamh and then he turned up the volume of the television so that I could hardly hear what she said. I told her that I'd book us a manicure together next week and then, after about 20 minutes, the atmosphere was so strained with Patrick sitting right next to us and the television blaring, that I said I would go. Niamh said she would walk me to the door but, as soon as I got up to hand her the Zimmer frame, Patrick leapt up and got between me and her and practically elbowed me out of the way to get her to her feet. Then, as she was shuffling towards the door:

P: So what's going to happen about this key?

Me: You heard your mum, she'd rather I hang on to it for emergencies.

N: Well, what do you think Patrick?

Me: This is your decision, love. What do you want?

N: Well, I don't want you two falling out. I think it might be better if Patrick has it.

And he gave me such a smug smirk I could have knocked his block off. So I handed it back but made a point of saying, "Now that means that I don't have an emergency key so, if I ring the doorbell, someone needs to get up and let me in!" And I glared at him.

But what it means is, he is effectively stopping me seeing her. If I ring the doorbell, he doesn't answer, he doesn't pick up the phone and now I can't let myself in if he goes out. What a fucking control freak! It's classic behaviour of an abuser: making sure the woman's friends are alienated; he's done it with most of her other friends and now me. I feel so unbelievably sad for her – and myself! I've known her over 20 years and don't know if I'll see her again – maybe when Aoife comes over. Although Niamh was saying that she didn't think Aoife was going to come anymore. I know Patrick had tried to stop her visiting last time, saying he didn't want her there.

When I got home I phoned Aoife – like she can do anything! Anyway, she was very understanding and said she wasn't happy about the care Niamh was getting from Patrick. This afternoon, there was blood all over the hall floor, walls and door because Patrick had cut himself and hadn't cleaned it up; there were 2 vases of dead flowers – not just wilting but properly dead by a couple of weeks; more tut all over the floor of the hall and sitting room, so that I was having to move things out the way so that she didn't trip as she came to the door with me – including a soiled incontinence pad – just lying in the middle of the floor! It's disgusting and that poor woman is trapped in that filthy house! Bless her – she deserves better.

Monday April 25th

Well, after much deliberation with Sam and Elaine *[who used to be a social worker]*, I've decided to report Patrick and Bob to Social Services under Safeguarding Vulnerable Adults. I told Aoife what I was doing and she's in full agreement saying that they were both bullying Niamh. I wrote out a long list of incidents with times and any witnesses. I hope it doesn't look as though I'm being vindictive – I was quite happy to carry on with the way things were but I am very concerned now that I have no access to her to check that she's OK and Patrick is becoming more and more controlling.

Thursday April 26th

Yesterday, a social worker phoned me. She said I'd made serious allegations and, as Niamh was of sound mind (the cancer has spread to her brain so, can she really be classed as being of sound mind?) if she didn't want anything to change, there was nothing social services could do, but they would do an investigation. I told her that Aoife was willing to speak to her and gave the social worker her number. Later in the afternoon,

Aoife phoned to say that the social worker had spoken to her and she's told her all her concerns that Niamh was married to Bob in name only and Patrick could no longer cope with being her carer. She said how grateful she was to me for starting the ball rolling but I still feel a huge sadness that it's come to this and I still question whether or not I did the right thing and whether or not Niamh will ever forgive me.

Bank Holiday Monday – May 2nd

What a crappy, fucking awful week!

Last Thursday I got a phone call from Aoife saying that Bob had been on the phone to her shouting at her and accusing her of going to Social Services. Jesus! So I immediately phoned Niamh. Patrick answered the phone and said, "Who is it?" He knows my voice but it's more controlling behaviour.

Me: It's Kate. Can I speak to your mum please?

Patrick: Mum, Kate's on the phone. Do you want to speak to her? (MORE controlling behaviour!)

Anyway, I spoke to Niamh and told her that it wasn't Aoife who'd spoken to Social Services, it was me. She asked why, so I told her that I didn't think Patrick was coping very well, to which she replied, "He's doing a wonderful job of looking after me."

Me: Well, my love, it's good that you think that but it doesn't look that way to me. (Or anyone else who cares about her.)

The Patrick piped up in the background, "Tell her I can't believe she'd be so underhand to go behind our backs."

Me: Niamh, I haven't been underhand – I'm telling you that it was me who spoke to Social Services. I did try to talk to Patrick about how he's been but he was very rude to me.

Niamh: What Patrick? What did he say?

Me: I really didn't want you involved in any of this. I did it because I care about you and I had, and still have, concerns about Patrick's ability to look after for you properly. I just wanted you to know that it absolutely was not Aoife and I didn't want anything to come between you and your sister.

I rang Aoife and told her but she said she was fed up with the whole business and had sat and cried all afternoon. She said she'd decided in October that she wouldn't come over to London anymore because Patrick made her feel as though she was intruding. At that point I had a call on my mobile from `Niamh Home' but when I picked up, it was Patrick, ranting and raving again, so I told him that I was not having the conversation and put the phone down.

I made a clear choice to back off from Niamh and her family. I feel so desperately sad that she's ending her life in such squalid conditions but if she thinks that Patrick is doing a wonderful job, there's nothing more to say. And, I felt a huge relief when I reached that decision. At least she's been flagged up with Social Services now, so they'll be keeping an eye on her – and Patrick! I cried, because I don't suppose I'll see her again but, it's a price I'd happily pay to know that social services are looking out for her.

Wednesday May 18th

I'm still in the throes of this horrible abyss of depression. I just keep crying. It's driving me nuts. I hate it. Nothing seems to shift it. Sam's being very good about it – probably because he's back in counselling for his own depression, so is able to support me better. What a pair: Mr & Mrs Misery! He is a good man. I lose sight of that when he's in the depths of his own crap and I get the brunt of it, but he is good and kind and very funny. I love him to bits and I get so sad about the fact that he has cancer and might die.

Friday May 27th

One of Niamh's friends and her husband called round on their way home. She said Patrick had been rude to her when they arrived and she'd challenged him about it but after that it was OK. Her husband had talked with Patrick about football and Niamh asked her to go into the front bedroom with her where she said, "I'm sorry about Patrick. I hope he didn't offend you. I can't afford to lose any more friends because of him." I was almost in tears. I do miss her so much. Such a sad situation.

Monday June 27th

On Saturday afternoon I got a missed call from Aoife. My heart sank when I saw who it was. I immediately thought the worst but she was ringing to say that she's coming over in July for a couple of days as Niamh's been asking for her and she'd like to meet up. I felt such relief. I thought she probably hated me after all the shenanigans with social services but she said she thought I'd got the poor end of the deal `after everything I've done to help Niamh and support her.' She thought I'd been treated very shabbily by Patrick and, when Aoife had asked

Niamh if she'd like to see me, Niamh said, "Well, I don't know because Kate said some horrible things to Patrick." What a bloody liar! I think liars are the worst sort of people because you just never know where you are with them. Anyway, Aoife and I are going to meet up in July and hopefully, she'll engineer it so that we bump into each other and I can see Niamh too. I hope that doesn't cause her too much distress but it would be lovely to see her one more time – even if it's the last time.

One Saturday morning as I was driving along the High Street, I passed a charity shop with a hot tub outside. I parked up and ran across to have a look. It was an inflatable one, all boxed up and in good condition so, after a (very quick) phone consultation with Sam, I bought it! That particular hot tub died the following year but we have since bought two others and I confess, they are the best things I've ever bought. I love my hot tub with a passion and go in it almost every day – even in winter. It keeps me sane.

Friday July 8th

On Wednesday I had a school visit! Yay! It was swelteringly hot and the train down was packed to the rafters. I walked from the station to the hotel with my suitcase full of books and a massive backpack on my back. I was knackered. Then my room was on the 2nd floor and there was no lift, the window was sealed shut and the air conditioning was rubbish. It was a single bed with a squodgy mattress that didn't do my back any favours at all.

It was a fabulous evening and I sat in the park and listened to a choir which was beautiful. The town was lovely and reminded me of York on a smaller scale with the bars – or gates – and medieval buildings. I really missed Sam. I'm usually OK when I go away on my own but I felt quite low and a bit lonely and just wanted to cuddle him.

The librarian picked me up at 8.30 and drove me to the school. The first group were Year 9 and I was teaching a workshop on Creating Characters. Then we went off to the drama theatre for a talk to Year 8. We were supposed to be in the hall but there was a dance exam in there, so we had to squeeze 6 tutor groups, 10 staff and me into the drama theatre which was cosy - in the same way sardines crammed in a can is cosy! Plus it was baking hot with no windows, no air con and 180 sweaty teenagers! Not the most fragrant experience ever.

The final group was another year 9 lower set and this lot were hard work! Oh my God, it reminded me why I'm no longer a teacher. Talk about playing to a graveyard. One girl had written nothing, so I went over and said, "So how's it going over here?" She looked at me, turned over her left wrist and, in big felt tip letters it said `FUCK U.' Nice!

The librarian gave me a lift to the station and, although my train wasn't till 4.20, the guard let me get the earlier one because there'd been a suicide on the track (a Year 9 teacher perhaps?) and all trains were delayed and being diverted. It was a 2 carriage train and I was the only one in my carriage with my plastic glass of Merlot that I'd got at the Pumpkin Cafe on the platform.

When I got home Sam told me he'd put the hot tub on. Oh yes! I walked in, dumped my bags and went straight in. Bliss! He brought me out a glass of wine and we ordered pizza. Felt 100% better.

Tuesday July 19th

Yesterday was another scorcher – up to 31°C and clear blue skies. And the hot tub got up to 38°C – unbelievable. I can't tell you how much I love it in there. Sometimes I have the bubbles on and sometimes I just wallow in the warm water. I am in Heaven. Sam came out to join me and we were still in there until 7.30 singing `On top of the World' by the Carpenters. It was such a magical moment – not sure the neighbours felt the same though!

Monday July 25th

Aoife is over and she called round. She'd bought us a millionaire's cheesecake, bless her. Apparently, Niamh had a fall about 3 weeks ago. She's damaged her spine and her legs don't work anymore. She'd also `had a funny episode where her right arm went numb and she couldn't speak' according to Patrick. Now, if that's not a TIA *[Transient Ischaemic Attack – a mini-stroke]*, I don't know what is. Apparently she's confined to her wheelchair even indoors and is very weak. But she says she misses me and would like to meet up so we decided to try and sort something out before Aoife goes home on Friday.

Thursday July 28th

Aoife rang: Niamh wanted to speak to me! She's in a dreadful situation where Bob and Patrick won't let her use the house phone and Patrick's taken her mobile, so she was having to use Aoife's in her bedroom and we all had to whisper so that Bob and Patrick couldn't hear who she was talking to! FFS! She's dying! Don't they get that? She sounded so weak and frail. I said I was so sorry for how things had turned out. She said she missed me and I said I missed her and would she like it if we could somehow meet up. She said he'd like that very much but she had to go as someone came to the door. I then spoke to Aoife and we arranged that if she could get Niamh out of the house without the men finding out where she was going, we could meet up. But about an hour later she rang back to say that the district nurse had been and Niamh's foot was swollen, blue and cold and she was calling the doctor. She rang back again to say the GP had called an ambulance as she didn't like the look of Niamh's foot and thought it might be DVT. So I didn't get to see her after all.

Monday September 5th

I went down to the allotment and picked masses of beans, blackberries and Swiss chard and then got a phone call from one of Niamh's friends to say that they were in a coffee shop in the High Street and would I like to join them? Felt so emotional!

I stopped what I was doing and dashed home, quick change and headed up there. On the way, I passed Patrick, who'd clearly been with them and he gave me such a look but I just looked away. Then I was worried that he'd find out where I was going and try to stop me. When I got there, two of her friends were with her and Niamh was in a wheelchair at the end of the table, sort of leaning to her right side. She had her plate on her lap and was trying to eat a sandwich but struggling with the crusts. I just went up and kissed her and said, "Hello, my love. How are you doing?" as though nothing had happened. She said she was OK but didn't smile and I wondered if I'd got it totally wrong.

They let me sit next to Niamh and I cut the crusts off her sandwich and then got her a drinking straw because she couldn't drink her tea. The four of us chatted about various things and I'd taken them all jars of homemade blackberry jam – but then I worried that if Patrick realised where it had come from, he might get arsy. How ridiculous for a grown woman of my age and experience to be frightened of a yard o' pump watter like him! But, it's not for myself: it's for Niamh because I don't want her any more distressed. I stayed about half an hour and then she said she was tired. Her friend said she'd call Patrick to come and help them get her into the car, so I said I would take my leave – I didn't want a scene in the cafe. When I went to kiss her goodbye I said, "Would you like to do this again some time?" And she said, "Oh yes, I'd love it." So I felt a bit better.

Friday November 4th

Yesterday Sam was at Perry's for his 4 monthly check-up. The doctor said that there was no palpable sign that the lymphoma was recurring and his bloods were normal, so he was very pleased and said Sam could lead a normal life. I don't even know what a normal life looks like. He can't go back to work because he forgets everything and his neuropathy is still very debilitating. Define normal, please!

Wednesday November 9th

As I came home today, I noticed that our dustbin lid was off. I went to put it back on and, on the bottom of the bin was a torn up card. I thought it was weird as I always put old cards in the recycling. When I looked closer, it was the birthday card I'd sent to Niamh. Patrick had obviously torn it up and put in our dustbin. Such a mean thing to do.

December

December was the usual round of charity events, although we didn't do a Christmas meal for families this year. But we did have another family Christmas in Wales. We hired a cottage on top of a hill in the Black Mountains and it was magnificent. Such a joy to be with all my family at Christmas.

2017

Several things changed this year: Sam got his SIA Security badge so that he could do as-and-when work, mainly at football stadia, and he also started feeding homeless people on a regular basis. There was quite a large community of rough sleepers living in a shopping mall near us, so he started taking them breakfast bags every Friday morning. On a Thursday, one of us would buy the shopping then I'd make up 30 sandwiches and Sam would put them in bags with crisps, biscuits, fruit and bottles of water. He, and sometimes I, would go out at 6 am on Friday and set up a stall in the shopping centre to distribute the food. We later expanded this to include: hot tea or coffee, hats, scarves, gloves, socks, toiletries, sanitary protection and underwear. And Sam increased his catchment area to include 4 or 5 other sites where homeless people lived.

We did this every week until March 2020 when Covid kicked in.

Thursday February 23rd

Sam was at Perry's today. The doctor couldn't feel any lumps anywhere and said that his bloods are still good so that's a relief. His liver functions are abnormal and erratic but they have been for several years, so there's nothing to worry about there and his para-proteins are still at 3, which is brilliant. Fingers crossed it stays that way.

Thursday March 23rd

I got back from Tesco at about 11 am and started to make up the `personal bags' for the homeless people. I made up 22 and each one contained: a bar of soap, a small shampoo, small toothpaste, toothbrush, tissues, a pair of underpants and a pair of socks. There were also some sanitary pads for the women. Sam got out a plastic box and a trolley and we loaded them into it.

Two women donated hats, socks, gloves and scarves last week and said they want to make 30 sandwiches and buy 30 bottles of water this week and every week for the foreseeable future. I felt a tad sad that my sandwich-making had been made redundant but, of course, there's no telling how long they'll last. Anyway, I asked Sam to contact them this morning and find out when they'd be bringing the stuff over so that we could make up the bags and identify what else needed to be bought to complete them. We try to make sure that each bag contains roughly the same things so that fights don't break out.

Tuesday March 28th

On Friday morning, we headed off to where all the homeless people sleep. We gave out all 30 bags of the breakfast food and all 22 personal bags. One man came up and kissed my hand. People are so grateful. One woman came and said she was allergic to eggs and would it be at all possible for her to change her food - as though it was in imposition. She was probably not much younger than me, bless her.

Friday April 14th – Good Friday

Aoife is over so, I went up to meet her in a coffee shop. It's so ridiculous – she picked the one furthest down the High Street, so that neither Patrick nor Bob would be likely to walk past and see us. I got there first and sat right at the back so that we weren't seen entering together, and when she left, she asked me to wait about 5 minutes before leaving so that we weren't seen coming out together. It's like something out of a John le Carre novel – except no national security depends on it: just two nasty men who would stop Aoife seeing her dying sister if they thought she'd met up with me!

She says Niamh can't move now at all: she's totally bed ridden and can't eat or drink by herself. Even if someone feeds her she only nibbles tiny bits of food. And her mind's going. When Aoife said something about me, Niamh said, "Oh yes. I had a friend called Kate who was always round at my house, but I haven't seen her for a long time – not since I came here." Apparently she thinks she's in some sort of home. The NHS has cut the funding for her carers and asked Bob for £500 per month about which he's on the warpath. Niamh's pension will be more than that. Anyway, he's reduced her 2 carers to 1 now – even though she needs 2 people to move her. Aoife said the house is disgusting but, thankfully, Niamh's unaware of it. She said the whole business was so appallingly sad but then she said, "You know what, Kate – Niamh's won. Her cancer's stable, so she could go on like this for years unless she gets an infection and, as long as she's alive, Bob can't sell the house and has to keep coming over here, so she's won. It's her ultimate revenge." We chatted for over an hour but, as she was about to leave, she saw a missed call from Niamh's landline which must have been either Bob or Patrick, so she left quickly and asked me to wait behind for a while.

Yesterday morning I got up early and went up to the surgery to queue for an appointment with the doctor. Luckily I got Dr K and she listened to my chest and said, "Oh goodness, you are very wheezy. Your right lung in particular is very tight. There's very little movement there." She said that I was already on the maximum asthma medication and, although she would give me antibiotics, I needed Prednisolone as well *[a systemic steroid.]* I was gutted. She also said that, currently, my chance of heart attack and/or stroke is 9%!!! My blood pressure was through the roof (179/90) and it's usually very low but she said that could be because I'm, so ill. I need to carry on losing weight and have my BP checked again in a couple of weeks by the nurse.

Saturday April 22nd

Yesterday afternoon I phoned the doctor again and said that things were not progressing as well as I'd hoped. Dr K rang me back at about 7pm and said she'd send an electronic prescription over to the chemist for me to collect in the morning – more Prednisolone! This time it's a 2 week decreasing dose. She's also told me to increase my inhalers – double the steroid inhaler and increase the other by 50% until my peak-flow improves.

On a slightly positive note, one of my story ideas has been accepted. They want lots of changes and a first draft by May 15th. Eeek! We're away from May 7th – 14th and Alice and I are supposed to be going away next weekend to Bournemouth. I'm panicking again.

Alice and I had signed up for the Great East Swim in June and Alice was concerned that she might not be able to manage a mile in open water. I'd done the Bournemouth pier-to-pier swim a couple times, which is 1.4 miles, so I suggested having a girly weekend and swimming from Bournemouth to Boscombe as a practice run.

Friday April 28th – Sunday April 30th

Oh my days – what a bonkers weekend! Alice and I headed off to Bournemouth. Got to the hotel at about 8.45pm, then went down to the surfers' bar by the beach for a drink - intending to go to bed at about 10. Which actually turned into 11.30. Ooops!

On the Saturday morning, I woke up at about 6am but let Alice sleep until 8 as she'd had a bad night. Then we had a picnic breakfast in the room and got into our wetsuits. I've actually lost more weight since I bought mine, so it went on really easily which was a relief. We walked down to the beach just as the tide started to come in. My dad always used to say: if the tide's coming in, jump in: if the tide's going out, stay out. So we'd planned our swim accordingly. I'd bought a small backpack and wrapped everything in zip up plastic bags and put them inside it – money, phones, Fitbits and microfiber towels. We left some warm clothing in a carrier bag on the steps of the lifeguard hut with a notice saying we were sea-swimming and then we went in the water – me with the backpack on. OH! MY! GOD! It was 10°C and, even though we had wetsuits on, our hands were freezing. In fact, they turned purple. (Afterwards I found out that no open water swimming takes place in the UK in below 12° and it was saying all wetsuits should be 5/6mm thick, whereas mine is 1.5mm and Alice's 3mm! It also said gloves should be worn – another ooops!)

I'd taken some money to buy ourselves hot drinks when we got out but my hands were so cold, I couldn't open the bag. I had to toss it at the woman in the kiosk and tell her to take out what she needed. Then we walked back along the beach and picked up our warm clothing from the lifeguards before heading back to the hotel. On the way, two women stopped us and said they'd been watching us swim and how impressed they'd been, which was lovely. And, later on, two other women in the hotel said the same thing. Seems we were some sort of mini celebs :).

We went down to the spa and went in the steam room and sauna and then headed back to the room for a bath and down to the beach for a picnic lunch. While we were sitting there, Alice looked up at the zip wire and said, "OK – so I swam the pier-to-pier, how about you going on the zip wire?" No way! I felt ill. We got all harnessed up and then had to climb to the top of this enormous tower on the end of the pier - which was already swaying in the wind. Then, when we got to the top, you were supposed to just launch yourself off this wooden platform. OH MY GOD! It was horrendous. Alice went off like she was in the SAS - no problem. But I stood there and thought: I can't do this. I've got to get down. I'm going to die. There were kids behind me going, "Go on! Hurry up lady!" In the end, I just stepped off and went. I was spinning round and round so that I couldn't see anything and I don't think I breathed the whole way down. I ended up on my knees and the two guys had to help me to my feet. Awful, awful, awful! But I did it! Yay!

Afterwards we walked into town and got a drink at the wine bar in the centre of town, then back to the hotel for some hot tub.

In the evening Alice pointed out the new big wheel down by the beach and said if it cost less than £5, she'd pay for us to go on it. Oh my days! She's such a thrill seeker. It was a howling gale and I didn't even have a coat but, as it only cost £5 each, I'd agreed to do it. I must be mad!

When we got off there was a couple who'd been in the pod behind us and we got talking. They suggested going for a drink and it turned out they were multi-millionaires: she owns a haulage company and he owns a security company. They'd gone to Bournemouth to test drive a £270K Bentley – which she had no intention of buying because she only buys Porsches: she's got a black one and a white one and she's thinking of getting a red 4x4!!! They were great fun. It was a totally mad evening and we didn't get back to the hotel till midnight – totally hammered!

Had a good journey back on Sunday but, when I got home, Sam was in agony with pain in his head and behind his eye – again. He couldn't move his head to the right at all. I offered to take him to A&E but he wouldn't go. Oh my days!

Tuesday May 2nd

I am so gutted right now. Sam, finally, went to the doctor this morning and she's told him that, in her opinion, he's too ill to travel on Sunday. *[We'd had a holiday booked to Portugal for several months.]* I have been so looking forward to this holiday. It would have been our first holiday abroad for 7 years and now we've got to cancel it. I'm also worried sick about Sam. He's such a bloody idiot about his health. Three weeks I've been telling him to go to the doctor and now look!

1.25pm

I've just cancelled the whole bloody holiday. Ryanair need a doctor's letter and then they'll decide whether or not to reimburse us but the hotel's agreed to a full refund and we've got cancellation insurance. Some consolation but it's hardly the same as a week on the Med!

Wednesday May 3rd

Sam went for blood tests and an X-ray yesterday and he's at the eye-clinic at Raphe's at the moment because of the pain behind his eyes. He's worried that he's going blind: I'm worried that it's a thrombus and we're both worried that it's the lymphoma coming back! Mind you, my chest still isn't 100% but at least my peak-flow is back to normal.

Thursday May 4th

Sam was out most of yesterday at Raphe's. They did another X ray – of the back of his eyes this time – and said that they don't think it's the glaucoma. But he's not satisfied with that, so he went off to Moorfields this morning to their A&E and see what they say. They've done some more tests including an ultrasound scan and so far the doctor doesn't think the pain is related to either his glaucoma or lymphoma. They've given him some pain killing eye drops that have helped but he's still there, waiting to see the doctor again. What a blooming fiasco!

Later

Sam got home about 8.30 and could hardly walk he was so exhausted. No nearer knowing what's the matter but in less pain thanks to the drops.

Monday May 15th

Hallelujah! I am feeling better today – the first time for a month. On Thursday morning I went to the doctor again and I asked for the new inhaler that Liz recommended which is a combo and quite expensive. Anyway, he gave it to me and, so far, I can really feel the difference. I can breathe! Yay!

On Friday we got up at 5am and headed off to the mall to give out the breakfasts. There weren't many rough sleepers - Immigration had been, so many of the non-British homeless people have moved away. There's also been a lot of trouble and someone got stabbed. There were probably only about 15 people there altogether and they said that the council were trying to get it closed, so that they had nowhere to sleep. Where are these people supposed to go? There but for the grace... etc etc!

After lunch I went to Raphe's to get a chest X-ray done, but, after waiting about an hour, they announced that the computers had a virus. So, I went over to the audiology clinic to sort out my hearing aids but they had a virus too. And then, in the news, it said that a ransom-ware virus had affected 79 health services and over 100 countries around the world! Bloody hackers! People's lives are being put at risk because the entire health service relies on computers these days. It scares me how vulnerable we all are. Bring back good old paper and pens!

Yesterday I went over to the allotment for about two and a half hours and it was lovely. I was tired but I got my main crop potatoes planted, a second crop of beans, sweet corn and a second crop of salad, spring onions and spinach. I'm strong to the finish 'cos I eat me spinach!

Friday June 2nd

I got an appointment with my optician and she said that my macular degeneration had degenerated (how appropriate!) and also there was a film across the back of my eye. It was pointless prescribing different lenses, I needed to see a consultant but she couldn't guarantee that there was anything that could be done about it. It was a bit of a shock, to be honest. At the moment I have to watch TV and read a book with my right eye closed otherwise it's all blurred.

Monday June 5th

And, today, I slept till 10.45 this morning. I couldn't believe it. I rang Raphe's eye clinic to see why my eye appointment hadn't come through and they said that the GP hadn't sent it! I rang them up and they said that they had sent it. Jesus wept! Anyway, I told them to send it again. My right eye is getting worse, so that I'm having to close it most of the time.

Tuesday June 6th

I've got to go to the doctor to have an ECG and my BP checked. I must admit, I'm a bit anxious. Especially as I had some chest pains again this morning. Who wouldn't with everything that's going on at the moment?

Thursday June 8th

On Tuesday I phoned Raphe's again and they said they STILL hadn't had my referral for my eye. In fact, the guy said that, if the reception staff said that they'd had confirmation of the fax, they were lying because the faxes at Raphe's had been down since the cyber-attack on May 12th but they'd come on again that morning. So, when I went for my ECG, I asked the receptionist about it and she insisted that they'd sent lots of faxes and had receipts. Hmmm! Anyway, they sent it again and gave me a copy of the letter. I then went in to see the nurse and she said my ECG was OK and my BP was down to 130/80, which is still a bit high for me but much lower than it has been of late.

Yesterday, I was so pissed off waiting for Raphe's to get back to me that Sam and I went up to Moorefield's A&E. I know my eye problem isn't either an accident or an emergency but it's causing me real distress. It's like having bubble wrap over my right eye and, when I close it for reading, typing or watching TV, it's a real strain on my left eye. Anyway, we got there at 9.15 and I was seen pretty quickly. They did lots of tests – apparently, I have narrowing of the peripheral lens and my macular is all wrinkled. A film has formed across the macular – an epiretinal membrane. Plus, I've got a cataract. Great! She's referred me to one of the clinics and I should get an appointment through the post. So, although I'm not going blind imminently, my right eye is pretty buggered!

Then, about 6 pm I was just putting on my shoes to get the washing in when there was an almighty crash behind me and

Sam was lying on the floor clutching his right arm and moaning. I immediately thought he'd had a heart attack. He said he'd slipped on the floor and landed on his right arm, the one with the neuropathy and then he couldn't get up. I did help him up to his feet but the whole incident shocked and unsettled me. I was shaking like a leaf. I was really tearful afterwards. I feel as though we're living on the edge of a crisis the whole time and it does get to me.

Sunday June 11th

On Thursday evening, we were just about to go up to bed when, at 9.45pm the doorbell rang and it was a delivery of Indian food for the charity from 2 women who are supporting us throughout Ramadan. But it was hot! I said to Sam that there was no way we could keep it until the morning, and it couldn't be reheated as there was rice with it. So, we had to go over to mall at 10pm - in the rain – and deliver the food to the rough sleepers in the shopping centre.

When we got there, there was another group already giving out hot drinks and biscuits, but we all joined together and spread out the Indian food on some bin bags for people to come over and help themselves. Then another woman came over with Danish pastries, so it ended up being quite a party. One guy was sobbing his heart out to me and another guy kept cuddling me - and I got a proposal of marriage. It was a strange and emotional evening and we didn't get home till midnight. But, at least we could go home to a soft bed in a warm home and not have to hunker down on cardboard boxes in a shopping centre.

Wednesday June 21st

Well, what a week!

- On Tuesday morning I went to the hearing-aid clinic and got different inners for my hearing aids. I was a bit shocked when the woman said that they'd given me the wrong bits before: they'd given me ones for slight hearing loss and mine was profound! It's hard getting my head round all this medical stuff – hearing loss, sight problems, heart arrhythmia, Achilles tendonitis, eczema, asthma, EDS and on and on! Everyone focuses on Sam's cancer – and quite rightly – but I have health issues too and they, largely, get swept under the carpet. BUT – none of them is cancer, so I count my blessings.
- Saturday 17th – The Great East Swim!! Alice's and my wave was 11.30 and the water was 19.6o, so positively balmy compared to the English Channel in April. It wasn't at all as I'd expected. The water was very murky, so that, even with goggles on, it was impossible to see. Everyone was bumping and barging and I didn't like that bit of it at all. I'd tied green ribbon on Alice's and my wrists so that we could identify each other amongst the hordes of black wet suits and I did manage to keep her within eyeshot until the backstraight. I finished in 39 minutes 19 seconds (a PB) and Alice did 38 minutes 4 seconds. I was so proud of her. And the whole family turned out to cheer us on!

Thursday June 29th

Alice, Evan, Wynter & Pixie moved in with us. They've sold their house in Ipswich but the one they were buying in Wales fell through – twice!

Wednesday July 5th

Got a phone call from Aoife at just turned 7 pm to say that Niamh had just died.

Feel like shit! I said a prayer for her and lit some candles. I hope Niamh was looking down and smiling. She loved her candles, bless her.

Friday July 21st

Alice came with me to Niamh's funeral while Sam took Wynter to the park. He said he didn't want to even set eyes on Bob or Patrick. I decided that I was NOT going to skulk at the back of the church, so we went to the far side and sat near the front.

I didn't want to go to the wake, so Alice and I joined Sam and Evan in the pub and we toasted Niamh's release from pain. I know she would have approved – bless her.

2018

Sunday January 21st

This morning, Sam told me that he'd found a lump in his groin. My heart sank. It's only small – the size of a pea - but it's definitely there. And also, his right leg keeps collapsing on him: it did it again yesterday when he was doing security work. I came downstairs and heard a thud, thud, thud aaaaaaaagh! I ran out to the hall and Sam was at the bottom of the stairs saying that his leg had given way again. Christ on a bike, what the hell is this now?

Wednesday January 24th

Sam went up to Perry's and the oncologist said that there was definitely an enlarged lymph node, but his bloods were good. As all the scanners were booked up in advance, he couldn't be scanned, so she said to keep an eye on it and, if it gets any bigger, to go back. I told him not to feel it again for a couple of days, so that he could tell the difference if there was one. But, of course, human nature being what it is, he can't keep his hands off it and says it's getting bigger.

Sunday January 28th

I felt Sam's lump again on Thursday and it did feel a bit bigger. Shit!

On Friday, I had an ultrasound scan on my shoulder. I told the radiographer that the pain was spreading right down to my elbow, but she just did the actual shoulder. At the end she said that I'd got 2 torn ligaments and tendinopathy. Torn bloody ligaments! No wonder it's so painful. But, of course, with torn ligaments you're supposed to rest them and with tendinopathy, you're supposed to move and strengthen the joint. Catch 22!

Monday January 29th

Sam was so grumpy this morning. Apparently, he'd bumped into someone he used to know. He'd been standing in the rain while she told him to `be positive' about the lump in his groin and he needed to `stay upbeat.' I can understand why he was pissed off. People can be such bloody know-alls. Whenever anything unpleasant comes along – like cancer – they don't really want to know the full story, so they come out with these useless, avoidance platitudes like, `you've got to be positive.' Well, guess what? When you're dealing with life-threatening illnesses, there are times when it's very difficult to be positive. I do believe in the power of positive thought but NOT ALL THE TIME! No one can be positive all the time. Not if you want to be authentic anyway.

I looked across at Sam as he was talking and thought: he is one handsome, sexy, funny, kind individual who doesn't deserve all this crap and I'm so lucky to have him in my life. I know I don't always think like that but it's good to know that I can still find those feelings after everything we've been through.

Friday February 9th – 4am!

Have hardly slept all night and feel dreadful.

Yesterday Sam was at Perry's. It was the first time since he's been at Perry's that he didn't see a consultant but just a registrar. I followed him in, and the guy looked at me and said,

"Who are you?" Bloody cheek! I'm the person who'd been there with him - and for him - for the past 7½ years since he was diagnosed. Anyway, he examined Sam and said he could feel the lump in his right groin, plus another one in his right groin and one in his left groin. Fuck! He said they were small, and lymph nodes in the groin can be up to 2cm and still be `normal' but I was concerned that there were 2 new ones, so he's booked him in for a CT scan and he has to go back in 3 weeks. If it is a recurrence of the lymphoma, at least they've got it early.

Monday February 12th

Sam was doubled up with stomach pains for most of this morning. And, of course, he convinced himself that it was lymphomas in his stomach. Which it might be. But I think it was probably more to do with having a drink of cold water after running in the icy weather, then doing half an hour on the stationary bike and having nothing to eat at all. I made him some toast and a cup of coffee to relax the muscles and that seems to have worked. However, I did notice several more lumps in his groin this morning – about 3 or 4 small ones in his right groin. I didn't feel the left one. His scan is next Wednesday – over a week to wait.

And tomorrow I've got my appointment with the rheumatologist, then next Tuesday I've got my eye operation, so I won't be able to go with him to the CT scan at City General. Our life is one long social merry-go-round!

Tuesday February 13th

In the afternoon, I went through to do my exercises in the sitting room and Sam was on the settee scrolling through the internet. He said, "Look, this article says that lymphoma doesn't show up in blood test but only in enlarged lymph nodes and I've got those."

In the end I stopped doing my exercises and said, "Hon, what is it you want from me?"

Sam: I want you to acknowledge that I've got the symptoms of lymphoma and I'm not making it up.

Me: OK – I am well aware that you have already outlived your prognosis by a good 3 years; I am also aware that you have enlarged lymph nodes on both sides of your groin; I'm aware that every time you get stomach-ache, it might well be enlarged lymph nodes in your stomach or spleen or liver and that when you get wheezy and you get a chest infection it might well be caused by enlarged lymph nodes in your lungs. I am aware of all this – OK? And, just because I choose NOT to go down the route of panic, making all that add up to a death sentence, but rather wait for the CT scan results so that we're dealing with reality and not speculation does not mean that I am unaware of what is going on. I have told you many, many times that, in that sacred space of `don't know' there is a bubble of hope and I want to hold on to that bubble. And, if I put up barriers to make sure that I can cling on to that for as long as possible, I have every right to do so without being harried and pressurised to get into collusion with you.

And then I burst into tears!

Anyway, he was very sweet and cuddled me and said that it was the first time I'd actually acknowledged what was going on (not true) and he'd needed to hear me say that (well, he should listen better!) But my mood had dissipated by then and I didn't have the energy or enthusiasm to continue with my exercises. I know he's scared but I try so hard to stay upbeat about everything that's going on, I really do not want to be drawn into catastrophizing.

Sunday February 18th – 3am!

On Wednesday it was Valentine's Day and Sam had said that we should make cards for each other this year. So, on Sunday evening, I started mine: a large heart completely filled with red doodles like henna designs. It took quite a long time. Sam started his on Tuesday evening and wanted glitter and glue. All I could hear from the dining room was groans and moans and curses. It was so funny. I went up to bed at 10 and had to ring downstairs at midnight for him to come up and he was covered in glitter and bemoaning his card-making efforts. It hadn't gone at all as he'd wanted, because his hands are too painful to hold scissors or pens. In the end, he went out to Tesco's at 5am and bought one!

I went down at 7 and the whole house was covered in glitter and sprinkles – tonnes of the stuff – in every room and all up the stairs! And there was his home made card – a roughly hacked out heart shape in the middle with 5 stick-on hearts: one in each corner and one showing through the middle. It was so funny. We both laughed until our sides hurt. And then he'd bought me one too and some flowers and some chocolates. I can't remember laughing so much in a long time. But I really love the card because he made it himself and we laughed so much about it. I'll treasure it always.

Sunday February 25th

Tuesday was my cataract operation. I was first on the list, so I was on the way home again by 10.30! It wasn't a particularly nice experience, but it was nothing compared to the retinal peel I had in October. But, of course, the trauma of that was still in my mind, so I was incredibly anxious and couldn't sleep the night before. But it wasn't too bad at all. Bog standard cataract surgery. It only lasted about 40 minutes and I managed to meditate myself back to the Maldives for most of it. Of course, I had a massive patch over it for 24 hours but then I could take it off – except at night. I have 2 sets of drops: antibiotics which I have to do 4 times a day and steroids which have to be done every 2 hours – and they mustn't clash. So, I've set my phone alarm for every time I have to do my drops, otherwise I don't think I'd remember half of them.

So, Tuesday I just sat on the settee and slept and watched Netflix: Wednesday I didn't even get out of my pyjamas – first time ever, I think! Sam went up for his CT scan at City General. He said there were 4 of them doing it but when he asked about the results, the woman just told him to discuss it with his oncologist. Of course, both our minds went into overdrive. That's another week of waiting.

Wednesday February 28th

This morning a doctor from Perry's rang and Sam put him on speaker phone. He said that there was no sign of the lymphoma coming back and there was nothing to worry about. So that was reassuring. But ... (why is there always a bloody but???) ... there was evidence that one of the bones in his spine was soft and cracked, which was sometimes an indication of prostate cancer so they would need to do more tests! So, why the fuck did he tell us that there was nothing to worry about? Honestly!

Sam underwent several more tests for prostate cancer but, so far, all have proved negative. Yay!

Wednesday October 10th

School visit today. Was shown into the hall which was very large with tiered seating – great for the talk. Then the librarian said, "And this is where we're having the workshop too." Not a desk or table in sight. How the hell were the kids supposed to do written work sitting in tiered seating? I was not a happy bunny.

The talk went OK – then we went off to the staff room for a half hour break but some little bugger set off the fire alarm! We all had to traipse out to the netball courts and line up and be counted. Although no one even asked my name or checked me off any list, so I could have been frying in the toilet for all anyone knew. That took about 15 minutes and then they said they'd go straight into the 30 minute break – reducing my workshop time by 15 minutes!

Then another woman came and took half the kids to do an exam in the hall, leaving me with the other half for my workshop – but with nowhere to do it. So, we had to go over to the canteen - another 15 minutes off the time. Of course, the canteen had no smart board, so no PowerPoint! Great! Acoustics were crap and the tables were all smeared with tea, coffee, sugar and crumbs. Soooo pissed off!

Then, my afternoon workshop was cancelled. Do they realise how much preparation goes into an author visit? Not only my time, but also the cost of printing out workbooks! But, on the positive side, I got to leave at 1 instead of 3pm. Although no one had seen my invoice so there was no cheque for me! Gggrr!

I got home and crashed out on the settee!

Thursday October 11th

Sam was at Perry's this morning and I had intended going with him, but he said he'd be fine and I should rest – which I did. I was still in bed when he phoned up, almost in tears. At first, I was: Jesus wept! Please God don't let it have come back. I was convinced it was bad news - but it was the opposite: his cancer has completely gone! HE IS 100% CANCER FREE! Bloody brilliant!

Apparently, it's unprecedented in his type of cancer – although Dr Dawn French now says he's had a combination of 3 cancers! We were told it was 2 different types. Eight years on and they're still changing their minds about what cancer he's actually got – sorry – HAD! Not that it matters now if it's all gone!

I was close to tears myself but couldn't quite get my head round it. Having lived with cancer hanging over us like a Sword of Damocles for eight and a half years, it's hard to just let it go.

And, of course I hadn't been with him so I kept thinking: has he misheard? Have they misread his results? Has someone put the wrong test results in his file – like they did at Raphe's? All those things went through my head.

That evening Sam ordered pizza for us and I got a bottle of Prosecco. We celebrated - which was lovely – but I was aware that I still couldn't relax properly. We've been told so many different things over the years, it's really hard to get to grips with the fact that this could be real.

Friday October 12th

I woke up feeling very anxious again. God knows why. I just couldn't let go of the fear that's dominated our lives for over 8 years.

I went to yoga and told the teacher about Sam and, of course, she was delighted. Then other people came in and I was telling them. The more people I told, the more I got it. Tears started pouring down my cheeks and suddenly I felt so much better. It was as though I'd been carrying an elephant on my back and then... it was gone! I was quite light-headed with relief.

Afterwards we went for coffee and I treated everyone as a celebration. I really breathed into it and finally started to fully experience the relief.

Part 4

Remission

October 2018 – Present Day

According to the NCI definition of cancer terms, remission is:

A decrease in, or disappearance of, signs and symptoms of cancer. In complete remission, all signs and symptoms of cancer have disappeared, although cancer still may be in the body.

And there's the rub! Although Sam's lymphoma is defined as NED [no evidence detected] it could still be lurking in his body somewhere, just lying in wait to rear up and ambush him when he's least expecting it. Obviously, the longer he goes with NED, the better his chances of long term survival. But the uncertainty is always present in our lives. The slightest pain, a raised temperature (and there are many of those), feeling tired (ditto times a thousand) and the cold, sick fear returns - until that particular crisis has been checked out and ruled out. Then, of course, there's another sigh of relief and we move on – until the next time.

So, we do our best to live in the moment. Easy to say but very tricky to do: wake up grateful for being alive and determined to spread kindness throughout the community; go to bed content to have done our best – most of the time. I'd like to say we never go to bed on an argument, but I'd be lying. We're only human!

On November 29th 2018, my 6th grandchild, and Alice's 2nd child, was born: Eli. No IVF this time and he completed my brood: 3 children, 2 stepchildren and 6 grandchildren! I love them all to pieces and they bring me more joy than I could ever have imagined.

Sam's charity continues to thrive. Every Sunday, Tuesday and Thursday evening, he collects end-of-day food from cafes in the High Street. And, pre-Covid, every Friday he got up at 4 am and made up breakfast bags and urns of tea and coffee. We took them to the shopping centre where up to 40 homeless people used to sleep. Quite often I would join him, but Sam went whatever the weather or temperature – or the state of his health. It was both eye-opening and humbling. Dozens of people – men and women – of all ages, quite literally, sleeping on pieces of cardboard on a concrete floor. They had nothing other than the clothes on their backs.

We would set up our tables at 6 am and, as the security officers were waking the rough sleepers, we would start: Sam doing the food and hot drinks and me on the clothing: underwear, socks, hats, gloves, scarves and sanitary protection. The vast majority of the people were inordinately grateful. Sam was respected amongst the homeless community and frequently calmed disputes. He was known as `Uncle' by many. Although I supported Sam, it was entirely Sam's brainchild, and my presence was minimal compared to his utter devotion to the people he supported. After the shopping centre, he would tour east London looking for other homeless individuals or communities. He would also source shoes and coats as well as *sleeping bags. And, at Christmas, we would take groups of homeless people for a fried breakfast with as much as they could eat and give each of them a wrapped gift of either a hat or scarf and a personal wash bag.*

When Covid struck and lockdown kicked in, things had to change. The shopping centre was shut and the vast majority of rough sleepers were housed in B&B accommodation. However, that didn't stop Sam. As restaurants, pubs and cafes closed, we found ourselves with van loads of fresh food being delivered to our home. We had a production line for sandwich making, buttering and filling up to 100 sandwiches an evening. Sam then delivered them to the local hospital for the night staff. We also made up food bags for families on low incomes or living in poverty and he drove round distributing those. Suddenly, within a few days, our beautiful 4 bedroomed home was transformed into a foodbank. Three of the four bedrooms were floor to ceiling with tins and packets of food.

People got bored at home and started clearing out their cupboards but, as the charity shops were closed, they brought their clothes and household goods to Sam to give out to families. And, of course, they were also stored in our house. We could hardly move.

2020

Monday February 24th

I've been writing – yay! And doing an abundance meditation – double yah! So, in addition to being let off the £90 fine from the train guard, *[I'd inadvertently got the wrong train and there was a £90 discrepancy in the fares– doh!]* a woman I've never met sent me 3 bunches of beautiful flowers on Thursday via Sam and then we won £2 on a scratch card. OK, so not exactly the Lotto but still – abundance comes in all forms.

On Friday, I got up at 4.20 and went out with Sam to do the breakfasts. It is certainly a humbling experience. I'm doing the abundance thing when, in fact, I have everything I could ever dream of – in abundance. These people have nothing whatsoever and most are friendly and grateful and soooo appreciative.

In December 2019 Covid was unlashed on the world. By early spring of 2020 it was raging through Europe and, on March 23rd 2020 in UK, total lockdown was scheduled to start. I had already begun self-isolating because of my asthma but Sam made no attempt to slow down his charity work at all. In fact, he stepped it up.

Sunday March 22nd – Mother's Day

Jesus Christ what a 24 hours! Yesterday afternoon, a friend of Sam's rang up to say he'd been contacted by a restaurant in Essex who had £500 worth of food that they couldn't use because all pubs, clubs, cafes and restaurants have to close tomorrow, including: 120 eggs, 4 x 1k roundels of Brie, 2x 1k logs of goats' cheese, sacks full of potatoes, leeks, spinach and rocket, bags of tomatoes and mushrooms and umpteen camembert – our kitchen was overflowing with food. So I began making up bags of fresh food for the nurses at Raphe's. Sam took them to the children's ward and they were overwhelmed and incredibly grateful. The supermarkets are now only open 8am – 8pm and those are the hours of a day shift for NHS staff so they can't buy food. After that, I had some dinner and went to bed at 8.30 while Sam went to the huge bakery in the shopping centre to pick up 50 sandwiches and 50 cakes.

This morning he went out at 6 and fed about 20 homeless people then took the rest of the sandwiches and cakes to the staff on 4 different wards at Raphe's. I made up food bags for the families he supports who are on low incomes – one has 4 children and another has 6 – then he took them out.

I got video calls from both Amy and Alice this morning and cards and letters from the grandchildren. I was holding up until then, but I just went – weeping copiously. Worst Mother's Day ever.

Quite early in Lockdown the shopping mall where we used to feed rough sleepers was closed and the benches removed. Many homeless people were offered B&B accommodation but not all. Most charities who went out feeding homeless people closed their services but there was one fairly near us that took end-of-day food from all the supermarkets and distributed it amongst families who were in dire straits. So, of course, Sam went to work there voluntarily. And, as well as delivering food to about 15 families on the estate, twice a week, it enabled him to source food for the families he was already supporting.

Sunday May 3rd

At 4pm, I walked round the corner to watch a concert given every Sunday evening by an opera singer and her musician husband from their front garden. Everyone was out with their masks and chairs and glasses of wine – keeping 2m apart - but I just stood there in the road. She was mesmerising. I'm not usually one for classical music and opera but it was wonderful – so moving and emotional. What a treat. She was supposed to be performing at Carnegie Hall in New York but, obviously, it's cancelled. Their loss: our gain! I felt as though I'd been transported to some ethereal plane.

Thursday May 21st

I went over to Amy's today for a socially distanced walk. I was worried about needing the loo and not being able to go into their house, so I took the grandkids' potty with me to use in the back of the car if necessary. Before I go there, I thought I ought to do a wee before we set off on our walk, so I found a quiet, unoverlooked spot and got into the back of the car. I sat on the potty and did my wee. Great so far. But, when I came to try and open the door, the bloody child locks were on. So, I was stuck in the back of the car, with a potty full of pee, trying to get into the front seat without knocking it over. The legs of my voluminous harem pants kept getting caught on the hand brake and I couldn't get my shoulders between the head rests. It was a nightmare. If anyone had been watching, they'd have been wetting themselves with laughter. (`Scuse the pun) In the end, I managed to prop the potty up so that it didn't spill and climbed over the seats to go round and open the back doors of the car. What an idiot!

Sunday May 24th

On Thursday evening we were in the hot tub when the opera singer started singing in the garden at the back of us. So, we were sitting in this warm water, I was lying back in Sam's arms, with the smell of the philadelphus and the sound of her voice with bees and butterflies drifting in the evening light. It was magical – one of the most wonderful evenings of my life.

2021

Thursday February 11th

Sam had his phone consultancy with Perry's at 9 am. It was the Big Cheese and he said that there'd been no evidence of anything coming back in his last blood tests (phew!) and he'd have to go up there for a physical consultation in August. Then I had my Covid jab at 10.30. It was very well organised and I was in and out within about 10 minutes. Brilliant!

Friday February 26th

Yesterday, Sam started with a temperature of 38.6 with the rigors and loss of appetite so I took him off for a Covid test last night and we're still awaiting the results.

Sunday March 7th

So, last week was pretty stressful. Sam's temperature stayed high for 6 days despite antibiotics. His Covid test was negative, thank goodness, but then he developed ulcers in his mouth, swollen glands around his neck (which are probably connected) and it was extremely painful to pee – plus he was off his food and was finding it hard to swallow. He did, finally, manage to get through to Perry's and his consultant is going to phone him on Wednesday, so hopefully they'll do blood tests – which the Big Cheese decided were unnecessary at his phone consultation about 3 weeks ago.

Monday March 15th

Sam's urine test came back negative, which Sam seemed to think was good news, but I found it a tad worrying. If it had been a urine infection, that would have explained his high temperature and a second bout of antibiotics could have hit it on the head but, the fact that it wasn't, means something else must have caused it. Anyway, a consultant from Perry's rang him and sent blood test strips which he had done today at Raphe's. Fingers crossed nothing untoward shows up.

[The blood tests were OK, but the bouts of high temperatures and non-specific illnesses continue to this day. In fact, as I write, Sam is in bed again with a temperature. It's become part of our lives but every time there's that nugget of fear niggling away at the back of our minds.]

As the grandchildren got older, we'd been talking about getting another dog. We decided against a rescue because, although all my other dogs have been rescue dogs, we didn't know their background and didn't want to risk having another unstable one with the grandchildren around.

Saturday April 25th

All my dreams have come true today. We took delivery of our gorgeous little puppy, Gaia. Oh my days, she is so unbelievably cute. A tiny little black Lab who crawls up on to my shoulder and snuggles into my neck. I am totally in love with her.

Sunday April 26th

Slightly less in love this morning after a night of howling and crying from Gaia. Came down to poo everywhere – her whole crate was caked in the stuff. All her bedding and toys had to go out and we had to disinfect the entire crate. The joys of puppy-parenthood.

Saturday June 12th

Last night the Queen's Birthday Honours List was announced and we could finally tell people that Sam's been awarded a BEM! *[British Empire Medal – we had a long conversation about the connotations of `Empire' but decided that it was an archaic name and the honour could only benefit the charity, so Sam decided it would serve no purpose to refuse it. It's not like he's John Lennon or someone like that.]* He got the letter back in April, but we were sworn to secrecy until now. So proud of him. It's for his work during Covid. And he's also been given two tickets to Centre Court at Wimbledon by Raphe's for his support throughout Covid. And also, he's been invited to the ceremony at St Paul's to commemorate the founding of the NHS and also to remember everyone who'd died from Covid. Talk about riding the wave! What a star!

Monday September 27th

Sam's investiture today – and it's peeing down! And me in my posh frock too.

It was in Westminster Abbey rather than Buck House because there were 4 lots of honours to be awarded, clearing up the backlog due to Covid: New Year's honours from 2020, Birthday honours from June 2020, New Year's honours from this year, and Sam's lot. Over 300 people. And it was the Lord Lieutenant of London giving them out rather than the Queen – presumably because of Covid too. Bloody virus has cocked up everything!

It was all very well organised. Everyone was seated in alphabetical order so Sam and I were on the 4th row with excellent views of everything that was going on.

There could be no handshakes or pinning on of the medal, so everyone had to wear theirs to walk up, then the Lord Lieutenant did Namaste and they stood next to him to have a photo taken by the official photographer. A very emotional day. Couldn't go out to celebrate afterward though as we had to go home to our gorgeous little Gaia.

2022

Saturday February 19th

[Sam had to have another operation to check for prostate cancer. Thankfully that came back clear too but...]

I picked him up the same day and the first night he was throwing up all night. Most likely the general anaesthetic but not helped by 2 bags of wine gums and entire packet of Jaffa cakes! And, because he had a catheter in, he couldn't move quickly so didn't always make it to the bathroom. Raises eyes to heaven. Then he said he could smell dog shit – great! I went downstairs to find Gaia had had diarrhoea all over the sitting room. My cup runneth over! Good job I'd bought a carpet cleaner. I was, literally, cleaning the carpets at 1am while Sam was throwing up upstairs.

And Gaia was the same the following night, although Sam wasn't throwing up by then thank God. I've cleaned every carpet downstairs in the space of 24 hours – although I still haven't gone upstairs where Sam was up-chucking. I still have that joy to look forward to.

Sam received another invitation to a Royal Garden Party. It was his third but the other two had been cancelled due to Covid.

Wednesday May 25th

The Royal Garden Party today. I was very excited: another new dress – plus hat! Compulsory item for `ladies.' But, gosh, what a shock when we got there. It's enough to turn anyone republican! But not in a Robespierre – `orf with their heads, sort of way! Just, maybe, get on your bikes and go down to Sainsbury's like they do in Holland.

All the roads around the palace were closed because they were getting ready for the Jubilee celebrations, so the cab dropped us halfway down The Mall and we started walking – miles! I was wearing my friend's mum's sparkly Italian sandals, which looked fabulous but, oh my days, did they hurt my feet. It took forever to find the end of the queue and then it started spitting with rain – not that it made a lot of difference. Once we got to the gate, our ID was checked and we were told to cross the forecourt without stopping to take photos. I'd really wanted one in front of the palace but there was no way I was going to argue with the man holding the submachine gun!

We went round the back to the gardens, which were HUGE! Acres and acres of perfectly manicured grounds – not a weed in sight. There were brass bands playing, taking it in turn to play different tunes - and snipers on the roof of the palace. We were immediately formed into two wishbone shaped corridors that converged at the end. People were picked out, not sure if it was pre-arranged or random, to stand in front of the general crowd and those were the ones who were chosen to be spoken to by the Royal Family. The rest of us watched as they walked along. Sam was gagging for some water *[Another legacy of chemo is a dry mouth. Suddenly, his whole throat can close up and he starts choking if he doesn't get some water]* but trying to cross the crowds to the refreshment tent was like trying to cross the Red Sea. In the end, I played the cancer card and found a guy in a top hat to guide us across and, sure enough, the crowd parted as if the bloke was Moses himself.

The Royals on one side of the wishbone were Edward and Sophie whilst the other side had Wills and Kate – there were a couple of Dukes as well, I think. But they had their own tea tent - The Royal Tea Tent! Then there was one labelled Dignitaries Tea Tent and then, at the other side of the garden, was the pleb's tent, which was massive. We had a couple of terrific downpours, but we were inside at those times so didn't get wet.

Wynter has been learning about the Queen and the jubilee at school so when Alice told him that Granny and Granddad Sam had been invited to have tea in the Queen's Garden, it blew his mind, bless him.

Epilogue

And, actually, it blows my mind too. How Sam survived a potentially fatal illness as a child, has overcome a background of poverty and homelessness, put himself through college as an adult to qualify as a social worker, come to terms with the death of a child and survived Stage 4 cancer is phenomenal. And then to go on and set up his own thriving charity, carry the Olympic torch, be awarded the BEM and attend a garden party courtesy of her Maj, is an amazingly impressive feat. I feel so proud.

As for me, my morning meditations have temporarily halted since the arrival of Gaia – trying to control an over enthusiastic Lab is not really conducive to clearing the mind, but I am writing again – hence this book. It was never meant for publication, but writing it was my salvation throughout Sam's illness and, preparing it for publication has been a much harder task than writing a novel from scratch. Hopefully, it'll get me back on track and my nursing career is well and truly over.

Some people are born to be carers: some have caring thrust upon them. I am definitely in the latter group. It's been an honour to have been part of Sam's roller coaster journey but fingers, toes, eyes and everything else crossed, let's hope the rest of our lives will be less of a Big Dipper: more a gentle merry-go-round!

On October 11th 2022, Sam was 4 years clear of cancer – Yay!

Thank you for reading our story.

Acknowledgements

First of all, from the bottom of my heart, I want to acknowledge the NHS and all the amazing people who work in it. Specifically: our GP, the brilliant Dr K and also, Claire, Sam's MacMillan nurse. There are many others, too numerous to mention individually, without whose knowledge and dedication Sam would not be alive today. And, had he not survived, many thousands of people would not have benefited from his amazing charity work. I know I've grumbled about certain aspects of the NHS in this book but, I believe that is not because of the service per se, it is because of the lack of funding from central government over decades. So, put your money where your mouth is, MPs, and restore our NHS to the jewel in the UK crown that it used to be!

I also want to thank Sam, first of all for beating cancer but also for giving his permission for me to publish his story. I know it wasn't easy for him to read again. I want to thank my family and friends for their love, laughter and unending support through one of the most difficult periods of my life. Without them I doubt I would still have my sanity.

And I would also like to express my gratitude to Caroline Montgomery, my long suffering agent, for her patience and understanding with getting this from diary to manuscript to book, and Fenris Oswin for his help with the formatting of it. I don't know where I'd be without either of them.

Thank you all!

No Easy Way to Say This

Printed in Great Britain
by Amazon

41928615R00218